'Scrupulous scholarship at its best. A for historical truth-telling of a sort immediately relevant to any.'
Alan Atkinson

'Avoiding big-picture generalisations, Bain Attwood has written a succinct and excellent close-grained study of the Djadja Wurrung people and their interactions with settlers and the Aboriginal Protectorate.'
Richard Broome, co-author of Mallee Country

'This is ... a deep local history that pays attention to the forces of time and place to explore how colonial relations evolved as they did in this region, and how Aboriginal people responded to the successive colonial processes of dispossession, institutionalisation, and assimilation.'
Amanda Nettlebeck, *Australian Book Review*

'Once you have this broad picture of, first, the Aboriginal nations' territory, then the overlay of the settlers' claims, you begin to see the land differently.'
Rosemary Sorensen, *Daily Review*

'Concise, focused on places and people and alert to the historiography ... exemplary in every way.'
Tim Rowse, *Australian Historical Studies*

'It is in his attentiveness to the finer textures of frontier relations that Attwood's book really shines.'
Russell McGregor, *Australian Journal of Politics and History*

ABOUT THE AUTHOR

Bain Attwood is a professor of History at Monash University. He is the author of many books, including *The Making of the Aborigines* (1989), *Rights for Aborigines* (2003), *Telling the Truth about Aboriginal History* (2005), *Possession: Batman's Treaty and the Matter of History* (2009), *Empire and the Making of Native Title: Sovereignty, Property and Indigenous People* (2020) and *William Cooper: An Aboriginal Life Story* (2021). He is also the co-author of *The 1967 Referendum: Race, Power and the Australian Constitution* (2007), and co-editor of *Frontier Conflict: The Australian Experience* (2003), *Frontier, Race, Nation: Henry Reynolds and Australian History* (2009), and *Protection and Empire: A Global History* (2017).

THE GOOD COUNTRY

The Djadja Wurrung,
the Settlers and the Protectors

BAIN ATTWOOD

MONASH
UNIVERSITY
PUBLISHING

Monash University Publishing
Matheson Library Annexe
40 Exhibition Walk
Monash University
Clayton, Victoria 3800, Australia
https://publishing.monash.edu/

First edition (C format) published in 2017 by Monash University Publishing.

Monash University Publishing titles pass through a rigorous process of independent peer review.

Monash University Publishing: the discussion starts here.

Series: Australian History

Series Editor Sean Scalmer

Design: Les Thomas

Cover image: Barramul (emu) Skirt created by Wendy Berick a proud Dja Dja Wurrung and Yorta Yorta woman

Author photo: James Braund

National Library of Australia Cataloguing-in-Publication entry

Creator:	Attwood, Bain, author.
Title:	The good country : the Djadja Wurrung, the settlers and the protectors / Bain Attwood.
ISBN:	9781922979070 (paperback)
Notes:	Includes bibliographical references and index.
Subjects:	Djadja Wurrung (Australian people).
	Aboriginal Australians, Treatment of--Victoria--History.
	Aboriginal Australians--Victoria--History.
	Frontier and pioneer life--Victoria--Social conditions.
	Frontier and pioneer life--Victoria--History.

Printed in Australia by Griffin Press

CONTENTS

In memory of John Hirst,

1942–2016

INTRODUCTION

On 27 February 1840 the Chief Protector of Aborigines for the Port Phillip District, George Augustus Robinson, wrote in his journal of a meeting he had had that day in a camp that part of the Galgal Balug clan of the Djadja Wurrung nation had made near a creek several miles from Mount Mitchell. Robinson distributed goods to this family group. He also introduced Edward Stone Parker to them and informed the Djadja Wurrung that Parker would come and be their protector, and that they should tell their countrymen. The Galgal Balug were apparently very pleased by this news. Their land was already occupied by squatters and sheep and they were being exposed to the ill treatment of every badly disposed white man who chose to molest them, or so Robinson reckoned.[1]

The Galag Balug recognised both Robinson and Parker and they reminded them that they had all met in Melbourne, that Robinson had given them food on that occasion, and that they thought that the Chief Protector had acted properly. Now it was their turn to be host as this was their country. The head of this family group, Nandelowwindic, a tall muscular man about thirty years of age, and his son, who could speak some English, asked Robinson and Parker to sit down with them and eat some of the murnong (yams) they had roasted. After they had eaten, Nandelowwindic stood up to speak. With a good deal of emotion, he stretched out his arm and said 'my country, merrygic barbarie, good country'. He told Robinson and

---

1   Ian D. Clark (ed.), *The Journals of George Augustus Robinson, Chief Protector, Port Phillip Aboriginal Protectorate, volume 1, 1 January 1839 – 30 September 1840*, Heritage Matters, Melbourne, 1998, entry 27 February 1840, pp. 180–82.

Parker the names of several prominent places, pointed in several directions, and repeated the names. This part of the country had two names, Korerpunerlite and Nollite, while the creek near where they sat was called Konedebit. Nandelowwindic was welcoming Robinson and Parker to his country.[2]

In this book the story I tell is largely that of a three-way relationship between the Djadja Wurrung, the British settlers who invaded their country, and the men who were appointed by the imperial and the colonial governments to protect the Aboriginal people. At the same time I try to indicate the relationship between the Djadja Wurrung and other Aboriginal groups, which was also crucially important to what happened after the European invasion. For too long we have tended to conceive of our histories of colonisation in terms of just two groups – the whites and the Aborigines – which is a result of our projecting onto the past racial categories that barely existed or were only in the process of being forged at the time we are investigating. In order to be able to recover the past adequately we must grapple with the ways that the different peoples on the frontiers of settlement – in this case the Djadja Wurrung, their nearest indigenous neighbours, the settlers and the protectors – conceived of themselves and perceived the others. If we cannot do this, we run the danger of producing a caricature of the past.

In part the story I tell will also be an *Aboriginal history*. In recent decades this term has been used so loosely that it has come to be applied to any historical work that considers the relationship between Aboriginal people and non-Aboriginal people in Australia, regardless of whether it concentrates on Aboriginal people and their

---

2   *Ibid.*

perspectives or not.[3] In thinking of this book as an Aboriginal history I have a particular meaning or set of meanings in mind, which are closely related to the ways that Aboriginal history was originally conceived in the mid 1970s by a particular group of whitefellas: the anthropologists, archaeologists, historians and linguists at the Australian National University who were responsible for founding a journal that they came to call *Aboriginal History*.[4]

For these white scholars Aboriginal history was to have several dimensions. First, they hoped it would expand the temporal sense of Australia's history because it would focus not only on the time that had traditionally preoccupied this country's historians, namely the era since British colonisation began in 1788, but also many years prior to this, which historians had long held to be the preserve of the discipline of anthropology.

Second, the founders of *Aboriginal History* emphasised that the principal historical subject and subjects of Aboriginal History would be Aboriginal people. This was in contrast to the research that had been done since the mid to late 1960s on the history of the relations between Aborigines and settlers, which was highly Eurocentric in nature as it was principally concerned with European colonisers as well as government policies and practices. It also tended to presume that British colonisation had simply led to the destruction, dispossession and degradation of Aboriginal people, whereas the founders of *Aboriginal History* assumed the survival of an autonomous indigenous world and sought to tell a story of its adaptation to the

---

3   See Gillian Cowlishaw, 'On "Getting it Wrong": Collateral Damage in the History Wars', *Australian Historical Studies*, vol. 37, no. 127, 2006, p. 182.

4   I discuss this in 'The Founding of *Aboriginal History* and the Forming of Aboriginal History', *Aboriginal History*, vol. 36, 2012, pp. 119–71. I have drawn on this article for the following several paragraphs.

colonial presence and the ways in which this had shaped Aboriginal people and their sense of themselves.

Third, the founders of *Aboriginal History* saw their task as one of presenting or re-presenting Aboriginal perspectives or points of view. This was to involve not only a shift in a moral viewpoint from the European to the Aboriginal, but also a shift in the sense of standpoint so that one looked over the shoulders of the indigenous people or even through their eyes. The founders of the journal insisted that non-Aboriginal scholars had to try to explain Aboriginal responses in Aboriginal terms; otherwise, they would simply continue to tell the history of Australia from a British or white point of view.

Fourth, the principal figures in the founding of the journal were committed to a goal of scholarly objectivity, and so they wanted Aboriginal history to tell a story of what had actually happened in the past, rather than what political advocates merely assumed had happened. At the same time they were aware that, whereas historians of late had tended to focus on the oppression and the consequent suffering of Aboriginal people and sought to not only instruct but reproach their readers, Aboriginal storytellers revealed a greater range of historical experience and feeling and were less inclined to pass judgement on those colonisers who acted badly. They wished to emulate this.

Fifth, *Aboriginal History* would pay considerable attention to the role that the culture of the Aboriginal people had played in shaping their post-contact history. This meant that the horizons of the discipline of history had to be broadened so that the historical sources would encompass non-European ones such as Aboriginal oral tradition, and the conceptual frameworks would embrace those of other disciplines such as anthropology.

Finally, and most importantly in respect of this book, the founders of *Aboriginal History* had a further definition of Aboriginal History in mind, namely a focus on the aboriginal in the sense of the local, as in the original Latin meaning of the word *ab origine*. They were critical of the work of historians such as Henry Reynolds who tended to advance sweeping arguments about the nature of Aboriginal culture and history rather than attending to its spatial and temporal variations. 'Although doubt has been cast on the validity and usefulness of national historiography itself', one of the founders of the journal was to remark in this context, 'there still seems to be a naïve need to generalise about "the Australian experience"'.[5]

In fact, the founding editorial team of *Aboriginal History*, which comprised the anthropologist Diane Barwick, the historian Niel Gunson, the linguist Luise Hercus, the archaeologist Isabel McBryde, and the historian Bob Reece, were critical of much of the research that historians had recently done. They were especially troubled by the dominance of the concepts of *the frontier* and *resistance*. In their view there had been too much emphasis placed on conflict, and this had overshadowed the fact that there was a range of ways in which the colonised and the colonisers had related to one another. At the same time they held that so much attention was being paid to the violence committed by Europeans that the phenomenon of Aboriginal people killing other Aborigines, which was largely the result of the nature of the relationships that had traditionally existed between most Aboriginal nations, had been overlooked. In keeping

---

5   Bob Reece, 'Inventing Aborigines', *Aboriginal History*, vol. 11, pt 1, 1987, p. 15. Recently, the historian Tim Rowse has made a similar call for the exploration of 'the geographical variety of Australia's colonial history' ('Indigenous Heterogeneity', *Australian Historical Studies*, vol. 45, no. 3, 2014, p. 297).

with this emphasis on the aboriginal in the sense of the local, the journal's founders adopted a policy of encouraging its authors to refer to Aboriginal people by their tribal, language or regional name.[6] In a sense the journal's editors were saying that tribal history was Aboriginal history par excellence and that it should comprise largely of local histories.

I have not only conceived this book in terms of the project of Aboriginal History whose features I have just delineated. I have also had in mind the challenge that has been mounted in recent years to the dominance of national history in historical inquiry. But whereas those responsible for that challenge have largely argued that the problem of national history is best addressed by projects that track experience and ideas across national boundaries (what has been called, for better or worse, transnational history), I have been more struck by a similarly revisionist project that has been mounted by historians such as Alan Atkinson, who have sought to reveal the multiplicity of nations that existed in the nineteenth century by recovering the history of colonies such as Tasmania.[7]

It might be said that this book also marks something of a *return* to a historical approach that emphasises the testing of one's arguments by undertaking a good amount of research in the records of the past. Much of the work recently done in the history of relations between settlers and indigenous people has been either highly conceptual

---

6   For a work that exemplifies the journal's conception of Aboriginal history, see the anthropologist Diane E. Barwick's *Rebellion at Coranderrk*, Aboriginal History, Canberra, 1998, and the archeologist M.A. Smith's *Peopling the Cleland Hills: Aboriginal History in Western Central Australia*, Aboriginal History, Canberra, 2005. For an example of a tribal history in another context, see Judith Binney, *Encircled Lands: Te Urewera, 1820–1921*, Bridget Williams Books, Wellington, 2009.

7   See Alan Atkinson, 'Tasmania and the Multiplicity of Nations', *Tasmanian Historical Research Association Papers and Transactions*, vol. 52, no. 4, 2005, p. 197, and his *The Europeans in Australia: A History*, vol. 2, Oxford University Press, Melbourne, 2004.

or historiographical in nature,[8] and has involved considerably less research (especially in official archives) than was true of the historical studies done on this subject matter in the 1970s and 1980s.[9] To my mind, a great deal of this work is overly programmatic in nature, adds little if anything to historical understanding, and renders the past a much less complex and messier place than it really was.[10]

The history told in this book is made possible by what amounts to an unusually rich historical record in the Australian context. For many parts of Australia, and especially in comparison to many other British settler colonies, historians struggle to recover what happened in the first couple of generations of contact between particular Aboriginal peoples and the newcomers, and especially so if they are seeking to do this from the Aboriginal side. But, in the case of the Djadja Wurrung, the invasion of their country more or less coincided with the establishment by the British government of an institution that was charged with the responsibility of protecting the Aboriginal people of the Port Phillip District of the colony of New South Wales

8   See for example the work of Dirk Moses in collections of essays such as *Genocide and Settler Society: Frontier Violence and Stolen Indigenous Children in Australian History*, Berghahn Books, New York, 2004; Patrick Wolfe, 'Settler Colonialism and the Elimination of the Native', *Journal of Genocide Research*, vol. 8, no. 4, 2006, pp. 387–409; and Lorenzo Veracini, *Settler Colonialism: A Theoretical Overview*, Palgrave Macmillan, Basingstoke, 2010.

9   For example, Penelope Edmonds, *Urbanizing Frontiers: Indigenous Peoples and Settlers in 19th-Century Pacific Rim Cities*, University of British Columbia Press, Vancouver, 2010, and Alan Lester and Fae Dussart, *Colonization and the Origins of Humanitarian Governance: Protecting Aborigines across the Nineteenth-Century British Empire*, Cambridge University Press, Cambridge, 2014, gesture towards vast official archives such as the records of the Port Phillip Protectorate and the British Colonial Office, only to decline to plumb their depths in any of their case studies. Cf studies such as Jessie Mitchell, *In Good Faith? Governing Indigenous Australia through God, Charity and Empire, 1825–1855*, Aboriginal History, Canberra, 2011.

10   Recently Philip Dwyer and Lyndall Ryan have made much the same points in their 'Reflections on Genocide and Settler-Colonial Violence', *History Australia*, vol. 13, no. 3, 2016, pp. 335–50.

(or what later became Victoria). The accounts of its officers, and especially those of Chief Protector Robinson and Assistant Protector Parker,[11] enable historians to recover something of what happened and provide some sense of the Aboriginal people's perspective of these events.

This said, it would be a mistake to exaggerate the richness of the historical record for this study. For most of the period considered in this book there are no primary sources penned by the Djadja Wurrung, since they had an oral rather than a literary culture, and there is no extant oral tradition because the depopulation they suffered broke the chain of remembrance it would have otherwise provided. Consequently, historians have to rely predominantly on primary sources created by the Europeans, and that means the indigenous voices we might hear are nearly always mediated by those interlocutors. An American historian, Richard White, has spelled out the implications of this in regard to the North American frontier. 'A large chunk of our early documents … are conversations between people who do not completely understand each other', he has written. 'We are connoisseurs of misreadings. We rarely know Indians alone, we always know them in conversation with whites'. This is surely true of the Australian frontier as well.[12]

---

11 For a brilliant account of Robinson's writing, or at least that in his journals, see Inga Clendinnen, 'Reading Mr Robinson', in her *Tiger's Eye: A Memoir*, Text Publishing, Melbourne, 2000.

12 Sylvia J. Hallam, 'A View from the Other Side of the Western Frontier: Or "I Met a Man Who Wasn't There …"', *Aboriginal History*, vol. 7, pt 2, 1983, p. 155; Richard White, 'Indian Peoples and the Natural World: Asking the Right Questions', in Donald L. Fixico (ed.), *Rethinking American Indian History*, University of New Mexico Press, New Mexico, 1997, p. 93.

Chapter 1

ENCOUNTER

In the mid 1830s the European invasion of what came to be called the Port Phillip District of New South Wales began. It amounted to a revolution for the Aboriginal nations of this area such as the Djadja Wurrung,[1] who for thousands of years had occupied the country that the colonial administration would soon appropriate as the Loddon District and which is now part of what is generally known as Central Victoria.

Mountains and river basins tended to define the territories of nations in much of Aboriginal Australia. In the case of the Djadja Wurrung their territory was marked by the basins of the Loddon River and the lower Avoca River. This estate amounted to some 2500 square kilometres and extended from Mount Macedon (Terrawait) in the south, north through Kyneton and Mount Alexander (Learganook), north-northwest to Boort in the lower Loddon basin, west-southwest to Donald in the Wimmera, and south between

---

1   According to the historical geographer Ian Clark, there are more than a hundred variants of the name for this Aboriginal nation (*Aboriginal Languages and Clans: An Historical Atlas of Western and Central Victoria, 1800–1900*, Department of Geography and Environmental Science, Monash University, Melbourne, 1990, p. 140). I have adopted the name preferred by the Australian Institute of Aboriginal and Torres Strait Islander Studies. Aboriginal nations called themselves by names that were derived from their words for 'yes' or 'no'. The Djadja Wurrung used *jajae* for 'yes'; *Wurrung* means 'language'. And so their name roughly means the Jaja speakers (*ibid.*). The first part of each clan name referred to a locality, the second part meant people (*baluk*) or men (*gundidj*).

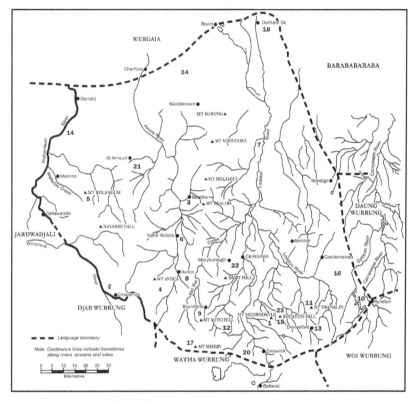

Djadja Wurrung language area and clans

1. Banebane baluk
2. Bargundidj
3. Bial baluk
4. Billawin gundidj
5. Bulangurd gundidj
6. Burung baluk
7. Catto's Run clan (Name has been lost)
8. Dirack baluk
9. Galgal baluk
10. Galgal gundidj
11. Gunangara baluk
12. Korerpongerlite gundidj

13. Kri baluk
14. Larningundidj
15. Leauragura baluk
16. Liarga baluk
17. Peerickelmoon baluk
18. Tanne baluk
19. Tardardyinlar
20. Tureet baluk
21. Wungaragira gundidj
22. Wurn baluk
23. Yarerinborin gundidj
24. Yung baluk

(Courtesy Ian D. Clark and Fred Cahir)

Ararat and Maryborough. It was a country that was quite diverse. For example, at its southern edge volcanic eruptions had created a staggering landscape of cones and basalt lava flows that was covered with sclerophyll forests, whereas in the northern reaches there were open woodlands and more patches of grassland. Most of this was good country and the Djadja Wurrung's wealth was all the greater because they held some rights to use a quarry at Mount William that provided the material for axes that were traded over a wide area in south-eastern Australia.[2]

Like other indigenous peoples in Australia, the Djadja Wurrung nation distinguished itself from other Aboriginal nations. They had a distinctive language and their own country, whose boundaries were well known, and each clan that made up the Djadja Wurrung nation could clearly point to land that they called their own. The Djadja Wurrung were bound to this land by religious beliefs that were expressed in the notion of the Dreaming. In the past, great ancestral beings had formed the land, created all species, and laid the foundations for their culture. The Djadja Wurrung clans, of which there seem to have been 24, adhered to a two-part moiety system: *waa* (crow) and *bunjil* (eaglehawk or wedge-tailed eagle). These clans were governed by a headman, designated by the title *neyernneyerneet*. His authority was recognised by all the clans and he was deemed to be the Djadja Wurrung's representative in its external affairs.

---

2   Robert Brough Smyth, *The Aborigines of Victoria*, vol. 2, Government Printer, Melbourne, 1878, pp. 154, 181; Isabel McBryde, 'Wil-im-ee Moor-ring: Or Where do Axes Come From? Stone Axe Distribution and Exchange Patterns in Victoria', *Mankind*, vol. 11, no. 3, 1978, p. 355; McBryde, 'Kulin Greenstone Quarries: The Social Contexts of Production and Distribution for the Mount William Site', *World Archaeology*, vol. 16, no. 2, 1984, pp. 269, 279; McBryde, 'Exchange in South-East Australia: An Ethnographic Perspective', *Aboriginal History*, vol. 8, pt 2, 1984, p. 142; Clark, *Aboriginal Languages*, pp. 151–52.

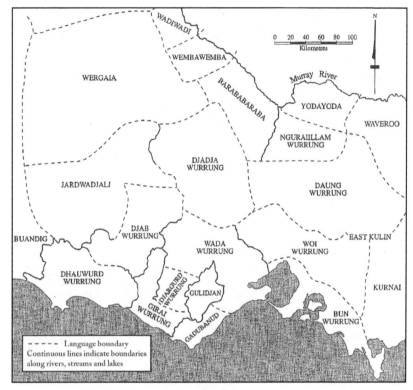

Map of the Aboriginal nations of the Port Phillip District of New South Wales

(Courtesy Ian D. Clark)

The Djadja Wurrung were on friendly terms with the nations to the north, south and west, with whom they intermarried, and they enjoyed good relations with the Woi Wurrung, who, like the Djadja Wurrung, were part of a larger grouping known as the Kulin. But many of the clans of the Djadja Wurrung were the enemies of the Daung Wurrung to the east and the Jardwadajali to the west. Indeed, they especially feared and loathed the former. One of the Djadja

CHAPTER 1: ENCOUNTER

Wurrung once told Edward Parker: 'They are foreign in speech, they are foreign in countenance, they are foreign altogether, they are no good'. The Djadja Wurrung had long suffered raids into their territory in which women were stolen, resources such as stone axes seized, and many killed. For example, in about 1832–33 most of the Gunangara Balug clan had apparently been massacred by Daung Wurrung.³

In Central Victoria, as elsewhere on the Australian continent, the Aboriginal nations had extensive trade and communication networks that connected them to Aboriginal peoples beyond their neighbourhood. Through these the Djadja Wurrung arranged marriages, traded commodities, exchanged decorative goods, and swapped news about strange goings-on. By these means the Djadja Wurrung probably heard of the white man long before they encountered these strangers.⁴ John Hunter Kerr, one of the pastoralists who later came to know the Djadja Wurrung well, was told as much. Similarly, as in many parts of the continent, an array of European commodities, such as iron, tin, glass, cloth, and axes, preceded the colonists. In 1836 the first European to explore this territory, Major Thomas Mitchell, found an iron bolt in an Aboriginal dwelling near

3   Edward Stone Parker, Census, February 1841, New South Wales State Records, NRS 905, Item 4/2472.1; Parker to George Augustus Robinson, 5 January 1843, New South Wales Legislative Council, *Votes and Proceedings*, 1843, Return to an Address, Dr Thomson, 29 August 1843, p. 46; Extract from Report by Parker, January 1845, New South Wales Legislative Council, *Votes and Proceedings*, 1845, Report from the Select Committee on the Condition of Aborigines, p. 53; Edward Stone Parker, *The Aborigines of Australia: A Lecture Delivered in the Mechanics' Hall, Melbourne, Before the John Knox Young Men's Association, on Wednesday 10 May 1854*, Hugh McColl, Melbourne, 1854, pp. 11–13; Brough Smyth, *Aborigines of Victoria*, p. 155; Edgar Morrison, *The Loddon Aborigines: "Tales of Old Jim Crow"*, s.n., Yandoit, 1971, p. 6; Clark, *Aboriginal Languages*, pp. 140, 154–69; Diane E. Barwick, *Rebellion at Coranderrk*, Aboriginal History, Canberra, 1998, p. 9.
4   Yet, a writer by the name of William Westgarth claimed that a Djadja Wurrung man, Beernbarmin (Tommy Farmer), told him in 1857 that his people had never heard of the white man before they set eyes on the explorer Major Thomas Mitchell (*Victoria and the Australian Gold Mines in 1857*, Smith, Elder and Co, London, 1857, p. 223).

Mount Arapiles (in north-central Victoria). Often Europeans were preceded by their animals as well. Creatures such as cattle and horses must have been mysterious to Aboriginal people. John Hepburn, one of the first pastoralists in Djadja Wurrung country, recalled meeting a group of Aboriginal people on a river near their territory. After a brief exchange of words, in which neither party understood the other, they had felt the skin of Hepburn's horses, presumably in an attempt to fathom the nature of these strange animals. Kerr wrote of such an encounter: 'The appearance of a man on horseback created the most profound astonishment, till it was ascertained that horse and man were distinct organisations'. In some instances at least, astonishment was surely matched by apprehension. An Aboriginal man who had seen Mitchell's expedition later apparently told Kerr: "Me big one frightened – think it all one fellow". Explorers and settlers were inclined to exaggerate the surprise that these encounters involved for Aboriginal people.[5]

The same networks that conveyed European commodities and information about these pale-faced newcomers brought devastation to Aboriginal communities long before first contact. Two smallpox epidemics, in 1788–89 and 1829, swept through south-east Australia prior to the first encounters. It is now thought that the Aboriginal population of the Port Phillip District might have been 60 000 prior to 1788 but that by 1835 it had been halved twice to 15 000. In other words, smallpox had drastically reduced the Aboriginal population in the Port Phillip District even before British colonisation began.

---

5   T.L. Mitchell, *Three Expeditions into the Interior of Eastern Australia*, vol. 2, T. & W. Boone, London, 1839, pp. 194–95; John Hepburn to Charles Joseph La Trobe, 10 August 1853, in Thomas Francis Bride, *Letters from Victorian Pioneers* (1898), Heinemann, Melbourne, 1969, pp. 67–68; John Hunter Kerr, *Glimpses of Life in Victoria* (1872), introduced by Marguerite Hancock, Miegunyah Press, Melbourne, 1996, p. 141; Brough Smyth, *Aborigines of Victoria*, pp. 154, 181 footnote.

In the case of the Djadja Wurrung they might have numbered three or four thousand in 1788 but there were only between 900 and 1900 by 1840. Such a ravaging disease as smallpox not only wreaked havoc but prompted a need among the survivors to understand or give meaning to what had happened. They seem to have done so by formulating mythic narratives. According to Parker, the Djadja Wurrung told of a large serpent called *Mindi* or *Myndie* which had unleashed this plague in the form of a dust they called *monola mindi*. They described the blows this agent of destruction had inflicted in terms of dysentery, blindness and death.[6]

In the wake of this devastation, a party led by Major Thomas Mitchell explored what became central and western Victoria and penned an account in which he waxed lyrical about the prospects he thought it held for pastoral settlement: 'The land is, in short, open and available in its present state, for all the purposes of civilised man'. Mitchell had little sense that the lush plains he described were the result of Aboriginal people firing the land (or practicing what the archaeologist Rhys Jones famously called 'fire-stick farming').[7] As the historian A.G.L. Shaw once remarked, this was not the land as God had made it but a land that the Aboriginal people had made. And in doing so the way had been prepared for British settlers and the basis laid for the future wealth of the Australian colonies. Not only were those such as Mitchell blind to this fact; he and those who followed

---

6   Parker, *Aborigines of Australia*, p. 18; William Thomas to La Trobe, undated, in Bride, *Letters from Victorian Pioneers*, pp. 421, 425–27; Clark, *Aboriginal Languages*, pp. 17, 150; N.G. Butlin, *Economics and the Dreamtime: A Hypothetical History*, Cambridge University Press, Melbourne, 1993, p. 135; Len Smith et al., 'The Political Arithmetic of Aboriginal Victorians', *The Journal of Interdisciplinary History*, vol. 38, no. 4, 2008, p. 535.

7   For a recent discussion of this, see Bill Gammage, *The Biggest Estate on Earth: How Aborigines Made Australia*, Allen & Unwin, Sydney, 2011.

in his wake were unaware of the fact that the smallpox epidemics had cleared the land of a large Aboriginal population, thereby making the British occupation of the country relatively easy.[8]

In the course of Mitchell's journey he crossed through the Loddon District twice, in July and September 1836. He made some contact with Aboriginal clans to the north but there are no recorded meetings between his party and the Djadja Wurrung. Later the same year, an overlanding party led by John Hepburn, Joseph Hawdon and John Gardiner moved through the Djadja Wurrung's territory on their way to the settlement at Port Phillip. It would seem that there was no contact between these newcomers and the Djadja Wurrung either. However, some of the Djadja Wurrung might have observed the journeying of these intruders in their country. While many European explorers never recorded seeing or meeting any Aboriginal people, many of these parties would have moved under the watchful eyes of the traditional owners of the country.[9]

It was not long before the Djadja Wurrung did encounter white men. In investigating these encounters several historians have followed the lead of Henry Reynolds in his 1981 book *The Other Side of the Frontier* where he posed this question: how did Aboriginal people *perceive* these strangers at those first meetings. Reynolds suggested, on the basis of linguistic evidence and oral tradition, that many Aboriginal people on the continent initially regarded Europeans as men returned from the dead. In this case, two pastoralists seem to

---

8   Mitchell, *Three Expeditions*, p. 333; Butlin, *Economics and the Dreamtime*, pp. 226, 228; A.G.L. Shaw, *A History of the Port Phillip District: Victoria Before Separation*, Miegunyah Press, Melbourne, 1996, p. 109; Robert Kenny, *The Lamb Enters the Dreaming: Nathanael Pepper and the Ruptured World*, Scribe, Melbourne, 2007, pp. 182–85.
9   Hepburn to La Trobe, 10 August 1853, in Bride, *Letters from Victorian Pioneers*, p. 62.

have been told as much by the Djadja Wurrung. Alfred Joyce recalled that 'their explanation of the white man was "tumble down black fellow come up white fellow"', while Kerr asserted: 'They believed that after death they would commence a fresh existence with a white skin, or, as they expressed it, "jump up white fellow"'. It appears that Aboriginal people often defined whites in terms that variously meant ghost, spirit, eternal, and the dead. According to Parker, the Djadja Wurrung used the word *amydeet*, which meant 'the separate state of the spirit when the body is dead'.[10]

Historians such as Reynolds have argued that this designation is hardly surprising. Apart from anything else, white was the colour that Aboriginal people associated with death. Moreover, for Aboriginal people the spirit world was very real and always present: the deceased were able to pass into another world as spirits, but rather than remain there they moved about their country and were still able to communicate with the living. Hence, the argument goes, it is unremarkable that white men seen wandering in the bush were often regarded as spirits: this was a much more likely explanation of the presence of these strangers than one which grasped that they were beings from unknown countries beyond the horizon.[11]

More specifically it seems that in many areas of Australia Aboriginal groups considered whites to be not merely reincarnated Aborigines but the spirits of their returning ancestral kinsmen. Parker believed that was the case among the Djadja Wurrung. This too, it

---

10 G.J. James (ed.), *A Homestead History: The Reminiscences and Letters of Alfred Joyce, of Plaistow and Norwood Port Phillip 1843 to 1964*, 3rd edn, Oxford University Press, Melbourne, 1969, pp. 74–75; Kerr, *Glimpses of Life*, p. 18; Richard Broome, *Aboriginal Victorians: A History Since 1800*, Allen & Unwin, Sydney, 2005, p. 57.

11 Henry Reynolds, *The Other Side of the Frontier*, History Department, James Cook University, Townsville, 1981, p. 26.

might be argued, is hardly remarkable given that Aboriginal people assumed that people were attached to their country by powerful spiritual bonds. In other words, when whites came many Aboriginal people might have concluded that they must have once belonged to the country or at least known of it in a previous life. One of the pastoralists who occupied Djadja Wurrung land, Frederick Race Godfrey, later claimed: 'They used to think, when we first took up the country and came amongst them, that, from our knowledge of it, we must have been there as blacks; and I was even told my former name and cause of death'.[12]

However, at least one anthropologist has challenged the account that historians such as Reynolds have given of this matter, not least because it seems to imply that Aboriginal people could not have seen the pale-faced newcomers in any other way. 'It is a serious misrepresentation to suggest that Aborigines saw their invaders as "ghosts" or "spirits"', Tony Swain has argued. 'Certainly there may have been initial perceptual errors on both sides of the frontier but, like the European ethnoclassification of Aborigines with subhuman species, the identification of whites with deceased relatives was [actually] a *conceptual* equation'. Swain argues that Aboriginal people were engaged in a hermeneutic process in their first encounters with the white man and he has pointed out that there were actually several ways in which they interpreted the newcomer after British colonisation began. He suggests that Aborigines came to regard the classifying of whites as deceased relatives as the most satisfactory way of handling their presence, and that they subsequently passed this approach on from region to region. By defining these intruders

---

12 Parker, *Aborigines of Australia*, p. 25; Victoria Legislative Council, *Votes and Proceedings*, 1858–59, Report of the Select Committee on Aborigines, p. 60.

as deceased kinsfolk, Swain explains, Aboriginal people provided themselves with a mechanism for expanding their social order so as to accommodate these alien people. While it would have been logical to categorise whites as malevolent spirits, this would have had the effect of placing the white man outside the domain of the human relationships Aboriginal people sanctioned; by equating the invaders instead with departed relatives, Aboriginal people could invite them to establish a morally sound relationship with their putative former kinsfolk.[13]

Clearly the way in which Aboriginal people perceived or conceived of the pale-faced stranger had important consequences for both the initial and subsequent contact between members of the two groups. If Aboriginal people chose to consider a newcomer as a relative they might accept his presence; but if they did not they might regard a newcomer as a dangerous interloper and kill him. In many cases, though, it seems that Aboriginal people were initially unsure of who these strangers were, and so the most common reaction to explorers and early pastoralists was avoidance, as they puzzled over how to treat them and what their intrusion meant. Where meetings did take place between the Djadja Wurrung and the European explorers and pastoralists it is evident that the former were often extremely nervous, suspicious and fearful. And where they offered hospitality it was probably on the assumption, or in the hope, that these intruders would not stay.

---

13 Tony Swain, *A Place for Strangers: Towards a History of Australian Aboriginal Being*, Cambridge University Press, Melbourne, 1993, pp. 122–23, his emphasis.

Chapter 2

CONFLICT

For many years the imperial government prohibited settlement in New South Wales beyond what was called the limits of location, an official line that enclosed nineteen counties and within which land could be granted. However, in October 1835 the Governor of New South Wales, Sir Richard Bourke, seizing upon an opportunity that was presented by a projected land grab in Port Phillip by a Van Diemonian Company, sought to persuade the imperial government that it should change tack and sanction new settlement beyond that boundary. Consequently, in September 1836, pastoralists began to invade Port Phillip at an extraordinary speed. The historian James Belich has aptly described this general phenomenon as explosive colonisation. Indeed, the invasion of the lands of Port Phillip proved to be one of the fastest occupations of land known in the history of empire. By the close of 1838 there were more than 300,000 sheep grazing in the Port Phillip District, and by 1841 this number had tripled; and there were 78,000 cattle to boot. By the following year, pastoralists had occupied half of the district.[1]

---

1   Sir Richard Bourke to Lord Stanley, 4 July 1834, National Archives of the United
    Kingdom, CO 201/39; Bourke to Lord Glenelg, 10 October 1835, National
    Archives of the United Kingdom, CO 201/47; A.G.L. Shaw, *A History of the Port
    Phillip District: Victoria Before Separation*, Miegunyah Press, Melbourne, 1996,
    pp. 87, 89; Bain Attwood, *Possession: Batman's Treaty and the Matters of History*,
    Miegunyah Press, Melbourne, 2009, pp. 84–85; James Belich, *Replenishing the*

CHAPTER 2: CONFLICT

The invasion of the good country of the Djadja Wurrung began in 1837 after overcrowding in Port Phillip drove pastoralists northwards in search of new lands for their stock. In 1837–38 several of them established runs in the Loddon District, and during 1839 this occupation of their land intensified as it reached what the historical geographer Joe Powell has called the infilling stage of pastoral occupation. This process meant that in a few short years a large part of the Djadja Wurrung's country in its southern and central reaches had been taken by white settlers for pastoral runs. Edward Parker remarked acerbically in June 1839, after touring a considerable part of the Loddon District: 'The country around Mt Macedon, and for many miles to the north and west, I find to be occupied at present by a few wealthy sheep and stock holders'. Invariably pastoralists took the land that the Djadja Wurrung held most dear. Parker complained in April 1840: 'The very spots most valuable to the Aborigines for their productiveness – the creeks, water courses, and rivers – are the first to be occupied'.[2]

Earth: The Settler Revolution and the Rise of the Anglo-World, 1783–1939, Oxford University Press, New York, 2009, chapter 3; Lisa Ford and David Roberts, 'Expansion, 1820–50', in Alison Bashford and Stuart Macintyre (eds), *The Cambridge History of Australia*, Cambridge University Press, Melbourne, 2013, p. 130.

2   Edward Parker, Report to George Augustus Robinson, 20 June 1839, Public Record Office Victoria, VPRS 13172, Unit 1; Parker to George Augustus Robinson, 1 April 1840, *Historical Records of Victoria*, vol. 2B, Victorian Government Printing Office, Melbourne, 1983, p. 692; Thomas Learmonth to Charles Joseph La Trobe, 11 August 1853, and William J.T. Clarke to Charles Joseph La Trobe, 13 September 1853, in Thomas Francis Bride, *Letters from Victorian Pioneers* (1898), Heinemann, Melbourne, 1969, pp. 98, 279; J.M. Powell, *The Public Lands of Australia Felix: Settlement and Land Appraisal in Victoria 1834–91 with Special Reference to the Western Plains*, Oxford University Press, Melbourne, 1970, pp. 13–14; Powell, 'Squatting Expansion in Victoria, 1834–1860', in Robert Spreadborough and Hugh Anderson (comps), *Victorian Squatters*, Red Rooster Press, Melbourne, 1983, pp. xi, xiv.

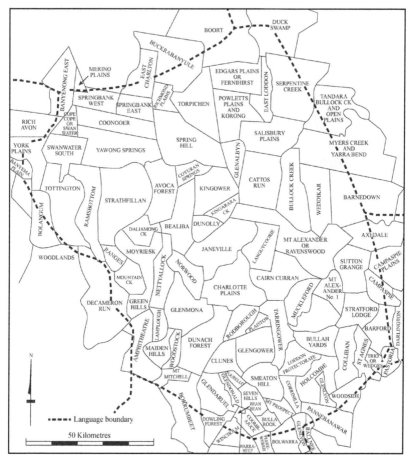

Map of Pastoral Runs in Djadja Wurrung country
(Drawn by Gary Swinton and Helen McFarlane)

Pastoralists intruding onto Aboriginal land were often welcomed by the senior men who were willing to share their country with small parties so long as the newcomers respected the land, especially its sacred sites. Aboriginal groups offered gifts to these strangers but expected that this would be reciprocated. In these ritual exchanges Aboriginal people were offering their resources in return for an acknowledgment of their ownership of the land. However, relationships between Aboriginal landowners and European intruders tended to break down quickly. Either it became apparent to the Aboriginal people that the newcomers were intending to stay on their land permanently and that their stock was having a major impact on their sources of food, or the pastoralists angered their Aboriginal hosts because they failed to understand or were unwilling to accept Aboriginal kinship rules that dictated an ethic of sharing and reciprocity. In this situation, Aboriginal people called upon the squatters to leave. In the Loddon District a headman of one of the Djadja Wurrung clans approached one of the first pastoralists, Charles Hutton, in the middle of 1838 to tell him that both the land and the water were his and to object to Hutton's remaining there. Later, this man was killed by pastoralists in an inexplicable manner. Aboriginal people also tried to acquire food by taking or killing the livestock that was displacing their game or by robbing homesteads and outstations for flour and other food. In turn, pastoralists and their employees often sought to punish those they assumed were responsible for these attacks on their property. Violent clashes between the two peoples tended to occur as a result. In this chapter I will principally seek to document this conflict, deferring any explanation of it until the chapter that follows.[3]

The Killing Times

In the first eighteen months of the pastoral invasion of the Djadja Wurrung's land we cannot be altogether sure about the nature or the number of the clashes that took place since there were no government

---

3   Parker, Report to Robinson, 20 June 1839; William Thomas to La Trobe, undated, in
    Bride, *Letters from Victorian Pioneers*, pp. 434–45; M.F. Christie, *Aborigines in Colonial
    Victoria 1835–86*, University of Sydney Press, Sydney, 1979, pp. 43, 51.

officials in the area to report them.[4] Yet, as noted earlier, we probably know more about this frontier than many in Australia as a result of the government's establishment of an Aboriginal protectorate in Port Phillip (which will be discussed at length in Chapter 4), since the assistant protectors were required to investigate any allegations of settlers mistreating Aborigines.[5]

The first violent clash seems to have occurred in March 1838 when two Djadja Wurrung men, one of whom was called Konokoondeet, were shot dead by a small party of white men who were exploring their country. This is all we know of this particular incident. In April William Bowman, who had formed a run (which later became Sutton Grange and Stratford Lodge) the previous month on the Coliban River on the Campaspe Plains, reported that Aborigines had committed several depredations on both his station and that of William Thomas Mollison. They had taken goods and thrown a

---

4 In his book *Scars in the Landscape: A Register of Massacre Sites on Western Victoria, 1803–1859*, the historical geographer Ian Clark provides an account of what he says were ten massacres in Djadja Wurrung country between March 1838 and August 1840. However, his tally can be faulted on several grounds: a massacre that he claims occurred in July 1838 is the same incident as one that he has taking place in February 1839; a massacre that he asserts took place in the winter of 1838 is probably the same massacre as one that he says occurred in June 1838; a massacre that he lists for June 1840 is the same massacre that he reports as having occurred in June 1838; and a killing that he states took place in December 1840 is the same killing as one that he believes took place in August that year (Australian Institute of Aboriginal and Torres Strait Islander Studies, Canberra, 1995, pp. 88–99). In other words, instead of the ten incidents Clark describes, no more than five or at most six occurred.

5 The pastoral map I have adapted here from R.V. Billis and A.S. Kenyon's *Pastoral Pioneers of Port Phillip* must be regarded as a snapshot of the runs in the area at a certain time. For more detail about the runs in the period under discussion as well as the location of some of the incidents of conflict that occurred, researchers and readers must consult the maps that appear in J.O. Randell, *Pastoral Settlement in Northern Victoria*, Vol. 1, Queensberry Press, Melbourne, 1979, between pages 60 and 61, 92 and 93, 116 and 117, 128 and 129, and 158 and 159, the maps in Randell's *Pastoral Settlement in Northern Victoria*, vol. 2, Chandos, Melbourne, 1982, pp. 70, 147, 158, 283, 412, and the two maps in Spreadborough and Anderson (comps), *Victorian Squatters*, an unpaginated section of maps for Western Port between pages 337 and 338.

spear at one of his shepherds. Bowman claimed that the attack on the shepherd had alarmed his men so much that they were reluctant to go out onto the run. He was puzzled about the attacks since he had instructed his men not to interfere with the Aborigines and believed that they had given them no cause to make these attacks. But perhaps the killing of the two Aboriginal men in March had provoked the Aboriginal attackers to retaliate the following month.[6]

In the middle of May some Aborigines drove away a flock of sheep on a run recently formed by William Henry Yaldwyn on land that adjoined Bowman's station, and the following day they killed and disembowelled one of Bowman's shepherds by the name of Thomas Jones and took a sheep and the bedding from a hut on the station. One of Bowman's shepherds claimed that the Aborigines had been very troublesome lately, and Bowman's overseer told William Lonsdale, the Police Magistrate in Melbourne, that the killing of Jones had provoked a great deal of fear among his men. In response, the pastoralists' men went out looking for the Aboriginal attackers but they failed to find them. Shortly afterwards, Lonsdale sent a party of the Mounted Police to patrol the area, instructing them to show themselves there for a short time in order to reassure the pastoralists and their men and to alarm the Aborigines.[7]

In the second week of June about twenty Aborigines attacked an outstation on Yaldwyn's run. They raided a hut and took away all the food. More significantly, after setting dogs on two flocks of sheep

6 Melbourne Court Register, 21 April 1838, *Historical Records of Victoria*, vol. 2A, Victorian Government Printing Office, Melbourne, 1982, p. 335; Parker to Robinson, 5 January 1843, New South Wales Legislative Council, *Votes and Proceedings*, 1843, Return to an Address, Dr Thomson, 29 August 1843, p. 60.

7 Deposition of Samuel Faloon, 28 May 1838, New South Wales State Records, NRS 905, Item 4/2423.3; William Lonsdale to Edward Deas Thomson, 3 June 1838, *Historical Records of Victoria*, vol. 2A, p. 336; Parker to Robinson, 5 January 1843, p. 60.

and pursuing their shepherds, they took the sheep, killed several, maimed many more, and rounded up the rest and secured them by making a bough or brush yard in the same manner that a white shepherd would. On learning that the flocks of sheep had been run off Yaldwyn's run, his superintendent, John Coppock, assembled and armed three men and set off in search for the sheep and the attackers. They were soon joined by four or five of Bowman's men. This party followed the tracks of the Aboriginal attackers and as dusk began to fall they found a camp where the Aborigines had corralled some of the sheep. One member of the white party seems to have fired a shot, apparently in the hope that this would scare the Aborigines. But the Aboriginal men immediately dared the white party to approach, shouting: "'Come on you white buggers" or "Come on white fellows"'.[8]

We cannot be sure what happened next.[9] Nearly three weeks later, Coppock gave a sworn deposition to the following effect. A pitched battle had ensued. The Aboriginal men, fortifying themselves behind fallen trees and sheets of bark, threw spear after spear, and the white party repeatedly fired. (One of this party would later inform Parker

---

8   Deposition of John Coppock, 29 June 1838, New South Wales State Records, NRS 905, Item 4/2423.3; Lonsdale to Thomson, 2 July 1838, New South Wales State Records, NRS 905, Item 4/2423.3; Deposition of Samuel Fuller, 7 July 1838, New South Wales State Records, NRS 905, Item 4/2423.3; Deposition of John Pittman, 7 July 1838, New South Wales State Records, NRS 905, Item 4/2423.3.

9   Ian Clark claims that a further massacre occurred in Djadja Wurrung country at much the same time as this incident, noting that James Dredge, the assistant protector for the Goulburn district, later reported that at a station near Mount Macedon, which was near Mount Alexander, he had been told by Thomas B. Alexander that Aboriginal people had taken away a flock of between 800 and 900 sheep from his master's station, Darlington, and seemed to suggest that a party of his men had caught up with them and shot thirteen dead (James Dredge to George Augustus Robinson, 23 July 1839, *Historical Records of Victoria*, vol. 2B, p. 674; Clark, *Scars in the Landscape*, p. 89). However, there seems to be no other evidence for this incident, and one should note that Clark's account, the place at which these killings are supposed to have occurred, and the estimated death toll are strikingly similar to the details for the incident in June 1838 that is being considered here.

that they had expended upwards of 90 rounds of cartridge.) The battle lasted for three quarters of an hour before the Aborigines beat a retreat and took some of the sheep. It was quite dark by this time and the settlers' men were afraid to pursue the Aborigines and so they returned to their stations. The following morning they went back to the camp to find the bodies of seven or eight Aboriginal men who they had killed in the conflict. The next day they returned again to discover that these bodies had been put on a fire but had only been partly consumed.[10]

It appears that Coppock and his fellow white men were less than candid in the accounts they gave of this incident in the depositions they swore in June and July 1838. A year later, Parker was told that they had slaughtered the Aborigines in great numbers. Furthermore, in January 1840 George Augustus Robinson visited the area and met a shepherd on a pastoral station now owned by Henry Monro, and it seems that this man took him to a place on a small hill where there was a deserted hut and a few hurdles and gave him an account of the killings, after which Robinson wrote in his journal:

> At the back of this hut on a small hill is the place where Bowman and Yaldwyn and Ebden's men shot the blacks down … [The shepherd said] when the men came up with the blacks, the blacks called to them to come on and they would fight them. There were, I believe, 16 white men all armed and for the most part mounted. They fired from their horses; the blacks were down in the hollow. They were out of distance of their spears. One old man kept supplying them with spears and was soon shot. Great many were shot. Some other blacks held up pieces

---

10 Deposition of Coppock, 29 June 1838; Ian D. Clark (ed.), *The Journals of George Augustus Robinson, Chief Protector, Port Phillip Aboriginal Protectorate, vol. 1, 1 January 1839 – 30 September 1840*, Heritage Matters, Melbourne, 1998, entry 25 January 1840, p. 139.

of bark to keep off the balls but it was no use. Some were shot dead with their bark in their hands.

The shepherd does not seem to have told Robinson how many Aborigines he believed had been killed but he might have told Parker, who had accompanied Robinson on this journey. At any rate, in a return Parker later made of the inter-racial killings in his district, he stated that about fourteen Aboriginal men had been killed in this incident.[11]

At much the same time as these killings took place, those responsible for the notorious massacre of twenty-eight men, women and children at Myall Creek on the Liverpool Plains in northern New South Wales sought to disguise their crime by burning the bodies of their victims. Subsequently, later that year, seven of those men were eventually found guilty, sentenced to death, and hung. This made frontiersmen very careful in their words if not their deeds. In January 1840 Robinson asked a shepherd whether he had been present at the shooting of Aborigines at Bowman and Yaldwyn's and was told: "what if I was, do you think I should be such a fool to tell you, to be hung?" The probability that a large number of Aboriginal men were killed on this occasion is lent further weight by the fact that the place of these killings quickly became known as Waterloo Plains or Waterloo Creek, named after the famous Battle of Waterloo. Such naming by white settlers was common on the frontiers of settlement in Australia.[12]

---

11 Parker to Robinson, 20 June 1839; Clark (ed.), *Journals of Robinson*, entry 18 January 1840, pp. 129–30; Parker to Robinson, 5 January 1843, p. 60.

12 Clark (ed.), *Journals of Robinson*, entries 17 January 1840 and 25 January 1840, pp. 128, 139. For accounts of the Myall Creek Massacre and the two trials, see R.H.W. Reece, *Aborigines and Colonists: Aborigines and Colonial Society in New South Wales in the 1830s and 1840s*, Sydney University Press, Sydney, 1974, pp. 34–42 and 145–66; Brian Harrison, 'The Myall Creek Massacre', in Isabel McBryde (ed.),

On learning of these deaths Lonsdale had sent a party of mounted police to gather depositions from some of the whites involved but he seems to have been reluctant to take any further action. He merely sent the depositions to the Colonial Secretary, Edward Deas Thomson, and asked for instructions. At the same time Lonsdale expressed the opinion that the Aboriginal people who had made the attacks on Bowman and Yaldwyn's stations were also responsible for a massacre on the Broken River (near present-day Benalla) on 11 April 1838 in which eight shepherds belonging to a party overlanding sheep for George and William Faithfull had lost their lives. For his part Coppock declared that he had been surprised by the attacks on Bowman and Yaldwyn's since there had been no intimate relations between the two parties and he was unfamiliar with those who were responsible for carrying them out.[13]

In the aftermath of the incident of June 1838 a party of the Mounted Police was stationed in the area, camping on Yaldwyn's Barford run. But, despite the provision of this protection to the pastoralists, it appears that Bowman felt it necessary to shoot every Aboriginal man, woman, and child whom he met on his run, or so his neighbour Yaldwyn (who was a magistrate) claimed in speaking to Parker a year later. Bowman soon gave up his run and left the district, perhaps

Records of Times Past, Australian Institute of Aboriginal Studies, Canberra, 1978; *Push From the Bush*, special issue, no. 20, 1985; and Roger Milliss, *Waterloo Creek: The Australia Day Massacre of 1838, George Gipps and the British Conquest of New South Wales*, McPhee Gribble, Melbourne, 1992, chapters 10, 17 and 18. There may well have been other killings for which no contemporary historical sources are available but in which cases the sites have been remembered in local folklore as sites of massacres. For a discussion of this phenomenon see for example David Roberts, 'Bells Falls Massacre and Bathurst's History of Violence: Local Tradition and Australian Historiography', *Australian Historical Studies*, vol. 26, no. 105, 1995, pp. 615–33, and Robert Foster et al., *Fatal Collisions: The South Australian Frontier and the Violence of Memory*, Wakefield Press, Adelaide, 2001.
13 Deposition of Coppock, 29 June 1838; Lonsdale to Thomson, 2 July 1838.

because he was apprehensive that he might be prosecuted for some bloody deed or another he had committed.[14]

In the next incident to occur, in the later months of 1838, it seems that Aborigines attacked three shepherds on a station called Smeaton Hill, badly wounding one of them. John Hepburn, who had established this station in April that year and recalled this incident fifteen years later, laid much of the blame for this attack upon his men or rather a man by the name of Knight. Knight was actually one of Bowman's men and probably a convict, and he had been amongst the Aboriginal people for several days prior to this attack. (The fact that he was later killed by Aborigines seems to confirm Hepburn's opinion that he was a troublemaker.) Yet, however critical Hepburn was of this man, he asserted that Knight had done him a good turn by making the Djadja Wurrung believe that he would kill them all. Moreover, he also recalled that he preferred to keep Aboriginal people at a distance and had himself called on his own men on several occasions to drive Aboriginal people off his run.[15]

In March 1839 two Djadja Wurrung men, one of whom was called Noorowurnin, were killed by two convict shepherds, John Davis and Abraham Brackbrook (or Braybrook), at their hut on a station called Maiden Hills, which was owned by a Sydney-based businessman Henry Boucher Bowerman, and managed by a man by the name of William Allen. The shepherds' hut was especially

---

14 Parker, Report to Robinson, 20 June 1839; Deas Thomson to Robinson, 17 July 1839, *Historical Records of Victoria*, Vol 2B, p. 672; George Brunswick Smyth to Brigade Major, 31 July 1838, summarised by Randell, *Pastoral Settlement in Northern Victoria*, Vol. 1, p. 36; Parker, Report to Robinson for 1 September 1839 – 29 February 1840, Public Record Office Victoria, VPRS 4410, Unit 2.

15 John Hepburn to La Trobe, 10 August 1853, in Bride, *Letters from Victorian Pioneers*, pp. 69, 91, 73–74, 76–77; Victoria Legislative Council, *Votes and Proceedings*, 1858–59, Report of the Select Committee on Aborigines, p. 87.

remote and lay on the junction of a creek that ran through a small plain bounded on two sides by wood-covered hills. The shepherds consequently felt vulnerable to attack by Aborigines and had been keen to forge a peaceable relationship with them. But it seems that they also wanted to have sexual relations with the Djadja Wurrung women. On two successive days prior to the killing, Djadja Wurrung men had come to the outstation and told Davis and Brackbrook that they would return shortly and bring their women kin. But Allen had ordered Davis and Brackbrook to tell him as soon as the Aborigines came near. On the following day he learned that one of the Djadja Wurrung men had been observing the outstation and so he went to the outstation, cautioned Davis and Brackbrook to be on their guard, and set off in search of the Djadja Wurrung party. He found a group of women several miles away coming towards the outstation. Allen told them they were not to come near the station. Perhaps this angered the Djadja Wurrung men. Shortly afterwards, a party of Djadja Wurrung men and women came to the outstation. It seems that the Djadja Wurrung wanted to offer the two shepherds sexual relations as a way of forging a relationship and that they expected Davis and Brackbrook to reciprocate. Moreover, it appears that sexual relations did take place that day but that there was a misunderstanding about the conditions of this arrangement.[16]

Reading between the lines of the depositions given after the event, this is how the events might have unfolded. Davis and Brackbrook both had sex with two of the Djadja Wurrung women; a Djadja

---

16 Pleas and Statements by John Davis and Abraham Brackbrook, 9 April 1839, *Historical Records of Victoria*, vol. 7, Melbourne University Press, Melbourne, 1998, pp. 310–12; Evidence of William Oliver, 10 April 1839, *Historical Records of Victoria*, vol. 7, p. 312; Deposition of William Allen, 8 April 1839, *Historical Records of Victoria*, vol. 7, p. 313–14.

Wurrung man took some of Brackbrook's clothes or more particularly his trousers from a watch-box outside his tent; Brackbrook called out to Davis in his tent twenty yards away to stop his clothes being taken; Davis tried to leave his tent to come to Brackbrook's aid but was pushed back by one of the Djadja Wurrung men; Davis himself now called out for help but on Brackbrook arriving there he was struck on the forehead and held by the same Djadja Wurrung man; Brackbrook panicked and called upon Davis to fire; Davis shot the Djadja Wurrung man dead, Brackbrook picked up his own gun, and both men rushed out of Davis' tent and shot dead a second Djadja Wurrung man. Whatever actually happened, we know that the following morning Allen returned to the hut with Davis and Brackbrook and ordered them to make a fire and burn the bodies of the two Djadja Wurrung men they had slain.[17]

This done, Allen rode to Melbourne to make a report to Lonsdale in which he claimed that the station had been attacked by Aborigines attempting to steal blankets and flour, and that in the affray Davis and Brackbrook had shot two of them dead. Allen was instructed by Lonsdale to tell Robinson what had happened, but he decided to make no further report about the matter in the hope that the killings might be concealed. However, Allen actually proceeded to tell several people of the clash during the following week, and Lonsdale heard that six or even eight Aborigines had been shot rather than two. Robinson got wind of this and ordered two of his assistant protectors, Charles Sievwright and Edward Parker, to investigate (since Maiden Hills lay near the boundary between the two areas to which they had been

---

17 *Ibid.*; Reverend Joseph Orton Papers 1825–1842 Mitchell Library, MS A 1715, Journal, entry 12 January 1841, summarising a report of Charles Sievwright dated 17 April 1839; Clark (ed.), *Journals of Robinson*, entry 2 March 1840, p. 192; Parker to Robinson, 5 January 1843, p. 60.

assigned responsibility). Sievwright journeyed to Maiden Hills to undertake the investigation. Davis and Brackbrook made no attempt to conceal the killings and confessed, and Sievwright took them into custody and charged them with murder. Sievwright claimed that the convicts employed at Bowerman's station all spoke of Aboriginal people in a most appalling manner. On Allen's hut at Maiden Bills as well as a hut on a nearby station the assistant protector had seen skulls placed over the doorways. He surmised they were those of Aboriginal people and had been put there 'to warn the lawful owners of the land at their peril to approach'.[18]

In May 1839 a further incident occurred on the run on the Campaspe River formerly owned by Bowman but now owned by Charles Hutton. A shepherd, Hugh Bryan, and a hut keeper, James Neill, were killed by a party of the neighbouring Daung Wurrung nation at a hut on Hutton's outermost station. Perhaps this was in retaliation for the killing of five Aboriginal people in the neighbourhood three weeks earlier by three white men. Bryan was brutally murdered, his skull fractured by a blow from a tomahawk, a spear forced into his body above the left shoulder, and the fingers on one hand cut off. At

---

18 Robinson to Sievwright, 1 April 1839, Documents Collected by Sir William Dixson regarding Aboriginal Australians in Victoria 1 April 1839 – 8 January 1850, Dixson Library, State Library of New South Wales, MS DLADD 86; Sievwright to Robinson, 2 April 1839, Documents Collected by Sir William Dixson regarding Aboriginal Australians in Victoria 1 April 1839 – 8 January 1850, Dixson Library, State Library of New South Wales, MS DLADD 86; Sievwright, Minute of Journeys Made, March–August 1839, Documents Collected by Sir William Dixson regarding Aboriginal Australians in Victoria 1 April 1839 – 8 January 1850, Dixson Library, State Library of New South Wales, MS DLADD 86; Clark (ed.), Journals of Robinson, entry 15 April 1839, p. 29; Sievwright to Robinson, 17 April 1839, Historical Records of Victoria, vol. 7, pp. 308–09; William Thomas, Journal, April 1839, Historical Records of Victoria, Vol 2B, p. 520; *Port Phillip Gazette*, 14 August 1838; Orton summary of Sievwright Report of 17 April 1839; *Port Phillip Gazette*, 21 September 1839; Clark (ed.), Journals of Robinson, entry 2 March 1840, p. 193; Lindsey Arkley, *The Hated Protector: The Story of Charles Wightman Sievwright, Protector of Aborigines 1839–42*, Orbit Press, Melbourne, 2000, pp. 25–26.

the same time the Daung Wurrung robbed the men's hut of all of its food, blankets, clothes, arms and ammunition, and ran a flock of 730 sheep off the property. On learning this, Hutton immediately set off with three of his men to try and recover the sheep. According to the accounts that he gave Lonsdale and Parker shortly afterwards, this party followed the tracks of the Aborigines and the sheep for up to 15 miles before they succeeded in coming upon a camp. But the Daung Wurrung eluded them by plunging into the deep bed of the Campaspe River. According to Hutton's account, he and his men recovered nearly all of his flock and part of the property that had been stolen, and destroyed all of the Daung Wurrung's property they had found in the camp.[19]

But is this all that happened?[20] More than a decade later a fellow pastoralist, William Thomas Mollison, told the Superintendent of the Port Phillip District, Charles Joseph La Trobe, that there was a local oral tradition about one and perhaps even two bloody encounters between Hutton's men and the Daung Wurrung. There seems to be little doubt that Hutton had a frame of mind that suggests that he could have been responsible for massacring Aboriginal people. In June 1839 Parker told Robinson: '[Hutton] frankly avowed that had he been able to get near them, he would have taken summary vengeance by their indiscriminate slaughter'; in August that year the assistant protector for the Melbourne and Westernport districts, William

---

19 Charles Hutton to Lonsdale, 6 June 1839, Public Record Office Victoria, VPRS 4, Unit 7; Deposition of James Cosgrove, 13 June 1839, *Historical Records of Victoria*, vol. 7, p. 323.

20 One can readily confuse, as I did in *'My Country': A History of the Djadja Wurrung 1837–1864*, Monash Publications in History, Melbourne, 1999, p. 9, this pursuit of Aborigines by Hutton with another pursuit a month later in which he also played a role, not least because Hutton himself conflated the two events in a deposition he gave in January 1840 (Deposition of Charles Hutton, 8 January 1840, New South Wales State Records, NRS 905, Item 4/2511).

Thomas, observed that Hutton had told him: 'if I [i.e. Thomas] would go in search of [the blacks] with the intent to exterminate them that he would undertake to say that he could get 30 at least of men in the surrounding district who would willingly volunteer in the service'; and in January 1840 Robinson noted two conversations he had with Hutton, in the second of which the pastoralist had 'assert[ed] as his firm opinion that the only way to govern the blacks was by fear and that no good would be done with them until they [were] served as the Murray blacks [were], one half destroyed'.[21]

More than a decade later, perhaps knowing of the oral tradition that connected his name to the massacre of Aboriginal people on his property, Hutton would strenuously deny that he had ever been involved in any wrongdoing. He wrote to La Trobe: 'as Your Excellency is about to leave the colony, and I may not have another opportunity, it is a satisfaction to myself to solemnly assure you that I never shot or otherwise destroyed one of them. I never even fired on one'. At the very least, Hutton's claim that the greater part of the Aborigines he and his men had pursued had 'suddenly disappeared' afterwards and died of influenza suggests a marked desire to deny or disavow any responsibility for what might have happened.[22]

---

21 Parker to Robinson, 18 June 1839, *Historical Records of Victoria*, vol. 7, p. 321; William Thomas Papers, Mitchell Library, State Library of New South Wales, uncatalogued mss, set 214, Item 9, Journal, entry 6 August 1839; Thomas to Robinson, 12 August 1839, *Historical Records of Victoria*, vol. 7, p. 341; Robinson to Edward Deas Thomson, 13 August 1839, *Historical Records of Victoria*, vol. 2B, p. 675; Clark (ed.), *Journals of Robinson*, entries 24 January 1840 and 29 January 1840, pp. 138, 146; Parker to Robinson, 5 January 1843, p. 60.

22 Hutton to La Trobe, 19 August 1853, in Bride, *Letters from Victorian Pioneers*, pp. 248–49; William Thomas Mollison to La Trobe, 22 August 1853, in Bride, *Letters from Victorian Pioneers*, p. 257. For a discussion of the phenomenon of disavowal, see my 'Denial in a Settler Society: The Australian Case', *History Workshop Journal*, no. 84, 2017 forthcoming.

Parker was instructed by Robinson to investigate these killings on Hutton's run and in the middle of June 1839 he reported that he had found Hutton's men greatly excited and avowing enormous hostility against all the Aborigines in the area, that Hutton had forcibly driven all of them away from his neighbourhood, and that some of Hutton's men were expressing their determination to shoot any Aboriginal man, woman or child they came across. Not surprisingly, the assistant protector was deeply concerned. He ordered a corporal and three members of the border police to move from their station near Yaldwyn's to Hutton's run and remain there until further measures could be taken by the Protectorate. In fact Yaldwyn had already ordered five members of the border police to move, but Hutton reckoned they were of no use as they lacked horses, and he had called for the better armed mounted police to come to protect his station.[23]

Shortly after this, the Commandant of the Mounted Police, George Brunswick Smyth, directed a party of his men under Sergeant Dennis Leary's command to go to Hutton's station and do what they could to *disperse* the Aborigines who were responsible for the attacks. *Disperse* was a term that was commonly understood to mean shooting Aborigines. As the historian Tom Griffiths has pointed out, this euphemism was part of a widely understood linguistic code in the Australian colonies that simultaneously pointed to and away from the violence settlers perpetrated on the frontiers of settlement. This kind of language was regarded by settlers, and more especially perhaps the officers of police and military forces, as necessary because the government had forbidden the use of force against Aboriginal

---

23 William Yaldwyn to Lonsdale, 29 May 1839, *Historical Records of Victoria*, vol. 2B, pp. 669, 672; Deposition of George Brunswick Smyth, 6 January 1840, New South Wales State Records, NRS 905, Item 4/2511; Parker, Report to Robinson, 20 June 1839.

people and so they were aware that their violent deeds could not be discussed openly. Yet, in this case, Smyth actually authorised Leary and his men to fire upon the Aborigines.[24]

On 21 or 22 June Leary and a party of five mounted police arrived at Hutton's run and shortly afterwards went out in search of Aborigines. They were guided – and no doubt urged on – by Hutton and his overseer, James Cosgrove. It was now four or more weeks since Bryan and Neill had been murdered and this party had to ride some distance before they encountered any Aboriginal people. But, after three or four days riding, they found a group of Djadja Wurrung who were camped near a creek on Campaspe Plains, perhaps 60 miles riding from the head station on Hutton's property.[25] In the depositions that four of this party were to give six months later, there was considerable disagreement about what happened next. The Djadja Wurrung might have thrown spears but almost certainly the mounted police (despite a later claim to the contrary by its commanding officer) charged without any warning and began firing on them. The Djadja Wurrung started to run away as fast as they could but the mounted police shot six of them dead and wounded several more.[26]

---

24 Smyth to Dennis Leary, 21 June 1839, included in Deposition of Smyth, 6 January 1840; Henry Reynolds, 'The Written Record', in Bain Attwood and S.G. Foster (eds), *Frontier Violence: The Australian Experience*, National Museum of Australia, Canberra, 2003, p. 84; Tom Griffiths, 'The Language of Conflict', in Attwood and Foster (eds), *Frontier Violence*, pp. 138–39; Tony Roberts, *Frontier Justice: A History of the Gulf Country to 1900*, University of Queensland Press, St Lucia, 2005, pp. 26, 57–58; Jonathan Richards, *The Secret War*, University of Queensland Press, St Lucia, 2008, pp. 77–78; Robert Foster, '"Don't Mention the War": Frontier Violence and the Language of Concealment', *History Australia*, vol. 6, no. 3, 2009, p. 68.2.

25 The members of the mounted police who gave depositions several months later provided conflicting information about both the time and distance they had ridden.

26 Deposition of Dennis Leary, 6 January 1840, Deposition of Edward Beach, 6 January 1840, Deposition of Hutton, 8 January 1840, and Deposition of James Cosgrove, 24

In the wake of this killing there were considerable rumours about how many were in fact killed. 'I am not at all satisfied about that affair of the six blacks being shot', Thomas told Robinson in July 1839, adding: 'tho' not enjoined in your letter of instructions to enquire into that affair, very much mystery surrounds it. I understand a letter was forwarded to Melbourne, that the police was sent down, with regular instructions, I think I know who wrote the letter [i.e. Hutton] tho' he wished not to say too much on the subject'. Later in the year Parker reported that the overseer of a neighbouring station had been told by someone that as many as forty Djadja Wurrung had been killed, but upon being asked by La Trobe to name his source of information (who was Cosgrove) and indicate why he regarded it as trustworthy, Parker faltered: on the one hand he declared that he was inclined to rely on this information since it was in the interests of the settlers and in fact their usual course to conceal these matters and that he saw no reason why the informant had any reason to exaggerate the number killed; but on the other hand he admitted that he did not regard Cosgrove as someone whose word could be trusted.[27] Parker would eventually report that Djadja Wurrung had informed him that six of their people had been killed in this incident. In the light of this testimony and the fact that guns were often unreliable and slow to reload, this is probably the correct death toll.[28]

January 1840, New South Wales State Records, NRS 905, Item 4/2511.

27 In October 1840 Parker would assert that it was Hutton who had stated privately that nearly 40 had been killed, forgetting that he had told by an overseer of a station neighbouring Hutton's that it was Cosgrove who had made this statement (Parker, Report to Robinson, 5 October 1840, New South Wales State Records, NRS 905, Item 4/2511).

28 Thomas to Robinson, 23 July 1839, *Historical Records of Victoria*, vol. 7, p. 333; Parker to Robinson, 5 November 1839, Public Record Office Victoria, VPRS 13172, Unit 1; Parker to Robinson, 13 December 1839, *Historical Records of Victoria*, vol. 7, pp. 361–62; La Trobe to Robinson, 31 December 1839, *Historical Records of Victoria*,

Robinson was outraged when he learned of these killings. 'Why were these Aborigines selected on whom to make an attack?' he asked. 'There was no proof that they were the guilty party, but on the contrary every probability that they were at least innocent at least of that outrage.' Parker agreed. He also insisted that it was illegal to fire on Aborigines in the manner that the mounted police had. Even Leary was apparently of the opinion that the attack was unwarranted. By contrast Hutton tried to claim that he had good reason to believe that the Aboriginal people whom the mounted police party murdered were those responsible since they had found them near the same place that he had recovered his sheep a month earlier.[29]

In another incident in July 1839 Aborigines harassed a shepherd and took a flock of over 600 sheep and several goods from an outstation on Sylvester Brown's Darlington run. In learning of this incident, Brown's overseer William Cox got a party together and went in search of the Aborigines to recover the sheep and the goods. Fellow pastoralist Alexander Mollison noted in his diary that the party came upon Aborigines at night as they were roasting several of the sheep, that they fled, and that Cox's men recovered the rest of the flock and all the goods. It is possible that Cox's party might have killed some of the Djadja Wurrung on this occasion but there is no contemporary historical record that reveals what happened. A local

---

vol. 2B, pp. 678–79; Parker, Report to Robinson, 5 October 1840. On the nature of gun technology, see David Denholm, *The Colonial Australians*, Penguin, Ringwood, 1979, Chapter 3, and Richard Broome, 'The Struggle for Australia: Aboriginal–European Warfare, 1770–1930', in Michael McKernan and Margaret Browne (eds), *Australia: Two Centuries of War and Peace*, Australian War Memorial/Allen & Unwin, Canberra/Sydney, 1988.

29 Robinson to La Trobe, 15 November 1839, Documents Collected by Sir William Dixson regarding Aboriginal Australians in Victoria 1 April 1839 – 8 January 1850, Dixson Library, State Library of New South Wales, MS DLADD 89; Deposition of Hutton, 8 January 1840; Parker, Report to Robinson, 5 October 1840.

historian, J.O. Randell, noted in the early 1980s that there was an oral tradition in the area that Aborigines were killed there and that their bodies were thrown into a waterhole.[30]

A day or so after this clash, Aborigines tried to run off a flock of sheep from one of Henry Monro's stations, which adjoined Darlington and stretched along both sides of the Coliban River and up the tributary creeks to Mount Alexander. Monro, his overseer Charles Christie and several of their men rode out in search of those responsible. They were unsuccessful but on their return they encountered a large party of Aboriginal men near the head station on the Campaspe Plains. Monro charged but his horse was speared and he was thrown from the saddle and speared. One of Monro's men charged in order to rescue his master and the two galloped away. The Aborigines pursued the party but Monro's men at the head station fired at them and they broke off. Several days later, some Aborigines speared a hut keeper, killed a dog, and robbed a hut of all that it contained at one of the outstations on Charles Ebden's Carlsruhe run. The hut keeper was unhurt and shot one of the Aborigines. He reported this incident but on going to investigate all that Mollison could find was their tracks, which suggested that the hut keeper had only wounded the man. Robinson directed Thomas to investigate this spate of attacks by Aborigines. The assistant protector concluded that attacks had been made on all the stations beyond Ebden's except for Yaldwyn's and was concerned that the settlers or their men would mount reprisals. 'I am extremely sorry also to report that the men at the various stations seem bent on revenge, some of their fellow

---

30 Alexander Fullerton Mollison, Station Day Book, Royal Historical Society of Victoria, MS 2506, Box 1, Item 2, entries 11 July 1839 and 12 July 1839; Randell, *Pastoral Settlement*, vol. 1, p. 134; Randell, *Pastoral Settlement*, vol. 2, p. 77.

servants being killed, their cry is that there is no satisfaction', he wrote. 'I am convinced no black could safely be seen near any of the stations where outrages have been committed', he added. Thomas returned to this point at the end of his report to Robinson: 'I have been able to discover among the men that the first black that appears near any of the stations where outrages have been committed will have no mercy'.[31]

The next several months seem to have been free of clashes between Aboriginal people and the settlers but in November 1839 there was a further incident on one of Monro's runs on the Campaspe Plains. A shepherd decided to move his flock after discovering a small party of Djadja Wurrung fishing in the Coliban River, but he became fearful once they began to follow him and fired at them several times, though apparently without injuring anybody. Parker, who was called to investigate, concluded that the Djadja Wurrung had expressed no hostile intentions and could readily have overtaken the shepherd and seized possession of his flock if they had wanted to do so. A few days later Monro reported one of his cows had been speared, claimed that one of his bullocks was missing, and blamed Aborigines for both these incidents. Parker was also told that some attacks had been made by Aborigines on a nearby run but he found this statement to be untrue.[32]

---

31 *Port Phillip Patriot*, 22 July 1839; Thomas to Robinson, 23 July 1839, *Historical Records of Victoria*, vol. 7, pp. 332–33; Thomas to Robinson, 12 August 1839, *Historical Records of Victoria*, vol. 7, p. 341; Clark (ed.), *Journals of Robinson*, entry 18 January 1840, p. 130; James Mouat, in T.W.H. Leavitt and W.D. Lilburn, *Jubilee History of Victoria and Melbourne*, vol. 2, Part V, Duffus Bros, Melbourne, 1888, p. 5.

32 Parker to Robinson, 3 December 1839, Public Record Office Victoria, VPRS 13172, Unit 1.

The Monro incidents

During a ten day period in mid to late January 1840 there were further clashes on one of the stations owned by Monro. I will recount these events at some length for two reasons.[33] Most of what happened during those ten days was, as the historian Marie Fels has suggested, typical as far as relations between Aborigines and Europeans on the frontiers of settlement go. Second, there is an extraordinarily rich historical record pertaining to this incident. This is a result of the fact that both Parker and Robinson were there, having been sent by La Trobe to investigate the killings that had occurred near Hutton's station eight months earlier. Robinson kept his journal as he always did, and Parker took numerous depositions (from pastoralists, their men, and the members of the border and mounted police) and made a report shortly afterwards.[34]

The month before this incident occurred, Monro had sent two flocks of sheep to two of Bowman's former outstations – the Twelve Mile Station and another one two miles beyond this (which was the third of Monro's outstations and so will be called here Hut No. 3) – which were the most remote outstations in the area. There was a drought and Monro felt he needed more feed for his sheep. A shepherd by the name of Archibald McCormick and a watchman cum hutkeeper, William Russell, went to the former station, while a watchman, James Howley, and a shepherd, John Preston, moved to the latter. On the evening of

---

33 The following account owes a great deal to Marie Fels, 'The Collision at Monro's Station', in Nicholas Clark (ed.), Aboriginal History and Archaeology in Djadja Wurrung Country (Central Victoria) Examining Mount Kooyoora, Mount Alexander and Mount Tarrengower, a report for the Bendigo Dja Dja Wrung Aboriginal Association, 2nd draft, March 1995, pp. 72–74, but Fels, as she acknowledges, was unable to trace all of the relevant depositions that have since been discovered in the New South Wales Records Office.

34 Fels, 'The Collision', p. 72.

17 January McCormick and Russell told the following story to Parker. On the afternoon of the previous day Russell had gone to the head station and McCormick was feeding his flock near the outstation hut at the Twelve Mile Station when he saw six Aboriginal men approaching. But one of Monro's junior overseers, Islay Liston, and a boy, cantered up on horses and the Aboriginal men ran off. At 9 or 10 o'clock the following morning, shortly after Russell returned, several Djadja Wurrung, including the headman Munangabum, came to the hut, and more arrived shortly afterwards until thirty of them gathered around it. Some crowded inside, took some meat and flour, knocked a cap off Russell's head, and pushed him and McCormick into a corner of the hut and held them there while the rest drove off a flock of 1500 sheep towards Mount Alexander. They were clearly aggressive but they did not strike the two men. As soon as they had gone McCormick and Russell walked back to the head station to report the incident. On learning of it, Monro armed his senior overseer, John Christie, Liston and two of their men and despatched them on horses to pursue the Djadja Wurrung and search for the missing flock. But the following morning Robinson and Parker met Christie as he was returning to Monro's head station and learned that his party had found one part of the flock near McCormick and Russell's hut and the rest nearby in the opposite direction to which McCormick and Russell claimed the Aborigines had driven off the flock. Christie told Robinson that Aborigines had not taken the sheep but that McCormick had left the flock and slept and that wild dogs had rushed the sheep and maimed some. It seems that McCormick and Russell had not been altogether truthful in the story they had told.[35]

---

35 Depositions of Archibald McCormick and William Russell, 17 January 1840, New South Wales Records Office, NRS 905, Item 4/2510; Clark (ed.), *Journals of Robinson*,

On the morning of 19 January Christie fell in with a party of Djadja Wurrung and they accompanied him to the Twelve Mile Station where they met Robinson and Parker. Robinson and some of this party had met before and they recognised each other. They embraced Robinson and said they were no longer frightened but that they had been when they met Christie and Liston an hour earlier. They denied taking any sheep and asserted that the shepherds were simply frightened and the sheep had run away. They offered to show Christie where they were. Liston and Parker tried to find these sheep but were unsuccessful. On their return Robinson told Christie that he should give this party some food so that he could send them away. Both Robinson and this party set off together. On the way they sang 'Hura Hura my boys, it's time for us to go. Bonny Highland Lassie', which they had apparently learned from McCormick, who was Scottish. Robinson suggested they go to the outstation nearest Monro's head station, the Five Mile Station, and encamp, but only five chose to do so. On the way there Christie told Robinson that Liston had that morning twice raised his gun to fire at the Djadja Wurrung but that he had called on him to stop. Robinson told Christie that Liston would have been put on trial for murder if he had shot any of the Aborigines.[36]

The following morning Robinson told Christie he wanted to buy some sheep to give to the Djadja Wurrung to eat. Christie doubted his master would be willing to agree. Robinson told him that Monro would have to pay for the consequences if he refused. Parker and his servant and three Djadja Wurrung men went to hunt kangaroo so

---

entries 17 and 18 January 1840, pp. 128–30; Parker to Robinson, 4 February 1840, Public Record Office Victoria, VPRS 11, Unit 4.

36 Clark (ed.), *Journals of Robinson*, entry 19 January 1840, p. 131; Parker to Robinson, 4 February 1840.

that the Djadja Wurrung had some meat to eat but they returned in the evening empty handed. It seems Robinson had promised they would get some sheep and that they were angry that there was none. They called on Robinson to try the shepherd James Howley and send him to gaol for refusing to give them any sheep. The white man's stock was destroying their traditional food and they expected to be given what they demanded. At the same time the Djadja Wurrung men sought to engage the whites in a kinship relationship by offering Djadja Wurrung women as sexual partners. Christie agreed to kill one sheep and this was distributed to the Djadja Wurrung but there was not enough to go around. This annoyed them. Throughout the day Robinson found this party of Djadja Wurrung very demanding. Probably more bemused than amused, he wrote in his journal: 'One wanted me to take off my shirt for him, another my trousers, another my shoes, indeed every article I had on. And so pressing that I scarcely knew whether I was to be left in a state of nudity or not'. The following morning the Djadja Wurrung told Robinson they were very hungry. 'It is astonishing the quantity of food they eat', he remarked. 'They were eating all day yesterday, and wanted still.'[37]

On the morning of 21 January Howley and Preston let their flock of sheep out of the fold at Hut No. 3 so they could graze. Shortly afterwards a party of seven Daung Wurrung men, whom they had never seen before, came out of the nearby mountains and asked for bread. In early January a Daung Wurrung party had raided Charles Ebden's Carlsruhe station and William Mollison's station near Malmsbury. They had been driven off by the border police and had now moved north. Howley and Preston gave them all the bread they

---

37 Clark (ed.), *Journals of Robinson*, entries 20 and 21 January 1840, pp. 132–33; Parker to Robinson, 4 February 1840.

had and tried to persuade them to leave but they refused. Shortly afterwards, a party of Djadja Wurrung men and women and a boy, whom Howley and Preston had seen two days earlier, arrived and sat down apart from the Daung Wurrung. The Daung Wurrung men asked for sheep and insisted they would not leave until they had some as they were very hungry. Howley told them that Parker and Robinson would come and give them food. There seems to have been a standoff for an hour and a half, during which time Preston went in search of Parker and Robinson and the Djadja Wurrung left though not before they told Howley that the Daung Wurrung were wild blackfellows and no good.[38]

At noon three Djadja Wurrung returned and one of them, Bootoogun, whom Howley knew as Jimmy, went to Howley and whispered: 'You brother belong me, bael you give it me musket – wild blackfellow tell me take it – must belonging to you – that wild blackfellow spear him you – you yabber plenty ball belonging to you'. In other words he told him to hold onto his gun as the Daung Wurrung would kill him and that he should threaten them. Howley took the hint and shouted that he had plenty of ball, that is cartridge. The Daung Wurrung reacted by seizing their clubs and calling again on Howley to give them sheep. Howley moved towards them but they seized hold of him, pulled up his clothes and felt his stomach and legs, suggested he would make good eating, and stripped him naked. Bootoogun intervened and restored Howley's clothes to him. (Howley thought Bootoogun had saved his life.) The Daung Wurrung now went to the sheep and each started to take one away.

---

38 Depositions of James Howley, John Preston, and Alfred Bridges, 22 January 1840, New South Wales Records Office, NRS 905, Item 4/2510; Clark (ed.), *Journals of Robinson*, entry 23 January 1840, p. 136.

Howley begged them to stop but they replied angrily 'spear him you' before leaving with two sheep.[39]

During this time the rest of the Djadja Wurrung had returned but they took no part in harassing Howley. At some point after Preston had returned, one of the Daung Wurrung men, whom he called Jacky Jacky, issued a threat to his master: 'White fellow matter (master) no good, plenty spear him' and put his hands together to suggest they would tie Monro up. After the Daung Wurrung had left, the Djadja Wurrung once more told Howley that they were wild blackfellows and no good. Shortly afterwards, the Daung Wurrung visited the Five Mile Station outstation and asked one of Monro's servants, Alfred Bridges, for sheep. Bridges tried to appease them but Jacky Jacky angrily told him: 'Master belonging to blackfellow give it jumbuk [sheep] boraik master belonging to jumbuk give it, white man no good'. The Daung Wurrung proceeded to rush the sheep, taking one or two and scattering the rest.[40]

On the evening of 22 January Robinson and Parker arrived at Monro's head station and found that Monro had sent some of his men out to the two furthest outstations to bring in the flocks and the hurdles to the Five Mile Station. Monro was incensed by what the Aborigines had done and had sent Christie to Melbourne to demand the protection of the mounted police. Parker sent a note to the border police at a crossing place of the Campaspe River on the Barfold run and wrote to the Commissioner of Crown Lands, Henry Fysche Gisborne (who oversaw the border police), to request his immediate intervention in order to apprehend the Aboriginal attackers, and that evening or the following one a corporal, James Hughes, and

39 Depositions of Howley, Preston, and Bridges, 22 January 1840.
40 *Ibid.*

two privates arrived. On the morning of 23 January Russell arrived at Monro's head station from his hut on Twelve Mile Station and told of how he had been bailed up two days earlier by Aborigines, and Howley and Preston arrived shortly afterwards from Hut No. 3 and related a similar story of what had happened there. Monro became increasingly agitated, complaining that the Aborigines had threatened his men and had vowed to seize and tie him up. Surely, he argued, the case was now so alarming that the protectors would render him some assistance. Two days later, La Trobe directed Smyth to dispatch a contingent of the mounted police to Monro's station and co-operate with Parker in taking measures to ensure peace in the area and prevent any further aggression or retaliation.[41]

Twenty-three and 24 January seem to have passed uneventfully but on 25 January the men that Monro had sent off in the company of Hughes and one of his men to Twelve Mile Station and Hut No. 3 to collect hurdles and move them to the Five Mile Station were overtaken by a party of Daung Wurrung who demanded to know where 'pickanniny lubra sat down' in the dray they were pulling. It seems that the Daung Wurrung thought that Monro's men might have abducted some Aboriginal women and were hiding them in the dray. Hughes told the Daung Wurrung that they could inspect the dray if they put down their spears. After inspecting it, they withdrew. Half an hour after the dray arrived at the Five Mile Station a shepherd reported that he had seen four Aborigines hiding nearby in the trees, which panicked the station. Russell was despatched to the head

---

41 Clark (ed.), *Journals of Robinson*, entries 22 and 23 January 1840, pp. 135–36; Parker to Henry Fysche Gisborne, 22 January 1840, New South Wales Records Office, NRS 905, Item 4/2510; Henry Monro to I. Hurd, 23 January 1840, *Historical Records of Victoria*, vol. 2B, pp. 684–85; La Trobe to Smyth, 25 January 1840, New South Wales Records Office, NRS 905, Item 4/2510; Parker to Robinson, 4 February 1840; Extract of Monro letter, 4 February 1840, *Port Phillip Herald*, 7 February 1840.

station to tell Monro that he had to send more men and arms or the sheep would be destroyed by the Aborigines.[42]

On the morning of 26 January Monro and Liston and three of their men made ready to leave the head station for Five Mile Station. It appears that Monro either sent a message to Hutton to ask him to send some of his men or that Hutton and some of his men came over to offer their help. Robinson was unwell but Parker seems to have realised that Monro had armed his men and that consequently he should go to the Five Mile Station. He set off before Monro and his men had finished their preparations. At the Five Mile Station that morning a party of a dozen or so Djadja Wurrung had come up to the hut and requested food. Hughes had asked them to put down their spears, and they had approached and sat down in front of the hut. Hughes had given them bread and ordered them repeatedly to go away and pointed out to them why his party of border police was there, but they refused to leave. Half an hour or so passed. Then, Monro's party galloped up. Monro called out to Djadja Wurrung party to stand, Liston fired over their heads, the Djadja Wurrung started to run, and one of the border police opened fire. Monro's party had overtaken Parker shortly before they reached the station but he heard the shooting, galloped up and ordered the police to stop firing and instead capture one of the Djadja Wurrung, who turned out to be Munangabum. As this was occurring, one of the border police pursued the rest of the Djadja Wurrung party and fired at them. It seems that he wounded several and at least one badly as they tried to escape across the Coliban Creek. One of Hutton's men was there and rescued one of the Djadja Wurrung men from drowning but he had

---

42 Clark (ed.), *Journals of Robinson*, entry 26 January 1840, p. 140; Parker to Robinson, 4 February 1840; Randell, *Pastoral Settlement*, vol. 1, pp. 143–44.

been mortally wounded and died that evening in agony. Hughes had given his men no orders to fire but they had done so nonetheless.[43]

After this incident Monro got together a larger party of men, which comprised some of his and Hutton's men and three mounted police, to pursue the Djadja Wurrung who had fled up the Coliban Creek. Before they rode off Monro promised Parker that the party would not fire on any Aborigines except in self-defence. They soon came across a group of ten or so Djadja Wurrung women who tried to flee. One of the party raised his gun to shoot a woman and her child but she cried out and Munro called on his man to lower his gun. Monro allowed this group to go and the party rode on to a Djadja Wurrung encampment seven miles from Twelve Mile Station. They found it had been deserted, though only recently. They then turned back. However, near the Twelve Mile Station they met a party of twelve Djadja Wurrung. Monro later claimed that they had tried to capture this party but that the Aborigines had presented too bold a front, that they had got behind trees and taunted them in broken English, that he had ordered his party not to fire but that one of the Djadja Wurrung had thrown a boomerang which narrowly missed one of the mounted police and that his party had consequently opened fire as they retreated. But this story seems to have been concocted. Certainly Robinson thought so. Whatever the case, Monro's party shot one young man dead and wounded several more, probably severely.[44]

---

43 Clark (ed.), *Journals of Robinson*, entries 26 January 1840, 27 January 1840, 28 January 1840 and 29 January 1840, pp. 140, 142, 145–46; Deposition of Ferrier Liston, 28 January 1840, New South Wales State Records, NRS 905, Item 4/2510; Deposition of James Hughes, 29 January 1840, New South Wales State Records, NRS 905, Item 4/2510; Parker to Robinson, 4 February 1840; Deposition of Parker, 4 February 1840, New South Wales State Records, NRS 905, Item 4/2510.

44 Monro to Frederick Brunswick Russell, 26 January 1840, *Historical Records of Victoria*, vol. 2B, p. 686; Clark (ed.), *Journals of Robinson*, entries 26, 27 and 29 January 1840, pp. 140–41, 143, 146; Deposition of Monro, 28 January 1840, New South

CHAPTER 2: CONFLICT

On the evening of 26 January the commandant of the mounted police contingent, Frederick Brunswick Russell, and four of his men arrived at Monro's. The following day this party as well as Robinson, Parker and Monro and some of his men all rode out together. It was only in the course of the morning that Robinson and Parker learned of the second episode of shooting that had occurred the previous day. Robinson was adamant that no further means be used against the Aborigines. As they rode, Monro, Russell, Robinson and Parker clashed angrily over what had happened. Monro sought to prejudice Russell's mind against the Aborigines and told Robinson that he had made a mistake in giving the Djadja Wurrung presents because this had emboldened them as they had assumed that he had done this out of fear. Russell seems to have agreed. He told Robinson that the Aborigines should be taught a lesson and that it was out of the question that station owners were to be disturbed by such wretches. He also suggested that Robinson had failed to act properly the previous day by failing to swear Monro's party as constables.[45] Robinson rejected these allegations. Indeed, he took umbrage. 'I said I would not yield my opinion to any man as to how the Australian blacks should be

---

Wales State Records, NRS 905, Item 4/2510; Russell to La Trobe, 30 January 1840, *Historical Records of Victoria*, vol. 2B, pp. 687–88; Parker to Robinson, 4 February 1840; Deposition of Parker, 4 February 1840, New South Wales State Records, NRS 905, Item 4/2510; Parker, Report for 1 September 1839 – 29 February 1840, *Historical Records of Victoria*, vol. 2B, p. 691.

45 It has been argued that Robinson could and should have prevented these killings, but one might doubt that his presence would have made any difference to a party of men filled with a murderous spirit. Robinson's biographer Vivienne Rae-Ellis has damned Robinson for what she regards as his cowardly behavior. However, so eager is Rae-Ellis to beat up her subject that she has Robinson refusing to accompany the armed party (*Black Robinson: Protector of Aborigines*, Melbourne University Press, Melbourne, 1988, pp. 203–05) when in fact his journal reveals that while he did express reluctance to join such a party at first he later reflected on the matter and resolved that he should go, and we know that he did (Clark [ed.], *Journals of Robinson*, entry 27 January 1840, pp. 140–41).

treated', he wrote in his journal that night. 'I had had eleven years of experience and knew what should be done, and what the blacks could do.' Robinson demanded to know why Russell had not issued warrants to apprehend the men responsible for the killings. For his part Parker stated that he would be making strong representations on the case. Monro said he did not care what Parker did, and claimed that Robinson had encouraged the Aborigines to steal sheep and had actually received them with open arms for having done so.[46]

On reaching the Five Mile Hut Robinson found Munangabum. His hands and legs were tied, and his arms pinioned. He told Robinson that he and his party had not stolen any sheep but that the Daung Wurrung were responsible and that they were no good. Parker learned that the previous day Monro had stood over Munangabum after he had been arrested, stamped his feet, gnashed his teeth, and told him he was a perfect savage towards Aborigines. The party next rode on to the place where the second killing had occurred. By this time both Monro and Russell had decided they had better try to appease Robinson and Parker. Monro apologised to Parker, and Russell suggested to Robinson that they could draw up a report jointly once they had returned to Melbourne. On reaching the place of the second shooting they found the body of the young man who had been killed. Russell suggested they could throw it in the creek, but Robinson insisted that he be buried. The Chief Protector seems to have been deeply pained by this killing. He wrote in his journal that evening:

> The circumstances attending this melancholy event led to deep and painful reflection. I thought of the right of these people, the right of the soil. I thought of the barbarity of my country,

46 Clark (ed.), *Journals of Robinson*, entry 27 January 1840, pp. 140–42.

that for a few scabby sheep two valuable lives (valuable no doubt to their tribe, and valuable to the God who called them into being). I thought of his helpless wife and offspring, of the deep lamentations among their tribe, at their bitter indignation against the white, and unrelenting persecution and oppression.[47]

After the young man's body had been interred, Monro and his men and Russell and his troopers got ready to return to the head station. Hughes' border policemen took the rope off Munangabum and handcuffed him. He struggled in protest and complained. It seems he was terrified. Some of the men in this party had been tormenting him by telling him that he would be shot or hung. On the way to the home station Robinson told Russell once more that enough had been done and that he would not agree to any further proceedings. Russell objected that the Aborigines responsible for the attacks on Monro's sheep had yet to be apprehended. Robinson seems to have lost his temper. Two lives had been taken, others had been wounded and one had been taken a prisoner. Was not this punishment enough, especially compared to the loss of a few scabby sheep? Besides, if those such as Monro wanted to expose their property by sending their sheep miles away when they had abundant feed nearer home they had to abide by the consequences. '[T]en individuals had the whole country, Mr Monro upwards of 100 square miles', he complained in his journal.

One more incident was to occur before the day was done. On the way to the home station Munangabum jumped off the back of the horse on which he was being carried and despite being handcuffed he seized hold of Parker's servant and pressed the muzzle of his musket

---

47 *Ibid.*, entry 27 January 1840, pp. 143–44.

against his body. He was about to cock it when one of Monro's men intervened and proceeded to beat him.[48]

That evening Russell went to Robinson's tent and tried to persuade him that he should not try to prosecute any of those responsible for the shootings but instead set the matter aside for a while, suggested that it would be best not to tell the story straight, and argued that Robinson and Parker should feel for the whites as well as the blacks. Robinson was unmoved, though he did call for the border police to be stationed permanently at or near Mount Alexander. The following day Parker took depositions, and several days later submitted a detailed report.[49]

Further conflict

In July 1840 more blood was again shed on the run known as Campaspie Plains, though it was now held by Daniel Jennings and George Playne rather than Hutton. In the last week of June two parties of Aborigines had visited two of its outstations but were driven away by Jennings, Playne and their overseer. One of the Aborigines shouted at Playne that he believed that the whites 'wanted to shoot blackfellows'. Three days later, a small party visited one of the outstations and was once more forced away. In early July a further party of Aborigines, who were Daung Wurrung, appeared. Several days later they approached a hut and asked the hut keeper for food. He gave them some damper and ordered them away. Sometime

---

48 Deposition of Daniel Jones, 26 January 1840, New South Wales Records Office, NRS 905, Item 4/2510; Clark (ed.), *Journals of Robinson*, entry 27 January 1840, pp. 143–44.

49 Clark (ed.), *Journals of Robinson*, entries 27 and 28 January 1840, pp 144–45; Robinson to La Trobe, 27 January 1840, New South Wales Records Office, NRS 905, Item 4/2510; Parker to Robinson, 4 February 1840.

later that day they attacked and killed one of the shepherds on this run, Alexander Mackenzie, took his gun, clothes and food, and tried to drive a flock of sheep across the Campaspe River. Jennings and Playne and their men rode out in pursuit of the attackers but failed to find them. Robinson later heard that one of Jennings' men had made war on the Aborigines, bragged of his prowess, and fired on them, and that Jennings was of the opinion that the Aborigines had consequently decided to kill this man. The same Aborigines might have been responsible for further attacks on Monro's station around this time but the fact that those responsible only took food rather than blankets, guns or other such commodities in two of the raids suggests that they were carried out by the Djadja Wurrung who were simply in need of food.[50]

In August a Djadja Wurrung man by the name of Pandarragoondeet (or Pandeloondic) seems to have been wantonly shot down by one of the assigned convict servants of Henry Dutton, William Darlot, and Don Simson, at Far or Fourteen Mile Creek (later Glenmona) on the Bet Bet Creek. It appears that the convict had enticed Pandarragoodeet to come to him only to shoot him dead once he was within shooting range. The killer absconded from the station shortly afterwards. The following month Daung Wurrung resumed their attacks. On 3 September they attacked one of the stations of the Learmonth brothers, which they called Black Hill,

---

50 Daniel Jennings to La Trobe, 21 July 1840, Public Record Office Victoria, VPRS 11, Unit 4; Frederick Armand Powlett to La Trobe, 30 July 1840, Public Record Office Victoria, VPRS 19, Unit 3; Deposition of Charles Bramley, no date [October 1840], Public Record Office Victoria, VPRS 11, Unit 4; Parker to Robinson, 2 October 1840, Public Record Office Victoria, VPRS 11, Unit 4; Powlett to La Trobe, 17 October 1840, New South Wales Records Office, NRS 905, Item 4/2511; Ian D. Clark (ed.), *Journals of George Augustus Robinson, Chief Protector, vol. 2, 1 October 1840 – 31 August 1841*, Heritage Matters, Melbourne, 1998, entry 24 October 1840, p. 20.

and forced them to move the flocks away from it. Earlier in the year one of their overseers had told Robinson that Aborigines had not troubled their runs since Allen had given them a lesson at Maiden Hills in March the previous year and he apparently exulted in what Allen and his men had done. After the attack in early September the Learmonth brothers spent a day searching for those responsible but could not find them.[51]

Later in September it appears that some Aborigines stole blankets and clothes from the hut of one of Mollison's hutkeepers. Shortly afterwards, a party of the Daung Wurrung harassed two men, James Rogers and Thomas Wheeler, on Lachlan MacKinnon's Tarrengower Station. A group of about thirty men and boys approached Rogers and Wheeler's tent and asked for damper. Rogers and Wheeler obliged but the Daung Wurrung proceeded to demand tea. They got this and made themselves a pot. Next they asked for flour. Wheeler told them that they could have some once a dray of supplies arrived, and asked one of the Daung Wurrung men to allow him to look at one of the several guns they were carrying. The man refused and Wheeler went into the tent to get his gun and to load it. A scuffle ensued as one of the Daung Wurrung seized Rogers but after Wheeler raised his gun the Daung Wurrung started to run. Rogers and Wheeler gathered up their belongings, got their sheep together, and started to drive them towards the head station. The Daung Wurrung followed, calling out, and fired at them three times. Rogers and Wheeler threw away their possessions in order to be able to move the sheep faster and

---

51 Clark (ed.), *Journals of Robinson*, vol. 1, entry 2 March 1840, p. 193; Ercildoun Homestead, 1830–1860, Thomas and Somerville Learmonth Station Diary 1839–43, La Trobe Library, State Library of Victoria, MS Box 102/9, entries for 3 and 4 September 1840; Parker, Quarterly Report, 1 December 1840 – 28 February 1841; Parker to Robinson, 5 January 1843, p. 60.

finally reached the safety provided by the head station. The Daung
Wurrung seized the men's possessions, which included clothes and
an axe. At some point in this month Aborigines also committed a
further robbery, on James Campbell's Bullarook Run on the Loddon
River.[52]

At this time, according to an oral tradition recounted by a local
historian, Edgar Morrison, a group of Jardwadjali murdered a former
convict who was the cook on the Glengower, a station which adjoined
Smeaton Hill on the north. The leaseholder, Lachlan McLachlan, is
remembered as a hard and ruthless exploiter of men and it is believed
that he led an armed party who overtook the murderers on the banks
of a creek several miles to the west and killed them as they sought
shelter in a large waterhole there. The place consequently came to be
known as The Blood-Hole.[53]

In February 1841 another incident occurred on Far or Fourteen
Mile Creek. It seems that four of the men on this run owned by
Dutton, Darlot and Simson had been sent to one of its outstations
to pursue Daung Wurrung after a Djadja Wurrung man had warned
that the Daung Wurrung were going to attack the station. Once there
they asked two Djadja Wurrung men, the headman Munangabum
and Gondu-urmin, if they knew where the Daung Wurrung were,
accused the former of sending them away, and told him they were
going to shoot him. Munangabum clasped one of the shepherds round

52 Deposition of Kenneth MacKenzie, 22 September 1840, Public Record Office
   Victoria, VPRS 11, Unit 4; Clark (ed.), *Journals of Robinson*, vol. 1, entry 29
   September 1840, p. 375; Deposition of James Rogers, 24 September 1840, and
   Deposition of Thomas Wheeler, 24 September 1840, Public Record Office
   Victoria, VPRS 11, Unit 4; Parker to Robinson, 25 September 1840, Public Record
   Office Victoria, VPRS 11, Unit 4; Clark (ed.), *Journals of Robinson*, vol. 2, entry
   25 December 1840, p. 45.
53 Edgar Morrison, *Frontier Life in the Loddon Protectorate: Episodes from Early Days,
   1837–42*, Advocate, Daylesford, 1967, pp. 12–13.

his neck and tried to get hold of his pistol. At the same time a party of Daung Wurrung men started to move towards the outstation. The overseer, Edward Collins, told Munangabum to let go of Morrison and threatened to shot him. Munangabum yelled repeatedly: 'Don't shoot, Neddy Neddy'. He finally let go but grabbed for Collins' gun. Collins fired on both Munangabum and Gondu-urmin, wounding the former and fatally wounding the latter, who died in the course of the following day. One of Dutton and co.'s men would later claim that shots had only been fired after the Daung Wurrung had launched spears at them, and another claimed that one of the shepherds fired at Munangabum and Gondu-urmin in self-defence. These shootings angered the Djadja Wurrung, and Munangabum and Gondu-urmin's kinsmen seem to have decided that they would try to revenge Gondu-urmin's death. At the end of March they murdered a hut keeper of Ebenezer Oliphant on the Mount Greenock (or Dunach Forest) run that had only recently been formed on the Loddon River. They had attacked him as he came up to his hut after shifting hurdles, and took all his provisions, clothing and gun.[54]

In the middle of April 1841 there was a further incident. Daung Wurrung mounted an attack on a station known as Mount Alexander, spearing the owner Richard Grice and his two shepherds, killing a horse, and driving off a large number of sheep, nearly all of which were soon recovered by Grice's men. One of the Port Phillip newspapers

---

54 Parker, Quarterly Reports, 1 December 1840 – 28 February 1841 and 1 June – 31
    August 1841, Public Record Office Victoria, VPRS 4410, Unit 2; Deposition of
    Patrick Clark, 8 February 1841, Depositions of William Martin, John Remington,
    William Jenkins, Joseph Maddox, Robert Morrison, and Edward Collins, 9 February
    1841, and Deposition of Henry Darlot, 12 February 1841, Public Record Office
    Victoria, VPRS 30, Unit 185, NCR 8; Parker to James Croke, 30 March 1841, Public
    Record Office Victoria, VPRS 21, Unit 1, Bundle 3; Parker to Robinson, 5 January
    1843, p. 60.

that was sympathetic to pastoralists claimed that Aborigines had committed further depredations in the neighbourhood and that consequently the country for miles around was in a state of alarm.

One of Grice's neighbours, Robert Pohlman, a co-owner of Glenhope which was formerly the northern part of Sylvester Brown's Darlington Station and the site of one of the possible massacres discussed earlier, called on Superintendent La Trobe a day after he heard of the attack in order to discuss what he called the troubled state of the country in the area. La Trobe showed him Parker's reports but these did not satisfy Pohlman. He complained in his diary: 'I [did not] hear anything of any effect being done hitherto for our protection but I was reminded, as before, that in advancing beyond the bounds of location, we estranged ourselves voluntarily from the protection of government and took upon ourselves a state of responsibility as well as risk'. Pohlman took umbrage at this. 'Yet I am edged in by settlers, purchased the station, have a government license, and I could not help quoting Blackstone that allegiance and protection were correlative terms and that government were bound to protect us'. Pohlman was a lawyer, and Sir William Blackstone's *Commentaries on the Laws of England* was an influential treatise on the English common law whose arguments about property were often quoted by settlers in intra-British debates about rights in land in the Australian colonies.[55]

At the end of April a small group of the Daung Wurrung men made an attack on a hut at Eighteen Mile Creek on Henry Bennett's Barnedown run, which had previously been held by Hutton.

55 Parker to La Trobe, 30 April 1841, Deposition of Richard Grice, undated, Public Record Office Victoria, VPRS 10, Unit 3; *Port Phillip Herald*, 30 April 1841; Robert William Pohlman Diaries, Royal Historical Society of Victoria, MS 000026, Box 12, Item 1, entries 29 and 30 April 1841; Wilfrid Prest, 'Antipodean Blackstone', in Prest (ed.), *Reinterpreting Blackstone's Commentaries: A Seminal Text in National and International Contexts*, Hart Publishing, Oxford, 2014.

Apparently they had been in and around the run for a month and had speared several sheep. On this occasion at least six Daung Wurrung men approached a shepherd, an assigned convict known as Long John Slattery. He ran, they pursued him, he fired at them, and they caught up with him and brutally murdered him, spearing him several times, slashing his head and knocking out one of his eyes. They also drove off more than 650 sheep. Thomas Thorneloe, four mounted policeman and several of Bennett's men went in search of the sheep. They found one of the Daung Wurrung men, who had a wound that seems to have been caused by Slattery's gunfire. He was arrested and sent to Melbourne to be charged.[56]

The district, if not the neighbouring regions, was quiet until January 1842 when a small group of Daung Wurrung robbed an outstation on Mollison's run. Two months later, a pastoralist by the name of Alexander Moffat Allan was killed on his run, which lay on the Loddon River between Languycorrie Station and Catto's Run. His killers were once more believed to be foreigners to the area. This proved to be the last Aboriginal killing of a white man on this frontier.[57]

---

56 *Port Phillip Herald*, 4 May 1841, 11 May 1841; Thomas Thorneloe to La Trobe, 5 May 1841, Public Record Office Victoria, VPRS 19, Unit 14; Randell, *Pastoral Settlement*, vol. 2, pp. 302, 414.

57 Parker, Quarterly Journal, 1 December 1841 – 28 February 1842, Public Record Office Victoria, VPRS 4410, Unit 2; Deposition of William Henry Allan, 17 March 1842, Powlett to La Trobe, 4 April 1842, La Trobe to Deas Thomson, 4 April 1842 and 21 June 1842, New South Wales Records Office, NRS 905, Item 4/2589B; Parker, Quarterly Report, 1 March – 31 May 1842, Public Record Office Victoria, VPRS 4410, Unit 2; Parker to Robinson, 5 January 1843, p. 60.

Chapter 3

FRONTIER

In the preceding chapter we saw that there was considerable conflict between the European newcomers and Aboriginal people in Djadja Wurrung country. In this chapter I will seek to account for that conflict. To begin, I will consider how historians have tended to explain conflict on the frontiers of settlement in Australia more generally. But before I do this, a word or two about the term *frontier* is in order. In Australian historiography this term has been especially ubiquitous and yet few if any of the historians who have used it over several decades, such as Henry Reynolds, have ever said what they mean by it. To my mind a frontier in a colonial context is best regarded as a place of encounter between groups of people of different societies and cultures in which there is no overarching source of power and authority. This is to say that it is a situation in which no one group, whether it be, for example, pastoralists, missionaries, protectors, or Aborigines, has sufficient power to be able to compel the members of the other groups to submit to their authority, and that as a consequence the resort to the use of naked force is common. A frontier can be said to close at the point that one or more of those parties has been successful in exerting their authority.[1]

---

1   I have drawn here on a recent discussion by Elizabeth Elbourne, 'Exploration, Conquest and the African "Frontier"', in *Frontier, Settlement & Borderland Encounters*, <www.amdigital.co.uk>, 2016, and especially her reference to the way that a fellow historian of South Africa, Herman Giliomee, defined frontier.

Many historians, including Michael Christie, the author of one of the first academic studies to investigate relations between Aborigines and Europeans in the Port Phillip District, have argued that a factor of primary importance in frontier conflict was the nature of the pastoralists. As these men set out to seize land they not only brought with them stock, tools and food but ideas, attitudes and experience that shaped how they regarded the new country and its indigenous people. As Angela Woollacott has shown recently, a good number of those who became settlers in the eastern Australian colonies in the early to mid nineteenth century had previously spent time in other places in the British empire, including North America, the West Indies and India.[2] More specifically, a significant number of the settlers had served in the British Army in India and elsewhere. It seems fair to assume, argues Woollacott, that these men had not only formed a particular understanding of racial hierarchies and systems of labour but that their participation in wars and their administration of enslaved peoples made them willing to countenance the seizure of the Aboriginal people's land and the use of the brute force that was necessary to wrest it from them. Some of the earliest pastoralists in Djadja Wurrung country had served in the British army or the British East India Company.[3]

A further consideration is the fact that pastoral settlement had been in progress in the Australian colonies for more than two decades by the time the invasion of the Port Phillip District began. Consequently, many of the pastoralists had already come into contact

---

2   This argument can be said to have been anticipated by A.T. Yarwood and M.J. Knowling. See their *Race Relations in Australia: A History*, Methuen Australia, Melbourne, 1982, pp. 19–20.

3   M.F. Christie, *Aborigines in Colonial Victoria 1835–86*, Sydney University Press, Sydney, 1979, p. 36; Angela Woollacott, *Settler Society in the Australian Colonies: Self-Government and Imperial Culture*, Oxford University Press, Oxford, 2015, chapter 1.

and even conflict with Aboriginal people and had developed firm opinions about how they should be treated. For instance, Thomas and Somerville Learmonth were determined to keep the Djadja Wurrung out and refused to allow them to enter their home station or their outstations. Moreover, some pastoralists had probably become hardened by the conditions of the frontier. George Augustus Robinson certainly believed that this was the case. 'It is a fact and deeply to be regretted', he remarked in his journal, 'that men, settlers, [who] go in to the wilds of Australia natural humans, at length become cruel'. He gave Charles Hutton as an example.[4]

The nature of the men that the pastoralists employed was undoubtedly an important factor in the violence that was wrought by whites on the frontiers of settlement. There were a great many workers on the pastoral frontier because pastoralism, and especially the grazing of sheep, demanded a good deal of labour. A flock of sheep (between 500 and 1000) usually required not only a shepherd and a hutkeeper but overseers, bullock drivers, carpenters and so forth. In the Loddon District the large pastoral runs employed between 20 and 50 men. Most of these men were ticket-of-leave holders, assigned convict servants, or freed convicts from New South Wales or Van Diemen's Land. Many of them were vicious and they treated Aboriginal people cruelly.[5]

4　Ian D. Clark (ed.), *The Journals of George Augustus Robinson, Chief Protector, Port Phillip Aboriginal Protectorate, vol. 1, 1 January 1839 – 30 September 1840*, Heritage Matters, Melbourne, 1998, entry 23 January 1840, p. 136; Clark (ed.), *Journals of George Augustus Robinson, Chief Protector, vol. 2, 1 October 1840 – 31 August 1841*, Heritage Matters, Melbourne, 1998, entry 7 August 1841, p. 371.

5　Edward Parker to George Augustus Robinson, 20 June 1839, New South Wales State Records, Series NRS 905, Item 4/2510; Charles Joseph La Trobe to Edward Deas Thomson, 12 February 1840, New South Wales State Records, Series NRS 905, Item 4/2510; M.B. and C.B. Schedvin, 'The Nomadic Tribes of Urban Britain: A Prelude to Botany Bay', *Historical Studies*, vol. 18, no. 71, 1978, pp. 260, 266, 275; A.G.L. Shaw, *A History of the Port Phillip District: Victoria Before Separation*, Miegunyah Press, Melbourne, 1996, pp. 93, 107, 136.

In addition to the nature of the pastoral labour force, the character of the police forces must be considered. The mounted police, which was formed in 1825 in order to bring order to the frontier, was recruited from regiments of the British army stationed in the colonies, and there is some evidence to suggest that it often made attacks on Aboriginal people. But even more problematic was the border police, a corps of mounted police that was established in 1839 for the purpose of preventing the aggression that was increasingly occurring in the absence of legal control on the frontiers of settlement. Their conditions of service were very poor: they got no pay and had no uniforms, though they did receive full rations. Moreover, the calibre of those who joined was the worst of the colonial police forces. The force was made up of prisoners of the Crown and their conduct was often poor. There are in fact many reports of the border police committing outrages against the Aboriginal people whom they were supposed to protect. As we saw in the last chapter, the Djadja Wurrung were among those who suffered at their hands. This said, it must be emphasised that the violence committed by whites on this frontier, as indeed on most frontiers in Australia, was by no means a monopoly of the state. Instead, it was mostly carried out by individual pastoralists and their men who had often struck out beyond the limits of settlement allowed by government.[6]

Scientific ideas about race might have played a role in the brutal attacks that pastoralists, their men and the police forces made on the Djadja Wurrung. Historians such as Henry Reynolds have argued that such ideas were widely disseminated in the Australian colonies in the 1830s and 1840s, that is, at the very time the Port

---

6   Robert Haldane, *The People's Force: A History of the Victorian Police*, Melbourne
     University Press, Melbourne, 1986, pp. 5, 16–17; Woollacott, *Settler Society*, p. 158.

Phillip District was being colonised. But what was probably more important was a deeply rooted settler conviction that they belonged to a superior race. Indeed, one senses that settlers were often violent towards Aboriginal people simply because they wanted or needed to demonstrate this claim of superiority. This claim was also expressed in the form of a belief that Aboriginal people were savages. Charles Ebden, one of the pastoralists in the Loddon District, seems to have regarded the Djadja Wurrung in this way, calling them 'those incorrigible and damned blacks'. Many settlers, in accordance with this view of Aboriginal people as savages, held that Aboriginal people had not worked the land and so had not acquired rights of property in it, which meant they could claim that the country had no owners and was therefore free to be taken. Charles Hutton, for example, asserted that 'it was never intended that a few miserable savages were to have this fine country'. Hutton's choice of words suggests that he held that this was the design of God. If this is so, he was by no means alone in citing this source of authority in order to excuse his thieving.[7]

These views of Aboriginal people and their rights were a major factor shaping relations between settlers and Aborigines on any frontier. They served to exacerbate tensions between members of the two groups and were used by frontiersmen to justify the harsh treatment they often meted out to the Aboriginal people. There seems to be little doubt that this was true of at least some of the pastoralists and their men in the Loddon District. One pastoralist, who had been appointed by the government as a magistrate, told Edward

---

7   Charles Ebden to James Donnithorne, 4 February 1839, reproduced in J.O. Randell, *Pastoral Settlement in Northern Victoria*, vol. 1, Queensberry Press, Melbourne, 1979, p. 50; Clark (ed.), *Journals of Robinson*, vol. 1, entry 25 January 1840, p. 139; Henry Reynolds, 'Racial Thought in Early Colonial Australia', *Australian Journal of Politics and History*, vol. 20, no. 1, 1974, pp. 45–53.

Parker soon after the assistant protector had arrived in the district that 'one half of the Aboriginal population must be shot, before we could subdue and keep in order the other half'. The pastoralists if not all their employees were certainly equipped to do this, as they were nearly always armed to the teeth. Robinson remarked in his journal in March 1840 as he journeyed through Djadja Wurrung country: 'I cannot conceive of what use so many loaded firearms are kept in these huts except to destroy blacks'.[8]

A further cause of the violence committed by white men on the frontiers of settlement sprang from the fact that few of the pastoralists and their men were accompanied by white women, which was a function of the nature of a pastoral economy since it tended to require the labour of men rather than that of families of men, women and children. Sexual relations between white men and Aboriginal women were a common feature of frontiers in the Australian colonies. Djadja Wurrung country was no exception. Generally speaking, Aboriginal people sought to incorporate the newcomers into their society by encouraging sexual unions in the expectation or the hope that the whites would become kinsmen and learn to behave as kin. But very few white men grasped that their acceptance of an offer of a sexual relationship with an Aboriginal woman meant that they had incurred obligations to the woman's kin, and when they failed to meet those obligations Aboriginal men were often angered and took punitive action. Furthermore, in many instances white men just kidnapped Aboriginal women and raped them.

8   Clark, *Journals of Robinson*, vol. 1, entries 17 January 1840 and 2 March 1840, pp. 128, 193; New South Wales Legislative Council, *Votes and Proceedings*, 1845, Report from the Select Committee on the Condition of Aborigines, p. 54; John Hepburn to Charles Joseph La Trobe, 10 August 1853, in Thomas Francis Bride, *Letters from Victorian Pioneers* (1898), Heinemann, Melbourne, 1969, pp. 71, 76.

There is considerable evidence that sexual relations between white men and Aboriginal women were a major cause of misunderstanding and friction in the Loddon District. For example, William Mollison assumed that the sexual relations taking place on his run occurred because the Djadja Wurrung women were being offered to his men for a very trifling sum, which is to say that he misconstrued these offers as a form of prostitution. Yet there were pastoralists in the district who were cognisant of the consequences of sexual relations between their men and Djadja Wurrung women and so tried to intercede. For example, when John Hepburn discovered that his men were having sexual relations with Djadja Wurrung women he tried to discourage the Djadja Wurrung from visiting his run and, when he learned that his men were holding the women contrary to his orders, he complained to Parker, who used his authority as a magistrate to fine them. The assistant protector was in no doubt that there would be less conflict if all the settlers adopted Hepburn's practice since he was acutely aware of the outrage that white men's sexual abuse of Aboriginal women provoked among Aboriginal people. In 1842 Parker claimed that nine out of ten attacks committed by Aborigines on whites could be traced to inter-racial sexual relations. He also believed that, while the labouring classes were the worst offenders, those who claimed the rank of gentlemen and even aspired to be administrators of the law were guilty of abusing Aboriginal women.[9]

---

9   Parker to Robinson, 20 June 1839; Clark, *Journals of Robinson*, vol. 1, entry 25 January 1840, p. 139; Edward Parker, Quarterly Journal, 1 December 1840 – 28 February 1841, Public Record Office Victoria, VPRS 4410, Unit 2; Parker, Quarterly Report, 1 March – 31 May 1842, Public Record Office Victoria, VPRS 4410, Unit 2; Parker to George Augustus Robinson, 18 December 1844, Public Record Office Victoria, VPRS 11, Unit 5; Parker, Answers to Questionnaire, n.d. (probably the 1845 New South Wales Select Committee on Aborigines), Public Record Office Victoria, VPRS 4410, Unit 2; La Trobe to Robinson, 19 August 1848, Public Record Office Victoria, VPRS 10, Unit 9; Hepburn to La Trobe, 10 August 1853, in Bride, *Letters*

A further cause of the attacks that settlers made on Aboriginal people on the frontiers of settlement was fear. Pastoralists and especially their men felt especially vulnerable as a consequence of their being in an unfamiliar environment and in the company of strangers whom they regarded as savages and to whom they attributed enormous capacity for cunning and treachery. As the historian Richard N. Price has reminded us recently, '[violence] is triggered when power is threatened or when it is believed to be threatened'. Pastoralists on the Australian frontier *expected* to be powerful, and they became anxious and fearful when they sensed or realised that they were not. This mental state could readily provoke pastoralists to be trigger happy, especially when they or their men had been injured or lives had been lost. This was evidently the case with those such as Henry Monro.[10]

An important reason for conflict between Aborigines and Europeans on the pastoral frontier, it has been argued, lay in the incompatibility between very different economic systems. Pastoralism typically requires large expanses of land, but this was especially true in the Australian case due to the arid nature of much of the continent. The pastoralists' cattle and sheep consumed the pastures on which native game fed, and they destroyed the yams and murnong roots that served as a staple in the Aboriginal people's diet. At the

from Victorian Pioneers, p. 78; Charles Hutton to La Trobe, 19 August 1853, in Bride, *Letters from Victorian Pioneers*, p. 248; William Mollison to La Trobe, 22 August 1853, in Bride, *Letters from Victorian Pioneers*, p. 258.

10 Parker to Robinson, 3 December 1839, *Historical Records of Victoria*, vol. 2B, Victorian Government Printing Office, Melbourne, 1983, p. 683; Clark, *Journals of Robinson*, vol. 1, entries 18 January 1840 and 3 March 1840, pp. 129, 195; Lieutenant F.B. Russell to La Trobe, 30 January 1840, Public Record Office Victoria, VPRS 19, Unit 3; Richard A. Price, 'The Colonial Frontier in Nineteenth-Century History and Beyond', in *Frontier, Settlement & Borderland Encounters*, <www.amdigital.co.uk>, 2016.

same time, the pastoralists' stock and Aboriginal people competed for water as well as the food sources that rivers and creeks could sustain, such as fish, eels and ducks. In regard to the Port Phillip District Christie concluded: 'Wherever the white man went, the native game was eaten out by sheep or shot for sport. Deprived of their former food sources, the Aborigines starved, moved into the more remote territory of neighbouring and possibly hostile tribes, or obtained food in some way or other from the whites'.[11]

Christie probably overstates the degree of incompatibility between a herding and a hunting and gathering economy but his point is well taken. Perhaps a more important factor lay in the pastoralists' determination to deny Aboriginal people access to their customary food sources. Parker observed in regard to the Loddon District: 'in many cases they [the Aborigines] are thus excluded from their favourite haunts and most suitable places of encampment. The game is extensively hunted by the white population, and, though not exterminated, is acknowledged by all to be greatly diminished. The *murnong*, their chief vegetable subsistence, is cropped off by the sheep, and it is exceedingly difficult, and in many cases impossible, for them to discover the valuable and nutritious root'. Parker went on to remark that the upshot of these circumstances was clearly evident: 'The unfortunate aborigines are in a state of destitution, deprived of much of their ordinary means of subsistence. It is acknowledged by the earliest settlers that the natives are now in a much worse condition, and present a far less robust appearance, than when they arrived'. Aboriginal people who were deprived of their traditional food resources often killed the white man's sheep and cattle and

---

11 Christie, *Aborigines in Colonial Victoria*, pp. 41–42.

raided supplies of flour and the like in order to meet their need for food. In doing so they probably held that these commodities were common property or that they had a right to compensate themselves for loss of food sources caused by the white man's occupation of their land.[12]

Many historians have characterised Aboriginal attacks of this kind as a form of physical resistance to the white invasion of their lands. Christie's account of the Port Phillip District exemplifies this approach. He claims that throughout much if not all of the district Aboriginal nations carried out an extensive campaign that involved disrupting stock routes, harassing shepherds and hut keepers, and running off sheep and cattle. More pertinent to this study, he argues that the part of the Port Phillip District that included the Djadja Wurrung's territory saw Aboriginal resistance on a similar scale to the Western District, where historians such as Peter Corris have argued it was exceptionally strong. As we will see in due course, it makes sense to characterise the attacks that some Aboriginal people launched on settlers in the Loddon District as resistance, but historians like Christie have tended to overstate the amount of determined and concerted resistance as well as the role it played in Aboriginal attacks. Other historians, such as Beverley Nance, have argued that there is considerable evidence that the reaction of most Aboriginal people in the Port Phillip District to colonisation was comparatively peaceful and that most of the attacks they made were prompted by hunger. This seems to have been true of most of the attacks the Djadja Wurrung made. Yet it is worth noting that hunger could often provoke anger among the Djadja Wurrung that the white

---

12 Parker to Robinson, 20 June 1839; William Thomas to Robinson, *Historical Records of Victoria*, vol. 7, Melbourne University Press, Melbourne, 1998, p. 332.

man was destroying their sources of food at the same time as they were refusing to share their food with them, and that this obviously led to conflict.[13]

The Monro incidents

I will now consider the possible causes of conflict in the Loddon District in greater depth by focusing on the clashes that occurred on Monro's station on 26 January 1840, which I described at considerable length in the previous chapter. These have been the subject of very careful analysis by the historian Marie Fels.[14] She has argued that several inter-related factors are essential to understanding this event. The first concerns the scarcity of food.

In the week leading up to the violent clashes of 26 January the Djadja Wurrung had been moving round the country, as they always did, seeking food. They were clearly hungry, or, to be more specific, they were hungry for meat. On 22 January Monro told Robinson that only eighteen months ago there had been millions of daisy yams all over the plains and kangaroo and emu so abundant that they came up to the tents but that now there were no yams because sheep had trampled the ground and consequently the kangaroos had been driven away. Robinson himself noted in his journal that he had not seen a kangaroo in all the country he had traversed around the Coliban and Campaspe Rivers. Two days previously, Parker and his men had been out hunting with three Djadja Wurrung men but had returned

---

13 Christie, *Aborigines in Colonial Victoria*, pp. 65–66; Beverley Nance, 'The Level of Violence: Europeans and Aborigines in Port Phillip 1835–50', *Historical Studies*, vol. 19, no. 77, 1981, pp. 532–52.

14 See Marie Fels, 'The Collision at Monro's Station', in Nicholas Clark (ed.), Aboriginal History and Archaeology in Djadja Wurrung Country (Central Victoria) Examining Mount Kooyoora, Mount Alexander and Mount Tarrengower, a report for the Bendigo Dja Dja Wrung Aboriginal Association, 2nd draft, March 1995, pp. 72–74.

unsuccessful. This had followed the assistant protector paying a visit to a Djadja Wurrung encampment seven miles west of the northern slope of Mount Alexander where there were several men and women and between thirty and forty children. The men were away hunting kangaroo and it seems they were unsuccessful. Hunting was men's business, and being able to catch game and provide it to women and children was an important source of manly pride and status. It appears that the men were angered by the loss of game and humiliated by their failure in hunting. At any rate they repeatedly called upon Monro's shepherds to give them sheep. On one occasion, a Daung Wurrung man, Jacky Jacky, demanded of one of Monro's shepherds that he give his people some sheep and asserted that the white man was no good because they failed to accede to his request. Robinson recorded in his journal that he found the Aborigines troublesome, noting, by way of explanation, 'They had been promised sheep and were jumpy and disappointed'.[15]

The second factor at play in this case concerns the response of pastoralists to the Aborigines' demands for food. This raises the question of the attitudes to the Aboriginal people of the white men who were key figures in the incident. Both Robinson and Parker claimed that in the Loddon District pastoralists held that the possession of a pastoral license or lease entitled them to expel the Aboriginal people from their runs. Parker spoke to Charles Hutton about what he called 'the rights of the natives to the soil' and was flatly told by him that 'he could not give in to that'. (Two years later a judge in the Port Phillip District would uphold Hutton's view by ruling

---

15 Clark, *Journals of Robinson*, vol. 1, entries 18, 20, 21, 22 and 26 January 1840, pp. 130, 132, 133–35, 140; Depositions of John Preston, Alfred Bridges and James Howley, 22 January 1840, New South Wales Record Office, NRS 905, Item 4/2510.

that it was lawful for a pastoralist to drive Aborigines from his run because they had no rights under the lease that he held to the land.) But the protectors were aware that the Aboriginal people deemed the land to be their property. Moreover, they endorsed their view of the matter. In June 1839 Parker remarked after travelling through Djadja Wurrung country: 'It is an important and unquestionable fact that the aborigines are not insensible of their original right to the soil'.[16]

A factor of major importance, perhaps even of overwhelming importance, in the violence perpetrated by whites on Monro's run was the nature of the two pastoralists, Hutton and Monro, who occupied the land in the neighbourhood where the conflict took place. Readers will recall that Hutton, who was formerly a captain in the British army, had been involved in collisions with the Aborigines that were under investigation by the Aboriginal protectors, most notably the one on Campaspe Plains in June 1839. He held especially harsh views as to the treatment of the Aboriginal landowners, Robinson remarking in his journal on 24 January 1840: 'Mr Hutton avowed his [approach to the natives] to be terror; to keep the natives in subjection by fear, and to punish them wholesale, that is, by tribes and communities. If a member of a tribe offend[s], destroy the whole. He believed they must be exterminated. This, in his opinion, was the best'. To make matters worse, most of Hutton's men were from Van Diemen's Land, where many convicts and former convicts were sent if they committed further offences in the Australian colonies and the site of an especially fierce war between settlers and Aborigines.[17]

16 Parker to Robinson, 20 June 1839; Parker, Quarterly Journal, 1 September 1839 – 29 February 1840, Public Record Office Victoria, VPRS 4410, Unit 2; Clark, *Journals of Robinson*, vol. 1, entries 17 January and 25 January 1840, pp. 128, 139; Richard Broome, *Aboriginal Victorians: A History Since 1800*, Allen & Unwin, Sydney, 2005, p. 84.

17 Clark, *Journals of Robinson*, vol. 1, entries 24, 25 and 29 January 1840, pp. 138–39, 146.

We know less about Monro. He had been speared by Aborigines six months or so prior to the incidents in question, was yet to recover fully from the wound, and was prone to fear and anxiety and liable to panic. He also had a reputation among his servants for being a hard master who cared more for his sheep than for his employees, which might suggest he had an even harsher attitude to Aborigines. In October 1840 Robinson remarked in his journal: 'He said he had been at war with them and since he had been in the colony he never allowed them to his station. He always detested them'. Monro's fear of the Aborigines undoubtedly spread to his men. Parker observed that there was great alarm on Monro's station as early as 23 January, and the commandant of the mounted police contingent, Frederick Brunswick Russell, remarked that everything was in a state of great confusion when he arrived there on 26 January. These feelings probably gave rise to claims by Monro's shepherds in the middle of January that 1500 sheep had been stolen by a large party of Aborigines who were said to have driven the sheep off in two flocks in different directions. This story, as we noted in the previous chapter, proved to be false.[18]

The anxiety and fear experienced by Monro and his men were exacerbated by the presence of a group of foreign Aborigines in the district whom Fels describes as a raiding party. According to the Mounted Police, they had attacked Charles Ebden's station at Carlsruhe, Mollison's station near Malmsbury, and John Howie's

---

18 Parker to Robinson, 3 December 1839; Clark, *Journals of Robinson*, vol. 1, entries 18 January 1840 and 21 January 1840, pp. 130, 134; Henry Monro to I. Hurd, 23 January 1840, *Historical Records of Victoria*, vol. 2B, p. 685; Monro to Russell, 26 January 1840, *Historical Records of Victoria*, vol. 2B, p. 687; Russell to La Trobe, 30 January 1840; Parker to Robinson, 4 February 1840, Public Record Office Victoria, VPRS 11, Unit 4; Clark (ed.), *Journals of Robinson*, vol. 2, entry 25 October 1840, p. 20.

station near Gisborne in the preceding week before moving north and encamping on Mount Alexander. The white shepherds there claimed that these Aborigines were quite unaccustomed to Europeans and their ways and were going to fight the Woiwurrung in Melbourne. These Aboriginal people were Daung Wurrung, who were the sworn enemies of the Djadja Wurrung.[19]

If the presence of this foreign party added to the tension felt by the pastoralists, so too did the presence of Robinson and Parker. The pastoralists had a very different vision about who should control what amounted to the spread of empire and what this would look like. Indeed, many pastoralists were extremely hostile to the Protectorate and its officers and complained that they were protecting the Aborigines when it was they who were most in need of protection.[20] (This matter will be discussed further in the next chapter.) Monro and Hutton were no exception. Most importantly, the pastoralists and the protectors had very different views about Aborigines' rights in land. Monro was typical in this regard: 'The blacks are still lurking about the creeks, and from what I have seen they will soon regain their lost ground and become again *heirs of the soil*, as the Protectors emphatically designate them', he complained in March 1840. 'I have been compelled to give up all my outstations, and have now the gratification to see my flocks and herds starving around me; how long this state of things may last you must be all well aware of'. More

19 Clark, *Journals of Robinson*, vol. 1, entry 23 January 1840, p. 136; Ian D. Clark, *Aboriginal Languages and Clans: An Historical Atlas of Western and Central Victoria, 1800–1900*, Department of Geography and Environmental Science, Monash University, Melbourne, 1990, p. 161.

20 For debate about the protectorate, see, for example, *Port Phillip Gazette*, 20 April 1839, 4 May 1839, 11 May 1839, 18 May 1839, 3 July 1839, 7 August 1839, 14 August 1839, 17 August 1839; *Port Phillip Patriot*, 13 May 1839, 22 July 1839, 5 August 1839; *Port Phillip Herald*, 4 December 1840, 8 December 1840, 11 December 1840, 8 January 1841, 15 January 1841, 21 May 1841, 7 December 1841.

specifically, he seemed to blame the protectors for this situation: 'We cannot defend ourselves now, the blacks are well aware we dare not shoot them, they have fresh courage put into them, if they have been taught nothing else'. The protectors undoubtedly contributed to this tension. Robinson in particular had an unfortunate tendency to overplay his hand. Among whites Robinson was stiff and awkward, and he tended to be highly competitive. In this situation he antagonised the pastoralists by making demands such as the one to provide Aborigines with sheep; and he raised the expectations of the Aborigines only for these to be dashed because he represented himself as their friend and protector and promised to obtain sheep for them.[21]

The importance of the local

The examination of the factors at work in the Monro incidents alerts us to the need to pay attention to the importance of local factors in considering the way in which relations between Europeans and Aborigines unfolded on the frontiers of settlement. As the discussion in the previous chapter suggested and the table below makes clear, nearly all the instances of conflict that occurred in the Loddon District took place on a small number of stations in its southern reaches. Furthermore, nearly all those stations lay in the same particular area, namely the Campaspe Plains. This requires us to consider the nature of this area.

---

21 Monro to Russell, 26 January 1840, *Historical Records of Victoria*, vol. 2B, p. 685; Extract of Monro letter, 4 February 1840, *Port Phillip Herald*, 7 February 1840, original emphasis; Robinson to La Trobe, 23 September 1840, New South Wales Record Office, NRS 905, Item 4/2511; Inga Clendinnen, 'Reading Mr Robinson', in her *Tiger's Eye: A Memoir*, Text Publishing, Melbourne, 2000, p. 209; Elbourne, 'Exploration'.

CHAPTER 3: FRONTIER

Documented incidents of conflict between settlers and Aboriginal people in Djadja Wurrung country 1838–42

Date	Pastoralist(s)	Pastoral run
March 1838	Unknown	Unknown
April 1838	William Bowman, and Alexander and William Mollison	Campaspe Plains (Sutton Grange or Stratford Lodge), and Coliban
May 1838	William Yaldwyn, and William Bowman	Barfold and Campaspe Plains (Sutton Grange or Stratford Lodge)
June 1838	William Yaldwyn, and William Bowman	Barfold, and Campaspe Plains (Sutton Grange or Stratford Lodge)
Later in 1838	John Hepburn	Smeaton Hill
March 1839	Henry Boucher Bowerman	Maiden Hills
May 1839	Charles Hutton	Campaspe Plains
June 1839	Charles Hutton, and the Mounted Police	Campaspe Plains
July 1839	Sylvester Brown	Darlington
July 1839	Henry Monro	Campaspe
July 1839	Charles Ebden	Carlsruhe (St Agnes)
November 1839	Henry Monro	Campaspe
January 1840 (twice)	Henry Monro and the border police	Campaspe
June 1840	Daniel Jennings and George Playne	Campaspe Plains
July 1840	Daniel Jennings and George Playne	Campaspe Plains
c. July 1840	Henry Monro	Campaspe
August 1840	Henry Dutton, William Darlot, and Don Simson	Far or Fourteen Mile Creek (near Loddon Protectorate)
September 1840	Thomas and William Learmonth	Maiden Hills
September 1840	Alexander and William Mollison	Coliban
September 1840	James Campbell	Bullarook
February 1841	Henry Dutton, William Darlot, and Don Simson	Far or Fourteen Mile Creek (near Loddon Protectorate)
March 1841	Ebenezer Olpihant	Mount Greenock (Dunach Forest)
April 1841	Richard Grice	Mount Alexander
April 1841	Henry Bennett	Barnedown
January 1842	Alexander and William Mollison	Coliban
March 1842	Alexander Allan	Between Languycorrie and Catto's Run

It turns out that the Campaspe Plains were rather singular in several respects. First, running through this area was Major Mitchell's Line along which many pastoralists travelled with huge parties of sheep, cattle, bullocks and horses. Several major conflicts took place along this route, beginning with the killing of seven of George Faithfull's men by Aborigines in April 1838. Second, this area lay on the boundary between the territory of the Djadja Wurrung and that of the Daung Wurrung. The anthropologist Norman Tindale once argued that boundaries between Aboriginal nations could comprise land that was the source of contention and dispute and so constitute what he called debatable ground. Perhaps this was true of the boundary between the Djadja Wurrung and the Daung Wurrung along the Campaspe River. I will return to the potential significance of this possibility later. Third, its topography was well suited to Aboriginal groups making raids on pastoral runs: they could readily come out of the mountain ranges, launch attacks, and retreat to this largely impregnable territory in the knowledge that it was very difficult for any whites to pursue them.[22]

Nearly all of the clashes on the Campaspe Plains involved the same protagonists. As we have already seen in the course of discussing the Monro incidents, the nature of the pastoralists was undoubtedly part of this equation. Certainly, it was Robinson's view that this was often the case: 'Parker said some of the settlers complain that the natives are troublesome, [but there are] others who say the blacks give them no trouble. The inference is that the settlers bring [it] on themselves'.

---

22 Parker to Robinson, 18 June 1839, *Historical Records of Victoria*, vol. 7, pp. 321–22; William Lonsdale to Thomson, 2 July 1838, New South Wales Record Office, Series NRS 905, Item 4/2423.3; Norman B. Tindale, *Aboriginal Tribes of Australia: Their Terrain, Environmental Controls, Distribution, Limits and Proper Names*, vol. 1, Australian National Press, Canberra, 1974, pp. 77–78.

Robinson believed that the pastoralists who took an interest in the welfare of the Aboriginal people and were willing to feed and employ them were rarely injured. But just as important was the nature of the Aboriginal people who were involved. In turns out that most of the attacks on pastoral runs that I have described were committed not by the Djadja Wurrung but by Aboriginal people belonging to other nations, especially the Daung Wurrung. Moreover, it was particular Daung Wurrung parties and even certain Daung Wurrung men who were responsible for these attacks on the Campaspe Plains as well as for many of those in neighbouring districts. The most important of these players was a Daung Wurrung man known variously by whites as Billy Billy, Billy Hamilton and Jimmy Cockatoo, who had a distinguishing feature, namely a defect in his left eye. Consequently, the Daung Wurrung were notorious among the pastoralists in the district.[23]

---

23 Parker to Robinson, 18 June 1839, *Historical Records of Victoria*, vol. 7, p. 322; Parker to Robinson, 20 June 1839; Clark, *Journals of Robinson*, vol. 1, entries 31 January 1840 and 27 February 1840, pp. 148, 181; Parker, Report 1 March – 31 May 1840, Public Record Office Victoria, VPRS 4410, Unit 2; F.A. Powlett to La Trobe, 18 September 1840, New South Wales Record Office, Series NRS 905, Item 4/2511; Deposition of James Rogers, 24 September 1840 and Parker to Robinson, 25 September 1840, Public Record Office Victoria, Series 11, Unit 4; Statement of Charles Bramley, no date, included with Parker to Robinson, 2 October 1840, and Parker to Robinson, 2 October 1840, New South Wales Record Office, Series NRS 905, Item 4/2511; Parker, Quarterly Journal, 1 December 1840 – 28 February 1841, VPRS 4410, Unit 2; Clark (ed.), *Journals of Robinson*, vol. 2, entry 25 December 1840, p. 45; Parker to Robinson, 31 December 1840, Public Record Office Victoria, Series 11, Unit 4; Parker to La Trobe, 30 April 1841, Public Record Office Victoria, VPRS 10, Unit 3; Parker, Quarterly Report, 1 March – 31 May 1842; Robinson to La Trobe, 9 April 1842, reproduced in Ian D. Clark (ed.), *The Port Phillip Journals of George Augustus Robinson: 8 March – 7 April 1842 and 18 March – 29 April 1843*, Monash Publications in Geography, Melbourne, 1988, p. 11; Parker to Robinson, 5 January 1843, New South Wales Legislative Council, *Votes and Proceedings*, 1843, Return to an Address, Dr Thomson, 29 August 1843, p. 45; John Hepburn to La Trobe, 10 August 1853, and William Thomas Mollison to Charles Joseph La Trobe, 22 August 1853, in Bride, *Letters from Victorian Pioneers*, pp. 77, 257, 77.

The finding that most of the violent clashes in this country took place in much the same locality and were perpetrated by many of the same settlers and the same Aborigines means that we have to reconsider the nature of the relations between the Djadja Wurrung and the pastoralists, and perhaps even the picture we have of the relationship between settlers and Aboriginal people on the frontier in the Australian colonies more generally. In this task the work of the historian Jan Critchett is instructive.

After studying the Western District of Victoria Critchett concluded that the Australian frontier was in fact highly local in nature, which is to say that relations could vary greatly from one area to another. But, more than this, Critchett pointed out the way in which the frontier, including its violence, could be said to have been intimate in character. She quotes a letter of the Superintendent of the Port Phillip District, Charles Joseph La Trobe, in which he remarked to a group of settlers: 'Even under circumstances far more favourable, both to the settler who seeks for protection and the government desiring to afford it – for instance, where a well-defined frontier or neutral ground could be interposed between the civilised and uncivilized – I need scarcely remind you how little real security has been enjoyed. Here, there is not even such a line; the savage tribes are not only upon our borders, but *intermingled* with us in every part of this wide district'. Critchett extrapolates:

> [The frontier] was represented by the Aboriginal woman who lived nearby and was shared by her Aboriginal partner with European men; it was the group living down beside the creek or river, as they did on many properties; it was the 'boy' used as a guide for exploring parties or for doing jobs now and then; and it was the 'civilised' Aborigine employed as a stockman. The 'other side of the frontier' was just down the yard or as

close as the bed shared with an Aboriginal woman. It was this intermingling of the races that determined when and where hostility was shown.

In the case of the Djadja Wurrung it is apparent that they and the settlers often knew one another and knew one another well enough to know one another's names. Readers will recall that in the incident in which Munangabum was wounded and Gondu-urmin was killed in February 1841 the former had called the man who seems to have been responsible for firing on them by his nickname.[24]

With these points in mind let us reconsider the historical record in regard to the Djadja Wurrung's relations with the pastoralists. Once we set aside the attacks that Daung Wurrung parties made on runs that lay on the boundary or in the border land between the two people's territory, the Djadja Wurrung response to the invasion of their lands seems to have been relatively peaceful, which is remarkable given that a large part of their country had been wrested from them. In 1853 the pastoralist William Mollison was to reminisce: 'The aborigines in our neighbourhood were from the first peaceable'. His recollection cannot be dismissed as an example of a pastoralist choosing to misremember or forget the nature of the Aboriginal response to his invasion of their lands. In 1841 his brother and fellow pastoralist, Alexander, had told a parliamentary select committee that they had employed four Aboriginal youths at different times to

---

24 Deposition of Edward Collins, 9 February 1841, Public Record Office Victoria, VPRS 30, Unit 185, NCR 8; La Trobe to the Gentlemen signing a Representation without date, 26 March 1842, British House of Commons, *Sessional Papers*, 1844, vol. 34, no. 627, Aborigines (Australian Colonies), Return to an Address, p. 214, my emphasis; Jan Critchett, *A Distant Field of Murder: Western District Frontiers 1834–1848*, Melbourne University Press, Melbourne, 1990, pp. 2, 21, 34, 46; Critchett, 'Encounters in the Western District', in Bain Attwood and S.G. Foster (eds), *Frontier Conflict: The Australian Experience*, National Museum of Australia, 2003, pp. 53–54.

bring in horses, run errands, strip bark, drove sheep, and guide them and their men, and that they had remained up to a few weeks at a time. Officials at this time support the gist of Mollison's account. In November 1839 Henry Fysche Gisborne of the Mounted Police reported to Superintendent La Trobe that he had found the country perfectly quiet on touring around it; in April 1840 Parker reported: 'many instances have come to my knowledge where [the Aborigines] have employed themselves to the satisfaction of the settlers and their own advantage'; and the following month Robinson observed that Djadja Wurrung were friendly with the Mollisons. Indeed, it seems that prior to March 1841 the Djadja Wurrung had never attacked any white men though they had been in the habit of taking sheep when the opportunity arose.[25]

How do we account for the relatively harmonious relations between Djadja Wurrung and the settlers for the period that all these sources reference, namely 1839–41? The first factor to consider is the impact of the pastoral invasion on Djadja Wurrung lands, particularly their food sources. While a large number of stations were established in the Loddon District, this occurred in stages, which contrasts with situations where the entire territory of a nation was taken up in a very short period of time. This meant that a good part of the Djadja Wurrung's territory remained unoccupied and thus relatively

---

25 Parker to Robinson, 18 June 1839, *Historical Records of Victoria*, vol. 7, p. 322; Parker to Robinson, 20 June 1839; Henry Fysche Gisborne to La Trobe, 7 November 1839, cited N.M. O'Donnell, 'The Australian Career of Henry Fysche Gisborne', *Victorian Historical Magazine*, vol. 5, no. 19, 1917, p. 120; Clark (ed.), *Journals of Robinson*, vol. 1, entries 21 February 1840 and 31 May 1840, pp. 176, 314; Parker to Robinson, 1 April 1840, *Historical Records of Victoria*, vol. 2B, p. 695; Parker to La Trobe, 30 April 1841; Mollison, Reply to a Circular Letter, 24 July 1841, New South Wales Legislative Council, *Votes and Proceedings*, 1841, Report from the Committee on Immigration, p. 47; Parker to Robinson, 5 January 1843, p. 45; Mollison to La Trobe, 22 August 1853, and Edward Dryden to La Trobe, August 1853, in Bride, *Letters from Victorian Pioneers*, pp. 257, 342.

unaffected by pastoral occupation. Consequently, the impact of the pastoral invasion on the Djadja Wurrung's sources of food might have been considerably less drastic than Robinson and Parker claimed, and as a result they might have had less reason to kill sheep and raid huts for food such as flour. Certainly this was the opinion of J.C. Riddell, a magistrate at Mount Macedon who was sympathetic to Aborigines. He told a parliamentary select committee inquiry in 1849 that while it was generally assumed that the food of the Aboriginal people was destroyed once settlers took possession of their country this was not necessarily the case, with the exception of kangaroos. (As noted earlier, the availability of kangaroo to hunt could be terrifically important to Aboriginal men for reasons of status.[26])

Other factors are probably more important in explaining the relatively harmonious relations during this period. The murderous attacks that settlers and police forces made in the district between 1838 and 1840 probably led the Djadja Wurrung to conclude that attacks on white settlers exacted a very heavy toll and that they were best to accommodate themselves to their invasion. At the same time the Djadja Wurrung might have decided that forming an alliance with the pastoralists could provide them with some measure of protection from their more powerful traditional enemies, the Daung Wurrung. There is evidence from other parts of the Australian continent of Aboriginal groups seeking to forge a relationship with settlers in these circumstances. Bob Reece notes that in the Swan River District of Western Australia in the 1830s and 1840s the Aboriginal people did not see whites as necessarily inimical to their interests and instead

---

26 New South Wales Legislative Council, *Votes and Proceedings*, 1849, vol. 2, Report of the Select Committee on the Aborigines and the Protectorate System, pp. 30–32.

saw co-operation with them as a means of either strengthening their position vis-a-vis Aborigines whom they regarded as their enemies or offering sanctuary against more powerful foes. Finally, there is also some evidence that the Djadja Wurrung aligned themselves with the Port Phillip Protectorate or more particularly its officers in the hope that this would serve their interests. On one occasion in 1841 a party of Djadja Wurrung described themselves as 'Jajouroung blacks belonging to Mr Parker'.[27]

The predominantly peaceful relations between the Djadja Wurrung and the settlers in the Loddon District continued throughout the 1840s. In June 1842 Parker reported that no complaint of any kind had been laid against Aborigines within Djadja Wurrung country, though outrages had occurred beyond their boundaries. One pastoralist who took land in February that year at Avoca, north of Henry Dutton, William Darlot, and Don Simson's station, where conflict had occurred the previous year, recalled that he had never had any trouble. And in summer of 1843 a small detachment of the native police led by William Dana that called at every station up and down the Loddon, Campaspe and Goulburn Rivers reported that a number of Aborigines were working there and were being treated well. There were only a small number of minor instances of conflict in 1842 and 1843. For example, two Djadja Wurrung men were apprehended for stealing sheep from a run in the Pyrenees in November 1843. Reports by government officials for each of the years 1845, 1846, 1847 and 1848 tell the same story. This is all the more remarkable given that the remainder of the Djadja Wurrung's land, which lay in the northern part of their country, was taken during these years as

---

27 Deposition of Collins, 9 February 1841; Bob Reece, 'Inventing Aborigines', *Aboriginal History*, vol. 11, pt 1, 1987, pp. 14–23.

pastoralists grabbed more land to form between twelve and fourteen new stations.[28]

In addition to the factors we have already noted, two more factors probably contributed to these peaceful relations. First, there is the presence of the protectorate station that Parker established. This will be considered in more depth in the next chapter but we can simply note here that a relationship grew up there between Parker and the Djadja Wurrung after 1841 that seems to have worked to ward off any trouble that was brewing between Aborigines and settlers on the pastoral stations. Second, there is the factor of the diseases that the white man had introduced. As we shall also see in the next chapter, these devastated the Djadja Wurrung, causing not only huge loss of life but enormous confusion.[29]

---

28 Parker, Quarterly Journal, 1 March – 31 May 1842; H.E.P. Dana to La Trobe, 5 April 1843, Public Record Office Victoria, VPRS 19, Unit 44; Parker to Robinson, 1 December 1843, Public Record Office Victoria, VPRS 4410, Unit 2; Extract of Parker, Annual Report for 1845, New South Wales Legislative Council, *Votes and Proceedings*, 1845, Report from the Select Committee on the Condition of Aborigines, p. 54; Leslie Foster to La Trobe, undated, Bride, *Letters from Victorian Pioneers*, p. 340; Clark, *Aboriginal Languages*, pp. 143, 145.

29 Parker to Robinson, 1 December 1843.

Chapter 4

PROTECTION

The Port Phillip District was settled at the time when philanthropic sentiment in regard to aboriginal peoples was at the height of its influence upon the British government. Evangelical philanthropists, after the triumphant conclusion in 1833 of their crusade to abolish slavery in the British Empire, had turned their attention to the plight of aborigines in Britain's settler colonies.[1] In July 1835 their leader, Thomas Fowell Buxton, persuaded the House of Commons to appoint a select committee to inquire into the conditions of indigenous peoples in Britain's settler colonies. This committee focused largely on the Cape Colony but it heard testimony about the devastating impact of British colonisation on Aboriginal people in the Australian colonies.[2]

1   In this book I follow the example of several scholars who on two grounds have expressed a preference for applying the term 'philanthropists' rather than the term 'humanitarians' to those who argued for the protection of aboriginal peoples: the use of 'humanitarians' or 'humanitarianism' can suggest a mistaken sense of continuity with the contemporary phenomenon that bears this name, and the term 'humanitarian' was not one that these people used for themselves, not least because it had unfavourable connotations at the time. See Claire McLisky, '"Due Observance of Justice, and the Protection of their Rights": Philanthropy, Humanitarianism and Moral Purpose in the Aborigines Protection Society circa 1837 and its Portrayal in Australian Historiography, 1883–2003', *Limina*, vol. 11, 2005, pp. 57–58; and Elizabeth Elbourne, 'Violence, Moral Imperialism and Colonial Borderlands, 1770s–1820s: Some Contradictions of Humanitarianism', *Journal of Colonialism and Colonial History*, vol. 17, no. 1, 2016, <https://muse.jhu.edu/article/613282>.

2   *British House of Commons Debates*, 14 July 1835, cols 552–53. For a discussion of the Committee's report, including its drafting, see Elizabeth Elbourne, 'The Sin of the Settler: The 1835–36 Select Committee on Aborigines and Debates Over Virtue and Conquest in the Early Nineteenth-Century British White Settler Empire', *Journal*

In respect of the Australian colonies the Select Committee insisted that the Aboriginal people were subjects of the Queen and consequently should be offered the protection of British law. The most important outcome of the committee's deliberations was the series of suggestions that included a recommendation to appoint protectors of Aborigines in the Australian colonies (which was no doubt influenced by the fact that there were protectors of apprentices in places such as British Guiana, following the abolition of slavery). Several months later, Lord Glenelg, the Secretary of State for the Colonies, made arrangements to implement this recommendation in a despatch to Sir Richard Bourke's successor as the Governor of New South Wales, Sir George Gipps. Although the Select Committee had implied that protectors should be appointed in all newly settled areas, Glenelg decided to appoint five protectors only and that their work should be confined to the Port Phillip District. Glenelg suggested to Gipps that their basic duties include guarding the Aboriginal people's rights and interests from the encroachment of settlers and acts of cruelty, injustice and oppression, representing their wants and grievances to the government of the colony, instructing them in Christianity, persuading them to live in one place, and teaching them the arts of cultivation and civilisation. He left it to Gipps to draw up more precise instructions.

It was Glenelg, however, who chose the protectors, albeit after seeking the advice of the former governor of Van Diemen's Land, Sir George Arthur, and Rev Jabez Bunting, the secretary of the

of Colonialism and Colonial History, vol. 4, no. 3, 2003, http://muse.jhu.edu/journals/journal_of_colonialism_and_colonial_history/v004/4.3elbourne.html; Zoë Laidlaw, "'Aunt Anna's Report': The Buxton Women's Political and Intellectual Contribution to the Aborigines Select Committee, 1835–37', *Journal of Imperial and Commonwealth History*, vol. 32, no. 2, 2004, pp. 1–28; and Elizabeth Elbourne, 'Imperial Politics in the Family Way: Gender, Biography and the 1836–37 Select Committee on Aborigines', in Bain Attwood and Tom Griffiths (eds), *Frontier, Race, Nation: Henry Reynolds and Australian History*, Australian Scholarly Publishing, Melbourne, 2009.

Wesleyan Methodist Missionary Society. He probably took charge of making the appointments because the Select Committee had held that the protection of Aborigines was a task that should be entrusted to the imperial government rather than colonial legislatures. To the position of Chief Protector Glenelg appointed George Augustus Robinson, who was famed for his role in conciliating Aborigines in Van Diemen's Land; and for the position of assistant protector he chose four Englishmen who had never been to the Australian colonies, James Dredge, Edward Stone Parker, Charles Sievwright and William Thomas. Sievwright was a former army officer, and Dredge, Parker and Thomas were school masters by profession. All were decidedly religious men with a missionary spirit.[3]

In June 1838 Gipps received a dispatch from Glenelg that not only told him that the imperial government had decided to appoint protectors of Aborigines but that the New South Wales Legislative Council would be required to vote the necessary funds for the upkeep of a protectorate on the grounds that the settlers had a responsibility to contribute to the protection and civilisation of the natives. By this time Aboriginal matters had become the source of enormous contention in the colony. Two months earlier, news broke of the massacre on the Broken River of eight white men belonging to the droving party of the Faithfull brothers; and in May and June there was further news of bloody attacks on pastoralists and their men in that part of the colony. In the wake of these reports, a large number of settlers, which included many of the colony's most wealthy and

---

3   British House of Commons, *Sessional Papers*, 1837, vol. 7, no. 425, Select Committee on aborigines in British settlements, pp. 77, 83–84; Lord Glenelg to Sir George Gipps, 31 January 1838, *Historical Records of Australia*, series 1, vol. 19, pp. 252–55; M.F. Christie, *Aborigines in Colonial Victoria 1835–86*, University of Sydney, Sydney, 1979, pp. 88–89; A.G.L. Shaw, *A History of the Port Phillip District: Victoria Before Separation*, Miegunyah Press, Melbourne, 1996, p. 117.

powerful, had presented a memorial to Gipps in which they expressed their alarm about the attacks committed by Aborigines, complained that settlers had been forced to abandon their properties, urged the adoption of coercive measures against the Aborigines, and warned that they would be forced to act themselves if the government failed to afford *them* protection. At least three of Sydney's newspapers published this petition and demanded that Gipps adopt measures to put a stop to Aboriginal attacks. Soon after this, the Governor was alerted to the shocking massacre at Myall Creek on the Liverpool Plains in the north-west of the colony in which twenty two of the Wirrayaraay people, most of them women and children, were believed to have been brutally slain. Gipps ordered a thorough inquiry and called for the perpetrators to be apprehended, charged and punished, but in mid August the members of his Executive Council attacked Glenelg's scheme of protectors and his requirement that the colony meet the cost of this new measure on the grounds that it was not only unworkable but too costly. A month later the government's inquiry into the Myall Creek massacre revealed that the death toll was actually as high as 28. Eleven of the twelve men suspected of committing the murders were arrested and charged. In the meantime Aboriginal people had been making increasingly widespread attacks on settlers on the Liverpool Plains to avenge the mass killing of their kin. This provoked further calls by settlers for their protection.[4]

---

4   Phillip Parker King and co to Sir George Gipps, 8 June 1838, New South Wales State Records, NRS 906, Item 4/1013; *Sydney Gazette*, 19 June 1838; *Australian*, 22 June 1838; *Colonist*, 23 June 1838; New South Wales Legislative Council, *Votes and Proceedings*, 14 August 1838; *Sydney Herald*, 15 August 1838; *Sydney Gazette*, 16 August 1838, 20 September 1838; *Australian*, 17 August 1838; S.G. Foster, 'Aboriginal Rights and Official Morality', *Push from the Bush*, no. 11, 1981, pp. 80–81; Roger Milliss, *Waterloo Creek: The Australia Day Massacre of 1838, George Gipps and the British Conquest of New South Wales*, McPhee Gribble, Melbourne, 1992, pp. 316–19, 390, 382, 395, 399.

The fact that Aboriginal matters were now attracting so much attention and causing so much acrimony was due largely to three factors. First, the House of Commons Select Committee report had represented the British settler colonies as sites in which men committed sin in an unchecked fashion by indulging in unrestrained appetites to have sex, exploit resources and kill aboriginal people, and the imperial and colonial governments had made clear that Aboriginal people had the same legal status as any British subject and so implied that they were in a sense part of the same cultural order as the settlers. This deeply troubled the settlers. As the historian Lauren Benton has observed, they believed that their standing, in both material and symbolic terms, rested in large part on cultural and legal distinctions being made between themselves and the Aboriginal people. Consequently, they felt threatened by a policy that emphasised that Aboriginal people had rights, and especially the right to protection under the law, and that drew into question the virtue of their enterprise.[5]

Second, the new Aboriginal policy adopted by the imperial and colonial governments helped to create discontent with the present system of government which was marked by imperial control over vital matters such as land and revenues. The new protectors were opposed not only because their task was to represent the interests of the Aborigines but because they were regarded as the appointees of a distant government and answerable only to the governor. This, too, provoked considerable alarm and resentment among the settlers of the colony.[6]

---

5   Lauren Benton, *Law and Colonial Cultures: Legal Regimes in World History*, Cambridge University Press, New York, 2002, pp. 184, 205, 208; Elbourne, 'Sin of the Settler', p. 28.

6   Ann Curthoys and Jessie Mitchell, 'The Advent of Self-Government, 1840s–1890', in Alison Bashford and Stuart Macintyre (eds), *The Cambridge History of Australia*, Cambridge University Press, Melbourne, 2013, p. 155–57.

CHAPTER 4: PROTECTION

Third, the settlers had a powerful weapon in the form of the colonial press.[7] In particular, the largest selling newspaper, the *Sydney Herald*, strove to form a body of public opinion favourable to the interests of the pastoralists as well as those of the settlers more generally. Its editor, Alfred Ward Stephens, was himself a major landowner as well as a champion of representative government, the appropriation of colonial revenue for emigration, and security of tenure for pastoralists. He penned leaders and published letters that mounted vitriolic attacks on the Aborigines but more especially on those he called 'black advocates' as he was particularly riled by the imperial government's appointment of protectors of Aborigines. In his view this new scheme was merely an expression of liberal sentiment and just one more example of a Whig (or liberal) job being done on the colonies by the mother country. In order to check the clashes between blacks and whites what was needed, Stephens insisted, was not protectors but a strong police force and an even-handed application of justice so that the sanctions of the law not only fell upon the settlers but the Aborigines as well. Unless the government provided this, he warned, the settlers would have to take up arms themselves against Aboriginal attackers and the result would be the waging of an exterminating war. In fact, once news of the Protectorate became public knowledge, nearly all of the colony's newspapers attacked the plan. Those critics included the *Port Phillip Gazette*. There can be no doubt that pastoralists who were invading areas such as Djadja

---

7 For a discussion of the colonial press at this time, see Alan Atkinson and Marian Aveling (eds), *Australians 1838*, Fairfax, Syme & Weldon, Sydney, 1987, pp. 198–205; Alan Lester, 'British Settler Discourse and the Circuits of Empire', *History Workshop Journal*, no. 54, 2002, pp. 25–48; and Anna Johnston, *Paper War: Morality, Print Culture, and Power in Colonial New South Wales*, University of Western Australian Press, Perth, 2012, chapter 3.

Wurrung country carried these attitudes towards the Protectorate with them. For example, Charles Ebden, who was among the *Sydney Herald*'s many readers, wrote from the Murray River as he overlanded stock to the Loddon District: 'If the government do not immediately give us the protection *we* require, we shall be compelled to turn out in a body against [the blacks]'.[8]

The protectors

On their arrival in Sydney in September 1838, Dredge, Parker, Sievwright and Thomas soon became aware of the antagonism of many settlers to the Protectorate and were greatly disturbed by it. To make matters worse, when they eventually arrived in Port Phillip in early January 1839 they found there was no one to greet them and that no arrangements had been made to accommodate them. Moreover, their immediate superior, Chief Protector Robinson, was not to arrive until the end of February and even though they had asked Gipps on more than one occasion for specific instructions regarding their duties none had been forthcoming. Robinson himself was unsure what their tasks should be. He only had Glenelg's list of duties, and Gipps refused to provide any instructions, perhaps in part because he had already concluded that the best kind of protection for Aboriginal people lay elsewhere, namely in the establishment of a more effective magistracy in the form of the Commissioners of

8 *Sydney Gazette*, 30 June 1838, 10 July 1838, 21 August 1838; *Sydney Herald*, 8 August 1838, 4 September 1838, 5 September 1838, 14 September 1838, 19 September 1838; *Australian*, 21 August 1838, 4 September 1838; *Sydney Monitor*, 3 September 1838; Charles Ebden to James Donnithorne, 4 February 1839, reproduced in J.O. Randell, *Pastoral Settlement in Northern Victoria*, vol. 1, Queensberry Press, Melbourne, 1979, p. 50, my emphasis; Alan Atkinson, 'A Slice of the Sydney Press', *Push from the Bush*, no. 1, 1978, pp. 82–84, 87, 94–95; Atkinson and Aveling (eds), *Australians 1838*, p. 204.

Crown Lands and the provision of police forces in the form of a border police force beyond the limits of location. (This, at least, is what he had concluded by April 1839.)[9]

Robinson fell back on Glenelg's rather vague list of duties and advice from Gipps, and decided that Dredge, Parker, Sievwright and Thomas should begin to move with the Aboriginal groups in order to learn their languages and culture and devise the best means of protecting and civilising them. In the last week of March he directed them to take to the field immediately, and after being prompted by his assistants he allocated each of them an area of responsibility. The task of protecting Aboriginal people in the northwest or the Loddon District fell to Parker.[10]

Parker was born in London in May 1802. He had been apprenticed to a printer but became a Sunday School teacher and a candidate for the ministry in the Methodist Church. However, in 1828 he broke the conditions governing the candidates for the ministry by marrying, and was suspended. Subsequently, he turned to teaching and was in charge of a Methodist day school at the point he was offered the position of assistant protector. Parker fervently believed

9   Gipps to Glenelg, 27 April 1838, *Historical Records of Australia*, series 1, vol. 19, p. 397; Assistant Protectors to Gipps, 1 October 1838, *Historical Records of Victoria*, vol. 2B, Victorian Government Printing Office, Melbourne, 1983, p. 384; Assistant Protectors to Edward Deas Thomson, 26 October 1838, *Historical Records of Victoria*, vol. 2B, pp. 385–86; Deas Thomson to George Augustus Robinson, 11 December 1838, *Historical Records of Victoria*, vol. 2B, p. 391; William Thomas Journal, entry 4 January 1839, *Historical Records of Victoria*, vol. 2B, p. 435; Robinson to Deas Thomson, 12 March 1839, *Historical Records of Victoria*, vol. 2B, p. 444; Gipps to Deas Thomson, n.d. [April 1839], *Historical Records of Victoria*, vol. 2B, p. 457; Gipps to Glenelg, 6 April 1839, *Historical Records of Australia*, series 1, vol. 20, pp. 90–92; Christie, *Aborigines in Colonial Victoria*, p. 91; Lisa Ford, 'Protecting the Peace on the Edges of Empire: Commissioners of Crown Lands in New South Wales', in Lauren Benton et al. (eds), *Protection and Empire*, Cambridge University Press, Cambridge, 2017.

10 Robinson to Deas Thomson, 12 March 1839, 21 March 1839 and 26 March 1839, *Historical Records of Victoria*, vol. 2B, pp. 444, 445 and 451.

Edward Parker

Of the men appointed as protectors, Parker was once regarded by historians as the one most sympathetic to Aboriginal people; William Thomas now seems to be more highly regarded in this regard.

(From Early Days in the Loddon Valley: Memoirs of Edward Stone Parker 1802–1865 *by Edgar Morrison (1966))*

that his responsibilities included the civilisation of the Aboriginal people and that this was best done by Christianising them.[11]

At the beginning of April 1839 Parker as well as Dredge and Sievwright were instructed by Robinson to proceed to their districts with the least possible delay and told they should provide a census of the Aboriginal population, a list of the groups and their boundaries, and a description of the relationships between the groups. This was easier said than done. The assistant protectors had to make

---

11 H.N. Nelson, 'Parker, Edward Stone', *Australian Dictionary of Biography*, vol. 5, Melbourne University Press, Melbourne, 1974, <http://adb.anu.edu.au/biography/parker-edward-stone-4363>.

arrangements for their families, and each of them had a large family. Parker and his wife Mary had six children and a seventh was on its way. The assistant protectors also had to obtain the necessary supplies and equipment. Further delay was caused by their haggling over the conditions of their employment, which included travelling expenses. The Police Magistrate William Lonsdale, who was in charge of the Port Phillip District until Charles Joseph La Trobe took up his appointment as Superintendent, was reluctant to make any decisions on these matters, and consequently the assistant protectors were left without the resources they needed in order to begin their work. (For example, they had each been promised four bullocks to cart their goods but these had been reduced to one.) The assistant protectors did start to learn the language of the Kulin peoples in the small town of Melbourne, and to provide religious instruction and issue medical supplies to them, but Parker, Dredge and Sievwright proved reluctant to move to the districts that Robinson has assigned them.[12]

The failure of the assistant protectors to go into the field soon attracted censure from Gipps but more especially the press in the Port Phillip District. In April the *Port Phillip Gazette* began to run a series of letters to the editor by a correspondent who called himself Humanitas.[13] The first of these letters was sympathetic to the Protectorate but argued that the measures devised for the attainment

---

12 Assistant Protectors to Robinson, 23 March 1839, *Historical Records of Victoria*, vol. 2B, p. 447; Robinson to Assistant Protectors, 1 April 1839, *Historical Records of Victoria*, vol. 2B, pp. 453–54; Dredge to Robinson, 15 April 1839, *Historical Records of Victoria*, vol. 2B, p. 455.

13 Letters to the editor of newspapers in the Australasian colonies were often written by anonymous and pseudo anonymous correspondents, and sometimes the authors were simply the editors of the newspaper in another guise (Russell Stone, 'Auckland's Political Opposition in the Crown Colony Period, 1841–53', in Len Richardson and W. David McIntyre [eds], *Provincial Perspectives: Essays in Honour of W.J. Gardner*, University of Canterbury Press, Christchurch, 1980, p. 19).

of its goals were inadequate. However, Humanitas soon became critical of the protectors themselves, making snide references to their accents, religious fervour and lack of practical skills, and eventually he made an outright attack in which he cast them as fools. By July the newspaper's editor, George Arden, was declaring that settlers were opposed to both the principle and the practice of the Protectorate, damned it as a waste of money, and attacked the assistant protectors as men totally unfit for their roles.[14]

Prosecuting settlers

Towards the end of 1839 Superintendent La Trobe began to call upon Robinson to investigate the clashes between settlers and Aborigines that were taking place in the interior, and the Chief Protector in turn charged Dredge, Parker and Sievwright with this task. It involved an attempt to bring to book the men who had harmed Aborigines and thereby give practical effect to the principle that Aborigines were British subjects and so had equal rights before the law. In the case of the Djadja Wurrung, Sievwright tried to prosecute Henry Bowerman's two assigned servants, John Davis and Abraham Brackbrook (or Braybrook), for the killing of the two Djadja Wurrung men in March 1839, and Parker tried to prosecute Henry Monro and his men for the killings of the two Djadja Wurrung men in January 1840 and five of Henry Dutton, William Darlot, and Don Simson's men, namely Edward Collins, William Jenkins, William Martin, Robert Morrison and John Remington, for the killing of Gondu-urmin in February 1841.[15]

---

14 Gipps, Minute, 28 May 1839, *Historical Records of Victoria*, vol. 2B, p. 459; *Port Phillip Gazette*, 20 April 1839, 11 May 1839, 18 May 1839, 1 June 1839, 3 July 1839.

15 In July 1839 Sir George Gipps demanded to know why Parker had failed to make a thorough inquiry into the killings of seven or eight Aboriginal men on Bowman's

In the first of these cases Robinson sent Sievwright's report and the depositions he had gathered to Gipps in April 1839. The previous year Gipps and his administration had incurred the wrath of pastoralists and much of the press in New South Wales when they tried to prosecute the men who were believed to be responsible for massacring Aboriginal people at Myall Creek.[16] This made the Governor and his officials very cautious in dealing with such matters. Gipps referred the material from Sievwright to his Attorney General, John Plunkett, who concluded that there was not enough evidence to warrant his putting Davis and Brackbrook on trial for murder. 'The circumstances attending their death, as detailed in the documents sent', Plunkett told Gipps, 'show it was in self-defence the aboriginal natives were shot by the prisoners, and there is no evidence to contradict the statements made'. Nevertheless, Plunkett held that Davis and Brackbrook's burning of the bodies of the two Djadja Wurrung men was a criminal act since cremation should be regarded as contrary to Christian beliefs and to the notions of British civilisation, and could be construed as an attempt to destroy the proof that was required to establish the cause of death and so amounted to an attempt to obstruct the course of justice. Plunkett asked the Colonial Secretary, Edward Deas Thomson, to call for further investigation into the circumstances with a view to committing to trial those responsible for the burning of the Aboriginal men's bodies. Plunkett insisted that

run in June 1838 (Gipps, Minute, 15 July 1839, on Robinson to Thomson, 24 June 1839, New South Wales State Records, NRS 905, Item 4/2510; William Lonsdale to Parker, 27 August 1839, Public Record Office Victoria, VPRS 4, Unit 7). Parker undertook to conduct such an inquiry but, as he remarked to Robinson, it seems likely that those who could have given evidence were now widely scattered over the Port Phillip District (Parker to Robinson, 27 August 1839, *Historical Records of Victoria*, vol. 7, Melbourne University Press, Melbourne, 1998, pp. 343–44).

16 For a recent discussion of this, see Rebecca Wood, 'Frontier Violence and the Bush Legend: The *Sydney Herald*'s Response to the Myall Creek Massacre Trials and the Creation of Colonial Identity', *History Australia*, vol. 6, no. 3, 2009, pp. 67.8–11.

it should be made known throughout the colony that the destruction of the bodies of people who died in such circumstances was a criminal act, least it be thought that such offences would be simply passed over by the government. Gipps agreed. Davis and Brackbrook were committed to stand trial. Lonsdale asked the Crown Prosecutor in Port Phillip, who revelled in the name of Horatio Nelson Carrington, to summons William Allen, the overseer of the two men, since both he and Plunkett had concluded that he was much to blame.[17]

In the week that the trial took place one of Melbourne's newspapers, the *Port Phillip Patriot*, took the opportunity to express its support for the Protectorate and more especially prosecutions of this kind. After attacking a demand that the *Sydney Herald* had made the previous month that Gipps ensure that the Aborigines were prosecuted for murdering whites and executed if they were found guilty, the *Port Phillip Patriot*'s editor, John Pascoe Fawkner, wrote: '[E]very murder of a white man [by the Aborigines] is trumpeted forth to the whole world by the press, but how many of the blacks are cut off by one, by two, and by larger numbers, and we are sorry to say, lately by the Mounted Police'. He continued: 'till of late they have had no person to report, or to call for either inquests or enquiry. That day is partly gone, and if the protectors do their duty, as we hope and trust they will, we pledge ourselves to bring before the bar of public opinion every offender'.[18]

At the opening of the trial both Davis and Brackbrook pleaded guilty but Carrington objected and the court's presiding official,

17 Robinson to Deas Thomson, 22 April 1839, *Historical Records of Victoria*, vol. 2B, p. 641; John Plunkett to Deas Thomson, 25 May 1839, *Historical Records of Victoria*, vol. 2B, pp. 642–43; Lonsdale to Plunkett, 2 July 1839, *Historical Records of Victoria*, vol. 2B, p. 643; Foster, 'Aboriginal Rights', pp. 68–98.

18 *Port Phillip Patriot*, 5 August 1839.

Edward James Brewster, agreed that they should change their plea. For the prosecution Sievwright told the court how the two men had confessed to burning the bodies of the two Aboriginal men but also observed that there had been no attempt on their part to conceal the fact that they had done so; and Carrington sought to the argue that the fact that the bodies had been burned so promptly revealed a consciousness on the part of Davis and Brackbrook that they had committed murder and needed to destroy the evidence of their crime. In their testimony Davis and Brackbrook claimed that they had burned the bodies on Allen's instructions and under the belief that cremation was consonant with Aboriginal custom. In summing up the case, Brewster advised the jury that the mere act of burning the bodies was only a criminal offence if it was done with an intention to obstruct the course of justice and that if they were not convinced that this was the case they should acquit the two men. The jury returned a verdict of not guilty. The protectors and their supporters were outraged. A Wesleyan missionary, Joseph Orton, wrote in his journal: 'In this case nothing more has been done than taking the depositions of the aggressors and murderers, there being no evidence but their own [i.e. that of the murderers] and that of the Aborigines – in the former case the accused cannot incriminate himself in a court of justice and in the latter Aboriginal evidence is inadmissible. Thus these miscreants elude justice and boast in their foul deeds, which accounts for the apparent frankness of their depositions'.[19]

In the case of the killings on Monro's run in January 1840, Parker's attempt to prosecute failed in large part because of the serious legal

---

19 *Port Phillip Gazette*, 14 August 1839; *Port Phillip Patriot*, 12 August 1839; Reverend Joseph Orton, Papers 1825–1842, Mitchell Library, MS A 1715, Journal, entry, 12 January 1841; Paul R. Mullaly, *Crime in the Port Phillip District 1835–51*, Hybrid Publishers, Melbourne, 2008, p. 676.

disability that Orton had criticised in the wake of the previous trial, namely the fact that any evidence Aboriginal people gave in a court of law was regarded as inadmissible because it was believed that they were ignorant of a supreme being and a future state and so could not take a valid oath.[20] In most cases the only eye witnesses whose testimony could be heard in court were the perpetrators of the crime, and there was a legal maxim that no man could be his own accuser. In the case of Monro and his men Parker referred the matter to the Crown Prosecutor for the Port Phillip District, James Croke. In Croke's opinion the case was serious enough to warrant his recommending to La Trobe that it be referred to Plunkett. Indeed, Croke seems to have believed that the admissions made by Monro and his party were enough to put them on trial. But at the same time he realised that prosecuting the case would depend on whether or not the confessions of Monro, Liston and Hughes were deemed to be admissible. La Trobe referred the matter to Gipps but in the end the case was dropped, presumably because the only testimony available was that of the men responsible for the killings. Parker had to be content with the prospect of pressing upon La Trobe the necessity of preventing these indiscriminate and murderous reprisals by whites and making Monro realise that his conduct was severely censured by the government.[21]

---

20 Gipps was anxious for cases such as this one to be prosecuted but he realised that it was difficult to do so until the law was altered so that Aboriginal testimony could be admitted (Gipps to La Trobe, 12 December 1840, A.G.L. Shaw [ed.], *Gipps–La Trobe Correspondence 1839–1846*, Miegunyah Press, Melbourne, 1989, p. 52). In October 1839 the New South Wales Legislative Council passed legislation to enable this but it was disallowed in August 1840 by the imperial government (see Russell Smandych, 'Contemplating the Evidence of "Others": James Stephen, the Colonial Office, and the Fate of the Australian Aboriginal Evidence Acts, circa 1839–1849', *Australian Journal of Legal History*, vol. 8, no. 2, 2004, pp. 237–83).

21 James Croke to La Trobe, 23 March 1840, Public Record Office Victoria, VPRS 19, Unit 4; Croke to Parker, 11 August 1840, Public Record Office of Victoria, VPRS 21,

In regard to the killing of Gondu-urmin on Dutton, Darlot, and Simson's run in February 1841, Collins, Jenkins, Martin, Morrison and Remington were apprehended and committed to stand trial for manslaughter. In submitting to Croke the depositions that he had gathered, Parker observed that there was a gross discrepancy between the account the accused had given and the one provided by some of the Djadja Wurrung. Moreover, he pointed out, the case would have had a more serious dimension if the Djadja Wurrung's evidence had been admissible. 'I am satisfied from the account given by the Aborigines, borne out as it is by the statement of the prisoner Collin[s], that the black Abraham [i.e. Munangabum] laid hold of the shepherd Morrison simply in self-defence, expecting he was going to be shot, and not with any hostile intent', Parker wrote. 'It is evident that the two blacks shot were *not armed*', he added. In other words, Parker would have committed the men to stand trial for murder rather than manslaughter if the Djadja Wurrung had been allowed to act as witnesses.[22]

On receiving the material for the case it appears that Croke concluded that all the depositions Parker had submitted were inadmissible because they were by the men who were alleged to have committed the offence. On being told this Parker pointed out that this was not actually the case: he had committed the men for trial solely on the basis of the depositions of two men who had been present but who were not on charge, Patrick Clark and R. Battenshell. Parker

Unit 1, Bundle 1; Parker to Robinson, 19 August 1840, Public Record Office Victoria, VPRS 11, Unit 4; La Trobe to Thomson, 10 October 1840, Public Record Office Victoria, VPRS 16, Unit 2.

22 Parker, Quarterly Report, 1 December 1840 – 28 February 1841, Public Record Office Victoria, VPRS 4410, Unit 2; Parker to Robinson, 12 February 1841, Public Record Office Victoria, VPRS 11, Unit 4; Parker to Croke, 1 March 1841, Public Record Office Victoria, VPRS 21, Unit 1, Bundle 3, his emphasis.

also informed Croke that a further witness might be called, a servant by the name of Joseph Maddox, who had stated that he was present and had fired on the Aborigines, but he conceded that Clark as well as the men charged had stated that Maddox only arrived after the fatal shots had been fired. It seems that Croke formed the opinion that Clark and Battenshell's evidence was also inadmissible. On 22 April he asked Justice John Walpole Willis to postpone the trial and the following day he more or less told Parker that he needed to procure additional evidence in order to strengthen the case. In the end, the case went to court on 18 May with Collins, Jenkins, Martin, Morrison and Remington charged with a lesser offence: shooting with intent to maim or shooting with intent to cause grievous bodily harm. It appears that the only witness was Maddox, who under oath made the outlandish claim that the party had been attacked by 150 Aborigines. At this point it seems that Croke decided to halt his prosecution of the case and Willis directed the jury to bring a finding that the accused were perfectly justified in shooting in self-defence, which is just what it did. To make matters worse for the Protectorate, Willis criticised Parker for taking sworn depositions from those he had charged, just as he had criticised Sievwright for this mistake earlier in this court's sittings. Finally, he rubbed salt into their wounds by expressing regret that the accused had had to spend so long in custody.[23]

Parker was livid. 'This witness [Maddox]', he complained, 'had stated in his deposition at the investigation of the case that there were *fifty* blacks only present, and even some of the prisoners had sworn

---

23 Parker to Croke, 30 March 1841, Public Record Office Victoria, VPRS 21, Unit 1, Bundle 3; Croke to Parker, 23 April 1841, cited Mullaly, *Crime in the Port Phillip District*, pp. 368–69; John Walpole Willis Case books, 1838–1843, Royal Historical Society of Victoria, MS 5181, Case Book No. 11, entry 18 May 1841; *Port Phillip Gazette*, 19 May 1841; *Port Phillip Herald*, 19 May 1841.

that no spears had been thrown'. Indeed, the assistant protector despaired that he would ever be able to prosecute the perpetrators of violence against Aboriginal people: 'Thus there is no chance of justice being obtained for these unfortunate people while their evidence is rejected. The witnesses are sure to be hostile and have only to swear hard enough, as in the present case, and the cause of the aborigines is put out of court'. Indeed, it seems that Parker came to conclude that the bar on Aboriginal people giving evidence meant that it was use-less trying to prosecute any pastoralists or their men for murdering Aborigines. In fact no white men would be successfully prosecuted for their killing of Aboriginal people in the Port Phillip District. Even where white man admitted that they had killed Aborigines, they were acquitted on legal technicalities. In one notorious case in 1842, in which a pastoralist had shot an Aboriginal man dead while driving Aborigines from his run with a whip, Justice Willis deemed the act lawful on the grounds that the Aborigines had no right to be there under the conditions of pastoral leases.[24]

Protecting Aborigines

In the course of the investigations that Parker conducted in Djadja Wurrung country in the middle of 1839 he grasped the nature of the threat that pastoral occupation was presenting to the Aboriginal people and began to form an opinion about the common causes of conflict between settler and Aborigine and what needed to be done to avert it. In June that year he argued that the Aboriginal people should be separated as much as possible from the convict shepherds

24 Parker, Quarterly Journal, 1 March – 30 May 1841; Suzanne Davies, 'Aborigines, Murders, and the Criminal Law in Early Port Phillip, 1840–1851', *Australian Historical Studies*, vol. 22, no. 88, 1987, pp. 313–36.

and hut keepers as well as others of their class. He also contended that the Aborigines had to be induced to give up their present practice of moving from pastoral station to pastoral station in search of food. But neither of these things could be done, he remarked, unless the protectors could hold out to the Aborigines sufficient inducement in the form of food, clothing, and shelter and place the Aborigines on tracts of land from which white settlers were excluded by law. Parker insisted that immediate measures of this kind were required for the preservation of the Aboriginal people.[25]

Yet Parker was slow to move to his district. Indeed he was the slowest of all the assistant protectors to shift to the districts to which they had been assigned. In September he moved out of Melbourne but only so far as Jackson's Creek (near present-day Sunbury), too far from the Aboriginal nations in his district. Parker pleaded that he was unwell and that his wife was confined for the birth of their seventh child, but he remained at Jackson's Creek once he had recovered and the child was born, and seemed reluctant to move any further.[26]

After a tour of his district Parker concluded that it was impossible for the assistant protectors to carry out one of the duties that Glenelg had originally set down for them, namely that of moving about with the Aborigines. In a report he submitted to Robinson in April 1840 he asserted that the protectors could not attach themselves closely and constantly to Aboriginal nations because they consisted of small groups and ranged widely in search of food. He suggested that it would be better if the assistant protectors could form protectorate

---

25 Parker to Robinson, 20 June 1839, *Historical Records of Victoria*, vol. 7, pp. 325–26.
26 Robinson to La Trobe, 23 September 1840, Public Record Office Victoria, VPRS 10, Unit 2.

stations to which they would strive to attract the Aborigines. In making this suggestion Parker made reference once more to the fact that many Aboriginal groups were being forced to try to acquire food from the pastoral runs, whether through begging, prostitution or the use of force. He stated again that this unsatisfactory situation could only be changed if the protectors were able to offer some inducement to Aborigines in the form of clothing, food and shelter. In short, Parker believed that concentrating the Aborigines on protectorate stations and providing for their needs would reduce the potential for conflict between the pastoralists and the Aboriginal people on the frontiers of settlement since it would both help guard Aboriginal people against injury by the settlers and secure the property of the settlers from attacks by the Aborigines. Recently, several historians have argued that the protection of Aboriginal people in the Australian colonies was a project that sought to govern Aborigines by bringing them under the authority of the colonial state.[27] This is undoubtedly the case but in regard to the Port Phillip Protectorate it must be recognised that those such as Parker seem to have concluded that the adoption of these measures was the only way to protect Aborigines because they realised that the state was either unable or unwilling to put a stop to the ravages of British colonisation.[28]

Parker concluded his argument with this emotional plea: 'But left in their present state to be beaten by the "white man's foot", to be excluded, perforce, from lands which they unquestionably regard as

---

27 See, for example, Jessie Mitchell, *In Good Faith? Governing Indigenous Australia through God, Charity and Empire, 1825–1855*, Aboriginal History, Canberra, 2011, and Amanda Nettelbeck, '"A Halo of Protection": Colonial Protectors and the Principle of Aboriginal Protection through Punishment', *Australian Historical Studies*, vol. 43, no. 3, 2012, pp. 396–411.

28 Parker, Report for 1 September 1839 – 29 February 1840, Public Record Office Victoria, VPRS 4410, Unit 2.

their own property, and from scenes as dear to them as our own native homes to us – despoiled – denied the rights of humanity – classified with and treated as wild dogs – I can entertain no other expectation that they will be driven to more frequent depredations and exposed to more rapid and certain destruction'. In the same report, Parker made clear the moral or philosophical basis of his belief that stations or reserves should be created:

> Are the territorial rights of the Aborigines to be set aside by violence? Appointed as I have been by Her Majesty's government specially 'to watch over the rights and interests of the natives', and to 'protect them from any encroachments on their property, and from acts of cruelty, oppression or injustice', I deem it my duty respectfully but firmly to assert the right of the Aborigines to the soil and its indigenous productions *until* suitable compensation be made for its oc-cupation by reserving and cultivating a sufficient portion for their maintenance.[29]

In the closing decades of the twentieth century historians such as Henry Reynolds drew attention to this kind of advocacy as part of a project in which they have sought to argue that there were enormous similarities between the rights in land that were claimed in the 1830s and 1840s by those they have called humanitarians and the rights to land that were claimed in the 1960s and 1970s by Aboriginal cam-paigners and their supporters.[30] It is undeniable that philanthropists in the 1830s and 1840s recognised that Aboriginal forms of land tenure existed, acknowledged that they were dispossessed, and held that they had rights of some kind on the grounds of their ownership of

---

29 *Ibid.*, my emphasis.
30 See Henry Reynolds, *The Law of the Land*, Penguin, Melbourne, 1987, and *This Whispering in Our Hearts*, Allen & Unwin, Sydney, 1998, chapters 1–4.

the land. However, the rights talk of the philanthropists in the 1830s and 1840s was rather different from that of the 1960s and 1970s. For the most part the rights they emphasised were civil rights rather than any right that could be claimed by aboriginal people alone; and those civil rights principally comprised a right to be protected from cruelty and oppression. In respect of any rights in regard to land the position the philanthropists took might be regarded as somewhat equivocal. They were principally concerned with the destruction of the Aboriginal people's food sources rather than the fact that the indigenes were being dispossessed of property in land; in any case they held that Aboriginal people were only entitled to small parts of their ancestral lands, such as reserves; and where they cast Aboriginal people as the original owners of the land they did so in order to create a case that Aboriginal people were owed some compensation for the means of subsistence they had lost, whether that be in the form of reserves or rations, which amounted to some kind of right to charity.[31] Certainly, as we saw earlier, this is what characterised Parker's position on the matter.[32]

Parker's plea that the assistant protectors be allowed to form stations was approved by Gipps at the end of April 1840. Each station was to have an inner reserve of a square mile, where cultivation should take place, and an outer reserve of five miles in radius, where hunting and gathering could occur. Gipps instructed the Commissioners of Crown Lands to refuse to allow any pastoral

---

31 For a recent discussion of this matter, see Mitchell, *In Good Faith*, pp. 98, 100, 105, 107–08, 113–14, 196.

32 This also seems evident in a report Parker gave in 1843: after referring to the provision given to some categories of Aboriginal people he remarked that 'in this way some compensation [is] made to these unhappy people for the loss of their country and the destruction of their original means of subsistence' (Parker to Robinson, 1 December 1843).

stations within five miles of a protector's residence. He also insisted that the assistant protectors take great care in choosing the sites for these stations, and that they should be as remote as possible from settled districts.[33]

Choosing a site for a station

Having argued that protectorate stations were desperately needed in order to save the Aboriginal people from extermination, Parker found it difficult to choose a site for a station in his jurisdiction. In February 1840 he and Robinson had travelled to the Loddon District on official business. During this trip the pastoralist John Hepburn had pointed out to them a place on the Loddon River several miles north east of Smeaton Hill that he thought might be suitable for a station. Robinson had immediately declared that there was no better site for a protectorate station: it had abundant kangaroos and large water holes that contained plenty of fish, it was not required by any pastoralist, it was readily accessible from Melbourne, and it was a favoured place of the Djadja Wurrung. However, the following month Parker told Robinson that he wanted to occupy a station in a central situation on the Loddon River some miles below Lachlan MacKinnon's station, Tarrengower, and sought permission to do this. It appears that the place Parker had in mind was a place that the Djadja Wurrung called Neura Mong, which meant 'hide here'. But Robinson informed Gipps that this was at a place crossed by Major Mitchell's line and the Governor refused to sanction Parker's

---

33 Parker to Robinson, 18 March 1840, Public Record Office Victoria, VPRS 11, Unit 4; La Trobe to Thomson, 3 April 1840, New South Wales State Records, NRS 905, Item 4/2628; Thomson to La Trobe, 28 April 1840, Public Record Office Victoria, VPRS 10, Unit 2; Robinson to Assistant Protectors, 11 June 1840, *Historical Records of Victoria*, vol. 7, pp. 368–69.

choice of site. Parker insisted that this was the best site for a station. Consequently, the matter seems to have stalled.[34]

In late September Parker went to the outstation on William and Alexander Mollison's run at a place called Lalgambook, which was on a creek of the Loddon River near Mount Franklin, to investigate whether it might be more suitable before proceeding down the Loddon River to Neura Mong where he once again concluded that it was peculiarly well suited for a station. However, there was a problem. It had been occupied recently by the pastoralists Darlot, Dutton and Simson. Parker decided he should postpone taking possession of it until he had secured La Trobe's permission, but after surveying the country on both sides of the Loddon River the following month he once more claimed that this was the most suitable site.[35]

In the middle of November Parker and several Aboriginal children in his care moved onto part of Darlot, Dutton, and Simson's run. In the course of the next few weeks a large number of the Djadja Wurrung visited Parker there. A few days after he had arrived Parker found to his surprise that the Commissioner of Crown Lands, Frederick Powlett, had failed to tell the pastoralists that a protectorate station was going to be created on part of their run. Consequently, Parker sent Darlot a letter advising the pastoralists that he had taken possession of a stretch of land along both sides of the river two

---

34 Parker, Report for 1 September 1839 – 29 February 1840; Ian D. Clark (ed.), *The Journals of George Augustus Robinson, Chief Protector, Port Phillip Aboriginal Protectorate*, vol. 1, 1 January 1839 – 30 September 1840, Heritage Matters, Melbourne, 1998, entry 14 February 1840, pp. 169–70; Parker to Robinson, 18 March 1840; Robinson to La Trobe, 31 March 1840, New South Wales State Records, NRS 905, Item 4/2628; Parker to Robinson, 6 July 1840, Public Record Office Victoria, VPRS 11, Unit 4.

35 Parker, Quarterly Journal, 1 September – 30 November 1840, Public Record Office Victoria, VPRS 4410, Unit 2; Parker to Robinson, 15 October 1840, Public Record Office Victoria, VPRS 10, Unit 2; Parker, Quarterly Journal, 1 December 1840 – 28 February 1841; Edgar Morrison, *Early Days in the Loddon Valley: Memoirs of Edward Stone Parker 1802–1865*, s. n., Daylesford, 1966, p. 14.

and a half miles below their head station and requesting that they immediately move their cattle so that he could begin cultivation.[36]

Not surprisingly, perhaps, Parker's missive riled the pastoralists. Darlot immediately appealed to Powlett. More importantly, the *Port Phillip Herald*, which was the principal organ of the critics of the Protectorate and which was co-owned by Dutton, seized upon the matter so it could mount another attack on the Protectorate. In a hyperbolic leader published in early December Arden claimed that Parker's assumption of land for a reserve was 'the most flagrant attempt to destroy legalised claims, and to substitute in their stead the caprice of the Protectorate'. He continued: 'We understand government have often asserted that they have a right to resume any station they may choose, upon giving three months' notice to that effect, although a regular license was held by the settler; but we never, until the last few days, imagined that they would enter upon such lands without notice, and in such a summary and arbitrary manner'. Arden insisted that the pastoralists had a license from the government to this land and that they had not breached any of its conditions. '[B]ut, in open defiance of this, Mr Parker has entered upon it with a tribe of blacks, and set himself down upon the very spot for which the license has been granted'. Arden went on to allege that Darlot had lost 650 cattle out of a herd of 800 at a cost of £4875 as a result of what he called Parker's wilful outrage and that this loss was only to be expected. 'It is well known to every settler, and cannot be a secret to Mr Parker, that cattle will not remain in the vicinity of

36 Parker, Quarterly Journal, 1 September – 30 November 1840; Parker to Darlot, 18 November 1840, reproduced in *Port Phillip Herald*, 8 January 1841; Parker to Robinson, 5 January 1841, Public Record Office Victoria, VPRS 11, Unit 4; Frederick Powlett to La Trobe, 8 February 1841, Public Record Office Victoria, VPRS 10, Unit 3; *Port Phillip Herald*, 4 December 1840.

the Blacks.' This was a formulation of a settler adage that 'blacks and cattle didn't mix'.[37]

If all these matters were bad in Arden's eyes what he next relayed was worse: La Trobe had confirmed what Arden called 'the black intrusion'. This amounted to an autocratic government trampling on the rights of the settlers: '*His* opinion of the law, or perhaps we should say *his law*, is that the government has a *right* to take possession, without previous notice, of any station whatever, independently of a regular license held by the then occupant, and that had Mr Parker seized the premises themselves, with all the improvements thereon, he would have been perfectly justified in so doing!!!' Arden concluded his argument thus: 'Let the aborigines be protected, and their every necessary want supplied to the utmost extent that humanity may dictate or justice demand, but never at the sacrifice of the pledged rights of the settlers'. In closing his editorial Arden claimed that Darlot was going to sue Parker for his serious loss.[38]

In the following number of the *Port Phillip Herald* Arden repeated his claims about the losses sustained by Darlot and alleged that settlers had joined forces and were planning a meeting at which they would 'remonstrate against the unprovoked injustice by which they were threatened'. At the same time he attacked what he called 'the omnipotence of the Protectorate' and asserted that the term protector had become a by-word in the colony for 'an aggressor and a destroyer' rather than 'a defender'. Indeed, he claimed that the case had provoked a crisis in the history of the colony. 'If Mr Darlot's case be allowed to remain a precedent – if he do[es] not receive ample compensation

---

37 *Port Phillip Herald*, 4 December 1840; Parker to Darlot, 18 November 1840, reproduced in *Port Phillip Herald*, 8 January 1841.

38 *Port Phillip Herald*, 4 December 1840, original emphases.

not only for his actual loss but also to mark *a principle* – the slavery of the slave will be the lot of our unfortunate colonists', he alleged. In the next issue Arden made much the same arguments, sprinkling his editorial with phrases such as 'the tyrannical despoilation of the Protectorate' and 'Black Protectors' (which was a term of abuse often used by the *Sydney Herald*).[39]

By this point in time Parker had already decided that the site he had occupied was quite unfit for the purposes of agriculture. In fact he had realised this the day after he arrived there in the middle of November. He had first seen the place after spring rain had created the appearance of rich soil but the onset of summer had revealed that the soil was sandy and only suitable for grazing. Parker sent his overseer, Bazely, to examine the land between Mackinnon's Tarrengower run and Lalgambook, and he reported that it was superior, but Parker decided that he had better stay put because La Trobe had sanctioned the site he was currently occupying. He hoped rain would come but by January these hopes had been dashed. Parker decided it was best to move to the site that Bazley had seen.[40]

This site had the advantage that it was preferred by the Djadja Wurrung. Aboriginal people played a role in choosing many of the places that protectors and missionaries nominated for reserves in Australia,[41] and this seems to have been the case here. In September a Djadja Wurrung man by the name of Yenebulluck had provided

39 *Port Phillip Herald*, 8 December 1840, 11 December 1840, original emphasis; *Sydney Herald*, 6 February 1839, 13 May 1839, 18 September 1839, 10 February 1840, 17 August 1840.

40 Parker, Quarterly Report 1 September – 30 November 1840; Parker to Robinson, 5 January 1841.

41 See, for example, Bain Attwood, *The Making of the Aborigines*, Allen & Unwin, Sydney, 1989, p. 4; and Heather Goodall, *Invasion to Embassy: Land in Aboriginal Politics in New South Wales, 1770–1972*, Allen & Unwin in association with Black Books, Sydney, 1996, pp. 77–79.

much valuable information to Parker and might have suggested that this was the best place for a station. Furthermore, one of the neighbouring Aboriginal nations had apparently told Parker that they would also be willing to settle at this place but that they were unwilling to contemplate any site further down the Loddon River. Parker informed Robinson that he was reluctant to move but argued that he had no choice. Perhaps part of his reluctance sprung from the fact that he knew that his new preferred site was on land occupied by a pastoralist, or in fact two pastoralists, Alexander Mollison (at Coliban) and Mackinnon (at Tarrengower), and was unwilling to have a further battle of the kind he had had with Darlot.[42]

Further battles

The pastoralists in the area soon learned of Parker's new plans and were quick to register their protests. At end of December 1840 D. Lyon Campbell at Bullarook complained to La Trobe that Parker's proposal would be a great injustice to him and his fellow squatters on the Loddon River. Campbell alleged that he had postponed setting up stockyards and huts for several months until Parker had decided where he would establish a station and that had only done so once the assistant protector had declared that he was going to establish a station on Darlot, Dutton and Simson's run. 'With all due deference', Campbell told La Trobe, 'I venture to remark that it surely never was intended that such power should be given the protectors: to run over the country dispossessing the settlers and as whim and other inducements may guide them, moving on from one settlement to form another'. A week later Mackinnon at Tarrengower complained

---

42 Parker, Quarterly Report 1 September – 30 November 1840; Robinson to La Trobe, 23 September 1840; Parker to Robinson, 5 January 1841.

to La Trobe that the interests of the settlers were being interfered with unnecessarily and demanded protection from what he called the 'ill-judged measures of these men immediately connected with the Protectorate'. Mackinnon also sought to persuade La Trobe that Parker's current site could not surpassed but that the site on part of his run was poorly suited because it was too close to Major Mitchell's line and thus the road to Melbourne.[43]

In the light of these appeals La Trobe asked Robinson to ascertain from Parker what his plans really were. Yet the Superintendent was largely unmoved by the pastoralists' pleas. He sought to reassure them that the government would take care to ensure that there was no unnecessary infringement of their interests but he also asserted that the moral and physical improvement of the Aborigines was of paramount importance. La Trobe might have resolved to take this position as a result of a further editorial in the *Port Phillip Herald* on the same day as he wrote to the pastoralists. Arden had turned his attack on the Protectorate onto La Trobe, alleging that he was responsible for Parker's incursion and should pay in full the losses Darlot had sustained. Shortly before going to press Arden had learned that Parker had decided that he needed to move his station to another site. He was scathing. Having inflicted so much damage on a pastoralist by seizing his land, now Parker was declaring these lands were not suitable for his purpose! At the very least this suggested that Parker was an unfit person to be selecting a suitable place for an Aboriginal reserve; at most the new plan suggested that La Trobe had acknowledged that he was in error and that the *Port Phillip Herald*

---

43 D. Lyon Campbell to La Trobe, 31 December 1840, Public Record Office Victoria, VPRS 19, Unit 9; Lachlan Mackinnon to La Trobe, 7 January 1841, Public Record Office Victoria, VPRS 19, Unit 10; Parker to Robinson, 5 January 1841.

had succeeded in upholding the rights of the settlers and foiling La Trobe's attempt to assume unconstitutional authority. As so often during this period, matters of Aboriginal policy were cast as a matter not of their rights but of the rights of the settlers.[44]

At the same time as La Trobe seemed willing to take a firm stand on the matter, he expressed concern to Robinson about the various charges that Arden, Campbell and Mackinnon had levelled. In regard to what had happened on Darlot, Dutton and Simson's run, he told Robinson that he had never been able to declare a reserve for the land Parker had occupied the previous November because the assistant protector had never provided any precise information that he had decided to occupy it. On the more general matter La Trobe reminded Robinson that the protectors would never want for his support while they took steps to promote the welfare of the Aborigines and uphold their rights, but cautioned him: 'you are not a stranger to my opinion that unnecessary collision with the settlers is to be deprecated for the good of the cause itself, and it is my decided impression that with the exercise of a proper discretion and judgement such collision could be altogether avoided without any sacrifice'. For the time being, given the concerns that Campbell and Mackinnon had expressed, La Trobe was unwilling to sanction Parker's request to move. He wanted more information and decided to send Powlett to get it.[45]

Parker was hurt by La Trobe's criticism. He told Robinson that he had given the Superintendent a clear description of the land he had intended to occupy, that he had proceeded there on the assumption

---

44 La Trobe, Minute, no date, on Campbell to La Trobe, 31 December 1840; La Trobe to Mackinnon, 8 January 1841, Public Record Office Victoria, VPRS 16, Unit 2; *Port Phillip Herald*, 8 January 1841.

45 La Trobe to Robinson, 9 January 1841, Public Record Office Victoria, VPRS 16, Unit 2.

that he had done all that was required on his part and that the necessary measures had or would be taken by the Commissioner of Crown Lands as a matter of course, and that he did not learn that this was not the case until after he had called upon Darlot to move his cattle. He also argued that there were several inaccuracies in MacKinnon's letter. Turning to the attack that had been made in the press, Parker complained bitterly of what he called 'the brutal prejudices with which the officers of this department have been assailed ever since the day of their arrival in the colony', and informed Robinson that he was prepared to refute the allegations that had been made in the press if he was required to do so by La Trobe. In fact, Parker had already done this in a letter he had sent to Arden. In concluding his letter to Robinson, Parker turned to the general issues that La Trobe had raised. 'In the considerations of this question I trust the paramount claims of the aborigines will not be overlooked. I must respectfully maintain on their behalf that they have a *right* to have the best land that can be obtained set apart to their use as permanent reserves', he began, before moving to the crux of the matter. 'I must beg, however, respectfully to call the attention of His Honor to the fact that every available spot in the Jajowrong [i.e. Djadja Wurrung] country has been occupied by squatters, mostly within the last year, and that, in my opinion, it will be quite impossible to form a suitable aboriginal reserve without disturbing some of the new occupants'.[46]

A couple of days later, Parker's letter to the *Port Phillip Herald* appeared prominently in its pages. Parker pointed out that he had recommended the site of the reserve in July the previous year and that

---

46 Ian D. Clark (ed.), *Journals of George Augustus Robinson, Chief Protector, vol. 2, 1 October 1840 – 31 August 1841*, Heritage Matters, Melbourne, 1998, entry 11 January 1841, p. 54; Parker to Robinson, 13 January 1841, Public Record Office Victoria, VPRS 11, Unit 4, his emphasis.

he had supposed the land to be unoccupied; that only a small number of Aboriginal people had accompanied him to the site and they were mostly children, that the pastoralists' cattle had not been disturbed by any of his people and that they had not even removed their cattle from the place Parker had chosen. In short, Arden's claims were wildly exaggerated. Parker refrained from addressing the matter of the rights of settlers under their squatting licenses on the grounds that this was beyond the scope of his duties, but he did raise what he called higher claims: 'I assert the paramount right of the original possessors of the soil, and I cannot but remark that it is a painful indication of the inhuman feeling prevalent towards the aborigines in this colony that as soon as they are concentrated and employed in raising the means of subsistence, private interests clamorously urge their exclusion from very spot calculated to yield a profitable turn, and it is sought to drive them back to the arid desert of the barren "scrub"'.[47]

This passionate defence of the Aboriginal people's rights to the land was grist to Arden's mill. He used the publication of Parker's letter as an opportunity to launch a further attack on the Protectorate and the government. In an editorial he entitled *The Protectors versus the Colonists*, Arden claimed that Parker's letter had undoubtedly been sanctioned by La Trobe, argued that Parker's statements in his letter only added to the proof of the terrible power Parker had assumed only to abuse it, and asserted that Parker's plan to abandon the station showed he was unfit for the office he held. Finally, Arden turned to the charge that Parker had levelled at settlers. 'We, on the part of our abused fellow colonists, indignantly deny that there is an "inhuman state of feeling prevalent towards the Aborigines in this

---

47 Parker to the Editor of the Port Phillip Herald, 9 January 1841, reproduced in *Port Phillip Herald*, 15 January 1841.

colony". There is not a settler in the wide range of the Port Phillip District who would not heartily rejoice at seeing the Aborigines really and well *protected*, and would not, in every way humanity might dictate or justice demand, contribute towards that desired end, but let us never measure our love of the blacks by our hatred of the whites. Justice to both is not incompatible with the duties of the Protectorate'. This was a common settler charge against the Protectorate. In concluding, Arden returned to the broader allegation he had made previously, namely that La Trobe's assumption of authority was unconstitutional.[48]

Parker's letter got him into hot water with La Trobe. By the end of the day that it appeared in the *Port Phillip Herald* La Trobe had called on Robinson to tell Parker that he had no authority to write to the newspaper. Soon afterwards, it appears that La Trobe asked Parker to answer specifically the charges Darlot had made. In reply, Parker informed Robinson that no more than twenty of Darlot's cattle were actually missing and alleged that Darlot's herd had never even moved away from the site Parker had occupied and had instead been trampling on the crops Parker had planted for the benefit of the Aborigines. Shortly afterwards, Crown Commissioner Powlett would confirm that Darlot's claims of injury were grossly exaggerated. Darlot's own overseer had told him that only thirty or forty cattle out of a herd numbering 1300 or 1400 were missing.[49]

In the middle of January 1841 La Trobe despatched Powlett to examine both the sites that Parker had first proposed to occupy as well as the one he now wanted to occupy. More especially he asked

---

48 *Port Phillip Herald*, 15 January 1841.

49 Clark (ed.), *Journals of Robinson*, vol. 2, entry 15 January 1841, p. 57; Parker to Robinson, 25 January 1841, Public Record Office Victoria, VPRS 11, Unit 4; Powlett to La Trobe, 8 February 1841, Public Record Office Victoria, VPRS 10, Unit 3.

Powlett to establish the exact distance between Parker's favoured site and the homesteads and outstations of the pastoralists that would be affected. It seems that Powlett might have agreed that Parker needed to move his station for the reason the assistant protector had stated. But Powlett appears to have been more concerned to try to heal the rift between the pastoralists and the assistant protector and was very conscious that runs were becoming more valuable in the district. Accordingly, he urged Parker to move further up the Loddon River or move westward. Parker was reluctant to adopt these suggestions. He claimed that Aborigines had told him they would refuse to go further than where the reserve was currently, and the Djadja Wurrung wanted nothing to do with the people of Aboriginal nations to the north. In the light of this but also in an attempt to choose a site that would interfere less with the interests of the pastoralists, Powlett recommended to Parker that he was best to settle on the part of Mollison's run at Lalgambook. Parker eventually acceded to this suggestion.[50]

This place was known by the Djadja Wurrung as Larrnebarramul (the home of the emu). This was their name for Mount Franklin, which resembles a huge emu nest.[51] It was in fact the place that

---

50 La Trobe to Powlett, 18 January 1841, Public Record Office Victoria, VPRS 16, Unit 2; Parker to Robinson, 26 January 1841, Public Record Office Victoria, VPRS 10, Unit 3; Powlett to La Trobe, 8 February 1841.

51 It appears that the emu was part of ceremonies that the Djadja Wurrung performed. A pastoralist in the area, John Hunter Kerr, noted that 'the natives were accustomed to bring [figures of an emu] into their night corroborees with great ceremony. It was nearly of life size, and was carried by a native who imitated the gait of a bird, while the others danced around' (in R.E. Johns, Scrapbook, Museum Victoria, vol. 1, ff. 241-42). Emus were also figured in bark etchings made by the Djadja Wurung. For a photograph of one of these, held by the British Museum, see <www.britishmuseum.org/research/collection_online/collection_object_details. aspx?objectId=512515&partId=1>; and for a schematic representation of it, see Elizabeth Willis, 'Exhibiting Aboriginal Industry: A Story Behind a "Re-Discovered" Bark Drawing From Victoria', *Aboriginal History*, vol. 27, 2003, p. 42.

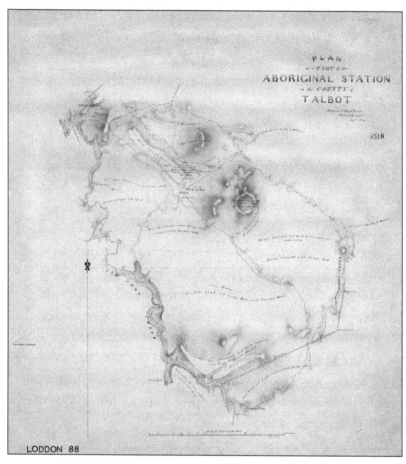

PLAN
of a PART of the
ABORIGINAL STATION
in the COUNTY of
TALBOT

8510

LODDON 88

A map of the protectorate station at Larrnebarramul,
drawn by a surveyor in 1854
(Courtesy Public Record Office Victoria)

Hepburn had pointed out to Robinson and Parker in February 1840 as a suitable site and which Robinson had urged Parker to select. As the Chief Protector was to note, it was surrounded by forested ranges that contained an abundance of game. Mollison called this place Jumcra, perhaps because he thought this was the Djadja Wurrung's name for it, but Hepburn called it Jim Crow Hill and while Parker's station became officially known as Mount Franklin Aboriginal Station (or Franklinford), Hepburn's naming stuck and became its nickname among many. There is some evidence to suggest that the Djadja Wurrung also adopted *Jim Crow* as its name. The historian Alexandra Roginski has reminded us recently that the name *Jim Crow* stemmed from 'Jump Jim Crow', a minstrel song that was first staged in the United States and which was seminal to a genre that relied upon caricatures that depicted 'dim-witted' Negro slaves. However, Roginski points out that many Aboriginal people nevertheless adopted 'Jim Crow' as their personal name and suggests that they might have done so because, rather than seeing the minstrel character as a racial joke, they could have regarded him as a famous figure who had been immortalised with his own song.[52]

At much the same time that Parker and Powlett settled on this site Gipps told La Trobe that he would not allow protectors to remove any pastoralists who had pastoral licenses. However, he also stated that there was no doubt that pastoralists had to give up land if the government decided this was necessary for a public purpose, as was

---

52 Clark (ed.), *Journals of Robinson*, vol. 1, entry 14 February 1840, p. 170; Ian D. Clark (ed.), *The Journals of George Augustus Robinson, Chief Protector, Port Phillip Aboriginal Protectorate, vol. 3, 1 September 1841 – 31 December 1842*, Heritage Matters, Melbourne, 1999, entries 19 and 20 November 1841, pp. 17–18, 20; Ellen to Parker, 10 June 1864, reproduced in Edgar Morrison, *The Loddon Aborigines: "Tales of Old Jim Crow"*, s.n., Yandoit, 1971, p. 93; Victoria, Legislative Assembly, *Votes and Proceedings*, 1877–78, vol. 3, Royal Commission on the Aborigines, p. 10; Robert Brough Smyth, *The Aborigines of Victoria*, vol. 2, Government Printer, Melbourne, 1878, pp. 159, 195; Edgar Morrison, *Frontier Life in the Loddon Protectorate: Episodes from Early Days, 1837–42*, Advocate, Daylesford, 1967, p. 41; Alexandra Roginski, *The Hanged Man and the Body Thief: Finding Lives in a Museum Mystery*, Monash University Publishing, Melbourne, 2015, pp. 6–7.

the case here. This said, Gipps called on La Trobe to do what he could to ensure that the interests of the pastoral license holders were consulted. In early March Gipps approved of Parker being put in possession of the land at Mount Franklin so long as he consulted the interests of the pastoralists who would need to be removed from the immediate neighbourhood. Powlett instructed Mollison to move his sheep from one of his outstations to make the establishment of the reserve possible. In fact there is no evidence to suggest that this pastoralist opposed the decision to create the reserve there. Moreover, most of the other long-term pastoralists in the area do not seem to have shared Mackinnon's animosity towards Parker and Robinson or the Protectorate. This was in marked contrast to the situation in some other districts, such as Portland, where the local protectorate's nearest neighbours were especially hostile. Finally, it seemed, Parker could begin on his work of seeking to Christianise and civilise the Djadja Wurrung.[53]

---

53 Thomson to La Trobe, 23 January 1841, Public Record Office Victoria, VPRS 10, Unit 3; Thomson to La Trobe, 6 March 1841, Public Record Office Victoria, VPRS 10, Unit 3; R.H.W. Reece, *Aborigines and Colonists: Aborigines and Colonial Society in New South Wales in the 1830s and 1840s*, Sydney University Press, Sydney, 1974, p. 201; Michael Cannon, *Who Killed the Koories*, William Heinemann, Melbourne, 1990, p. 20.

Chapter 5

REFUGE

By the time Edward Parker began to establish a protectorate station at Lalgambook in June 1841 he and the Djadja Wurrung were already pretty well acquainted with one another. At a meeting in February 1840 two groups of Djadja Wurrung had apparently told George Augustus Robinson that they were very pleased at the prospect of Parker coming to sit down among them and protect and care for them. They informed Robinson that they would make houses there and tell their countrymen about Parker's coming.[1]

In the following months Djadja Wurrung were to meet Parker in Melbourne and seek his help. For example, in March a group travelled there to seek the release of Munangabum, who, readers will recall, had been arrested in January in the midst of the Monro incidents. They were successful: he was discharged after Superintendent Charles Joseph La Trobe asked the Crown Prosecutor James Croke whether it was necessary to detain him given that his case had not been listed in the court's forthcoming sessions. However, in September some Djadja Wurrung told Parker that some of their fellow Aborigines were angered by the measures that the government was taking to exclude them from Melbourne and

---

1   Ian D. Clark (ed.), *The Journals of George Augustus Robinson, Chief Protector, Port Phillip Aboriginal Protectorate, vol. 1, 1 January 1839 – 30 September 1840*, Heritage Matters, Melbourne, 1998, entries 21 and 27 February 1840, pp. 175, 181.

by the treatment they were receiving from many of the settlers. 'I
have been plainly told', Parker wrote in his journal, 'that the natives
would, "bye and bye", take to the mountains and try to drive the
white fellows from their country'.[2]

In October the Djadja Wurrung and other Aborigines were enraged
when a contingent of soldiers and police led by Major Samuel Lettsom
raided an encampment comprising over 400 Aboriginal people from
different nations (who had gathered for ceremonial purposes and to
settle disputes), marched them into Melbourne, and held them at
the prison barracks stockade. Parker found thirty Djadja Wurrung
Aborigines there. They demanded to know why had they been driven
like sheep to this place and whether they were going to be shot. In the
aftermath of this incident Parker learned in confidence from several
Aborigines of a threat that the Daung Wurrung were making: a
sorcerer or clever man was going to call up the *Myndie* to bring about a
pestilence that would wreak destruction on all whites in Port Phillip,
even those whom they regarded as their friends.[3] In other words,
the *Myndie*, the large serpent that Aboriginal people, including the
Djadja Wurrung, associated with the smallpox that had devastated
their people in the recent past, was to be unleashed by Aborigines
upon the settler community in response to the mistreatment they had
received at the hands of Lettsom.[4]

---

2   *Ibid.*, entry 18 March 1840, p. 204; Edward Parker, Quarterly Journal, 1 March – 31
    August 1840, Public Record Office Victoria, VPRS 4410, Unit 2; Charles Joseph La
    Trobe to James Croke, 10 April 1840, Public Record Office Victoria, VPRS 21, Unit
    1, Bundle 1; Croke to La Trobe, 10 April 1840, Public Record Office Victoria, VPRS
    19, Unit 4.

3   This was not the first time such a threat had been made: see Clark (ed.), *Journals of
    Robinson*, entry 19 March 1840, p. 204.

4   Parker, Quarterly Journal, 1 September – 30 November 1840, Public Record Office
    Victoria, VPRS 4410, Unit 2; Edward Stone Parker, *The Aborigines of Australia: A
    Lecture Delivered in the Mechanics' Hall, Melbourne, Before the John Knox Young Men's*

CHAPTER 5: REFUGE

In the last week of November 1840 a large group of Djadja
Wurrung came to the station that Parker had begun to establish on
the Loddon River. Apparently they welcomed him and called him
Marmingorak or father and told him that many more of their people
were coming as news spread of the reserve. Indeed, the first week
of December saw a further group of Djadja Wurrung arrive. Parker
wrote in his journal: 'As they appeared to march in with some degree
of ceremony, I received them in a similar manner'. Parker went on to
note that they separated into particular sections and were formally
introduced to him by some of their number. And these speakers
reminded Parker that they had met previously at various places.
As scholars such as Sylvia Hallam have noted, meetings between
different groups in precolonial Aboriginal society were staged events
and tended to be highly structured, involving strict protocols in
regard to matters such as how they approached one another in order
to reduce the possibility of conflict. It is apparent that sometimes
they sought to apply these formalised and ceremonious proceedings
to their encounters with Europeans. The Djadja Wurrung must have
been very pleased by the fact that Parker responded on this occasion
in a way that they would have regarded as culturally appropriate. By
the end of December there were 170 Djadja Wurrung at the station.
They told Parker of how the white man had wantonly killed some of
their people, taken their land, and ordered them away from places
where they had long got food. By February the following year so

---

Association, on Wednesday 10 May 1854, Hugh McColl, Melbourne, 1854, pp. 17–18;
M.F. Christie, *Aborigines in Colonial Victoria 1835–86*, University of Sydney, Sydney,
1979, pp. 110–12; Robert Kenny, *The Lamb Enters the Dreaming: Nathanael Pepper
& the Ruptured World*, Scribe, Melbourne, 2007, pp. 190–91; Marie Fels, '*I Succeeded
Once': The Aboriginal Protectorate on the Mornington Peninsula 1839–40*, Aboriginal
History, Canberra, 2011, pp. 113–14.

many Aboriginal people had come that Parker had almost run out of food. Consequently, most of the Djadja Wurrung began to leave.[5]

Civilising

In June 1841 a large number of Djadja Wurrung accompanied Parker to the site of the new protectorate station, Larrnebarramul. There, what might be regarded as a naked power struggle began between Parker and the Djadja Wurrung. Parker had a missionary project to civilise and christianise the Djadja Wurrung, and this entailed an attempt to radically change their behavior. Parker insisted that they abandon their nomadic hunting and gathering and settle down on the station rather than continue to move about their country. To this end he sought to supply food in the form of rations. Parker believed that the Djadja Wurrung had some entitlement to rations on the grounds that they had been dispossessed of their hunting grounds, but this did not mean that he held that the government had an absolute obligation to provide rations. Instead, the supply of rations was contingent upon the Djadja Wurrung participating in station life. To be more specific, Parker expected the able-bodied Djadja Wurrung to work in return for the rations that he otherwise provided without condition to the young, the elderly and the sick.[6]

5   Parker, Quarterly Journals, 1 September – 30 November 1840 and 1 December
     1840 – 28 February 1841, Public Record Office Victoria, VPRS 4410, Unit 2; Parker
     to George Augustus Robinson, 31 December 1840, Public Record Office Victoria,
     VPRS 11, Unit 4; Sylvia J. Hallam, 'A View from the Other Side of the Western
     Frontier: Or "I Met a Man Who Wasn't There …"', *Aboriginal History*, vol. 7, pt 2,
     1983, pp. 134, 136.

6   Charles Joseph La Trobe to Edward Deas Thomson, 11 December 1840, New
     South Wales State Records, Series NRS 905, Item 4/2512.1; Thomson to La Trobe,
     6 March 1841, Public Record Office Victoria, VPRS 10, Unit 3; Parker, Quarterly
     Report, 1 June – 31 August 1841, Public Record Office Victoria, VPRS 4410, Unit
     2; Robinson to La Trobe, 11 December 1841, Public Record Office Victoria, VPRS
     10, Unit 3; Parker to Robinson, 1 December 1843, Public Record Office Victoria,

Parker, like other protectors and missionaries, assumed that work on the station would inculcate discipline and punctuality and lead to the acceptance of authority. More particularly, Parker wanted the Djadja Wurrung to till the soil. Evangelical philanthropists associated agriculture with moral improvement since it involved individual effort, regular labour, subjugation of nature, and the valuing of property. In support of this aim the government appointed to the station in 1841–42 white overseers, bullock drivers and farm hands. In urging the Djadja Wurrung to work Parker largely focused on the men but he also encouraged the women to make hats, baskets, covers and table mats in European style but out of native grasses, which he sent to Melbourne to be sold.[7]

Many of the Djadja Wurrung seem to have been willing to work on Larrnebarramul but some refused. Aboriginal attitudes to work were very different to those championed by the likes of the protectors. In traditional society they worked in order to be able to have food and fulfill religious and social obligations. Now, as they came in to white settlement, they followed much the same cultural imperatives. They were willing to work for various reasons, such as meeting a need for food, satisfying a desire for European commodities such as guns, forging a means to remain in their own country, and establishing a closer, reciprocal relationship with particular white individuals, rather than because they felt

VPRS 12, Unit 4; Parker, Report for 1 January – 30 June 1846, New South Wales State Records, NRS 905, Item 4/2474.

7   Parker to La Trobe, 21 March 1842, Public Record Office Victoria, VPRS 19, Unit 28; Parker to Robinson, 21 February 1843, Public Record Office Victoria, VPRS 11, Unit 5; *Port Phillip Patriot*, 22 May 1843; Parker to Robinson, 1 May 1845, Public Record Office Victoria, VPRS 11, Unit 5; Jessie Mitchell, *In Good Faith? Governing Indigenous Australia through God, Charity and Empire, 1825–1855*, Aboriginal History, Canberra, 2011, pp. 98–99.

a need to be industrious or valued the wages they might earn. Furthermore, they tended to find much of the work that whites required extremely tedious and boring and worked only in order to fulfill their immediate needs. And, since Aborigines shared with one other and expected whites to do the same, everyone got something whether they worked or not, and they saw nothing wrong in begging whenever they felt the need.[8]

In February 1842 several Djadja Wurrung men angrily told their kinsmen that they were fools to stop at the station and work. 'Why did they not go about as they used to do', they demanded to know. In fact most of the Djadja Wurrung were loath to embrace Parker's requirement that they work regularly. At one point he observed that it was essential that the Djadja Wurrung felt that the work they were doing was for their own advantage rather than that of anyone else, adding: 'They appear generally to feel that they owe us nothing and that they are under no obligation to work. If the suspicion therefore be aroused in their minds that they are working for the benefits of whites than their own advantage they will speedily recede from their employment'. On another occasion Parker observed that it was crucial that they were 'barely commanded'. As this suggests, Aboriginal people rejected the hierarchical ordering of colonial society and the demands that masters had for the obedience and deference of servants. Parker also realised that Aboriginal people expected to be properly rewarded for the work they performed. Those such as the Djadja Wurrung had become accustomed to working for pastoralists in a range of tasks and receiving some payment. At

---

8   Henry Reynolds, *With the White People*, Penguin, Melbourne, 1990, pp. 91–92, 97; Richard Broome, 'Aboriginal Workers on South-Eastern Frontiers', *Australian Historical Studies*, vol. 26, no. 103, 1994, pp. 207, 209, 216–17.

some points Djadja Wurrung complained that they only received rations in return for their labour on the station. On one occasion a Djadja Wurrung man indignantly questioned Parker why he had employed a white labourer rather than a Djadja Wurrung man, which was really to ask why the white man was getting paid and they were not.[9]

Parker not only sought to hold the Djadja Wurrung on Larrnebarramul by providing food but also by offering medical help. A medical officer, Dr William Baylie, was appointed to both the Loddon and the Goulburn protectorate stations to treat the alarmingly high level of illness among the Aboriginal people. As we noted in the first chapter, the Djadja Wurrung had probably suffered severe depopulation as the result of a smallpox epidemic prior to contact with the white man but there were still considerable numbers at the point that the pastoral invasion began. However, a further fall occurred as they came to live in proximity with Europeans. They succumbed to colds, bronchitis, influenza, chicken pox, measles, scarlet fever, and dysentery as they had little if any immunity to most of these illnesses. According to Baylie, the Djadja Wurrung welcomed his medical aid.[10]

---

9   Parker to Robinson, 1 April 1840, *Historical Records of Victoria*, vol. 2B, Victorian Government Printing Office, Melbourne, 1983, p. 695; Parker, Statement, undated, cited by Reynolds, *With the White People*, p. 96; Parker, Quarterly Journal, 1 September – 30 November 1841, Public Record Office Victoria, VPRS 4410, Unit 2; Parker, Quarterly Journal, 1 December 1841 – 28 February 1842, Public Record Office Victoria, VPRS 4410, Unit 2; Parker, Quarterly Journal, 1 June – 31 August 1842, Public Record Office Victoria, VPRS 4410, Unit 2.

10 William Baylie to La Trobe, 27 December 1841, Public Record Office Victoria, VPRS 4410, Unit 1; Baylie to Robinson, 24 January 1842, Public Record Office Victoria, VPRS 11, Unit 1; Parker, *Aborigines of Australia*, pp. 10, 17. For reports by Baylie's successor for 1844–45, see Public Record Office Victoria, VPRS 4410, Unit 2.

Syphilis and gonorrhoea in particular seem to have reached epidemic proportions along the Loddon River. Indeed, white men's lust killed many more Aboriginal people than did their guns. It had spread quickly amongst the Djadja Wurrung for the same reason it had elsewhere, namely the sexual relations that occurred between pastoralists and their men and the Aboriginal women. It was alleged that this was particularly so on Darlot, Dutton and Simson's run. One of their men, Patrick Clark, was known by the Djadja Wurrung as Fuckemall. ('I told them this was my name when I came here last July', he once stated.) In March 1840 Robinson observed that a couple of women and children had contacted the disease but by late the following year Parker reckoned that as many as nine-tenths of the Djadja Wurrung whom he had counted in a census at Larrnebarramul were suffering from syphilis. Indeed, he claimed that many were so debilitated by the disease that they were scarcely able to crawl. Baylie and Robinson confirmed its prevalence.[11]

Venereal diseases not only killed. They rendered Aboriginal women sterile and infected their babies, severely diminishing the possibility of an Aboriginal demographic recovery. In July 1842 Parker reported that a new-born child had died and another was seriously ill. He wrote in his journal: 'other children are likely to be born in a few weeks but from previous observations I do not expect any of them

11 Clark (ed.), *Journals of Robinson*, vol. 1, entry 7 March 1840, p. 197; Parker, Quarterly Journal, 1 December 1840 – 28 February 1841; Testimony of Patrick Clark, 8 February 1841, Public Record Office Victoria, VPRS 30, Unit 185, NCR 8; Parker, Quarterly Journal, 1 September – 30 November 1841; Baylie to La Trobe, 27 September 1841, Public Record Office Victoria, VPRS 19, Unit 24; Parker to Robinson, 15 October 1841, Public Record Office Victoria, VPRS 11, Unit 4; Ian D. Clark (ed.), *The Journals of George Augustus Robinson, Chief Protector, Port Phillip Aboriginal Protectorate, vol. 3, 1 September 1841 – 31 December 1842*, Heritage Matters, Melbourne, 1999, entry 20 November 1841, p. 20; Parker, Quarterly Journal, 1 June – 31 August 1842.

to be reared. The mothers, with one exception, have been or still are diseased, and it is melancholy to witness the effects of their wretched conduct in their offspring. In a few weeks, sometimes a few days, after their birth, the poor children become covered with the syphilitic eruption and speedily perish'.[12]

Parker did his best to administer to the Djadja Wurrung and many were prepared to try European medicine and even adopt European forms of healing in place of their own traditional ones. However, they were loath to abandon the beliefs that accompanied those practices. This infuriated Parker. In September 1841 he challenged a Djadja Wurrung doctor over the care of one of the sons of the headman, Munangabum, who was seriously ill with inflammation of the lungs, in large part because he was determined to show the Djadja Wurrung what he called the utter absurdity of their beliefs. The Djadja Wurrung doctor had claimed that he could take away the evil spirits that were the cause of the boy's illness. Parker told him he could treat the boy but that his cure had to work immediately and that if he failed the assistant protector would regard him as a great deceiver and punish him in some way. The doctor refused to proceed, Parker bled the boy and dosed him with an emetic, and he recovered in a few days. Parker claimed that this outcome shook the faith of the Djadja Wurrung in their doctor. This seems unlikely. Nevertheless, the Djadja Wurrung who came into contact with Parker and Larrnebarramul might have suffered a lower rate of mortality than the members of Aboriginal nations who had no resort to a protectorate station. Parker certainly believed this was the case.[13]

---

12 Parker, Quarterly Journal, 1 March – 31 May 1842, Public Record Office Victoria, VPRS 4410, Unit 2.

13 Parker, Quarterly Journal, 1 September – 30 November 1841, his emphasis; Parker, Report for 1 July – 31 December 1845, New South Wales State Records, NRS 905,

Christianising

Parker's principal goal at the station was reclaiming the Aborigines, whom he regarded as heathens, by preaching the Gospel. As he remarked in November 1841, 'It will be my main object to make known the truths and blessings of the religion of Jesus to these degraded and unhappy people'. This is hardly surprising. As noted earlier, Parker had undertaken some training in the Wesleyan ministry in England and was a member of a branch of the Wesleyan Missionary Society in Port Phillip. Evangelical beliefs were marked by an emphasis on the inherently corruptible nature of human beings, the accessibility of scripture, the doctrine of atonement, and the defining experience of conversion. Consequently, Parker's sermons focused on what he called the 'great and essential principles' of 'the fall and universal corruption of human nature, redemption by the advent and death of our Lord Jesus Christ, the necessity of change of heart or "new spirit" and of conformity to the will of God … and the certainty of a final judgement and state of eternal reward or punishment'.[14]

In the task of seeking to convert the Djadja Wurrung, Parker, in common with many missionaries at this time, believed that it was very important to preach in the people's own aboriginal language and to translate parts of the scripture into that language.[15] He set about trying to do this but soon encountered a considerable difficulty, at least

Item 4/2742.

14 Parker, Quarterly Journal, 1 September – 30 November 1841, Public Record Office Victoria, VPRS 4410, Unit 2; Parker, Journal 1 June – 31 December 1849, Public Record Office Victoria, VPRS 4410, Unit 2.

15 See Alan Atkinson, *The Europeans in Australia: A History*, vol. 2, Oxford University Press, Melbourne, 2004, pp. 41–43; Kenny, *The Lamb*, 104–05; Hilary M. Carey, 'Missionaries, Dictionaries and Australian Aborigines, 1820–1850, <https://downloads.newcastle.edu.au/library/cultural%20collections/awaba//language/linguistics.html>, and 'Lancelot Threlkeld, Biraban, and the Colonial Bible in Australia', *Comparative Studies in Society and History*, vol. 52, no. 2, 2010, pp. 447–78.

in his mind. 'Up till now I have experienced insuperable difficulties in finding expressions designatory of moral qualities and actions', he remarked in July 1842. 'For physical objects and their attributes, the language readily supplies equivalent terms, but for the metaphysical, so far as I have been able to discover, scarcely any'. A few years later Parker simply despaired that this work of translation could be undertaken. 'What can be done', he complained, 'with a people whose language knows no such terms as holiness, justice, righteousness, sin, guilt, repentance, redemption, pardon, peace, and c., and to whose minds the ideas conveyed by those words are utterly foreign and inexplicable?'. But Parker probably undermined any chance of success in converting the Djadja Wurrung as a result of the approach he took. This included his denouncing those cultural practices that he considered an obstacle to their conversion and warning that God would punish them severely for their misdemeanours.[16]

In the early years of his protectorate Parker often reported that many of the Djadja Wurrung had attended his religious services and were willing to follow some of the forms observed at Christian religious services such as standing and kneeling at certain times. But the interest they expressed was seldom what it seemed to be. In the beginning at any rate the Djadja Wurrung were perplexed by Parker's religiosity. 'At an early period of my experience', he was to recall some years later, 'I found them much puzzled to understand how it was that I should be so urgent with them to come to "God's house, and hear his

---

16 Parker, Quarterly Journal, 1 March – 30 May 1841; Parker, Precis of Journal for
    1 March – 31 August 1841, Public Record Office Victoria, VPRS 4410, Unit 2;
    Parker, Quarterly Journals, 1 September – 30 November 1841; Parker, Quarterly
    Journal, 1 June – 31 August 1842; Parker to Robinson, 1 December 1843; Extract
    from Parker Report, January 1845, New South Wales Legislative Council, *Votes
    and Proceedings*, 1845, Report from the Select Committee on the Condition of
    Aborigines, p. 50.

book" when on no other station in the district they ever observed any prayers or Christian ordinances'. It is clear that the Djadja Wurrung maintained their own traditional religious practices, and often used the station for this purpose. Indeed, Parker came to realise that most of the Djadja Wurrung were unmoved by his proselytising. In the middle of 1846 he reported: 'Some openly express their disbelief of what is taught. Others seem to assent for the time but do not exhibit any decidedly beneficial results in their pursuits'; and a few years later he remarked: 'The mass of the Aboriginal population of this district remains unchanged in their characteristic habits and inclinations, and in some instances I have witnessed more determined hostility to religion, and more inveterate attachment to their own sensuality and superstition than ever'.[17]

In the project of seeking to civilise Aborigines, missionaries typically came to focus on children and youths. Parker did the same. In the early years he adopted several Aboriginal children who in his eyes were orphans. One of them was a boy by the name of Kolain. Parker took him into his family some time in 1840 and began to teach him the rudiments of Christianity, and during a visit to the station in May 1842 the Wesleyan missionary Francis Tuckfield baptised him. Parker sought to persuade the Djadja Wurrung youth to settle on the station and adopt European ways by building themselves houses, working regularly, and attending school lessons. To help in the process of civilisation Parker also tried placing several of these youths with local pastoralists as shepherds, bullock drivers and domestic servants.

17 Parker, Quarterly Journals, 1 September – 30 November 1840 and 1 December 1840
    – 28 February 1841; Parker, Report for 1 January – 30 June 1846, Public Record
    Office Victoria, VPRS 4410, Unit 2; Parker, Report for 1 January – 30 June 1848;
    Parker, Report for June to December 1849, Public Record Office Victoria, VPRS
    4410, Unit 2; Parker, *The Aborigines*, p. 27; *Mount Alexander Mail*, 23 August 1883.

By the middle of 1842 he reckoned that several young couples were staying steadily at the station and were saying that they wanted to settle there permanently.[18]

A struggle for power

The Djadja Wurrung seem to have been willing to come to Larrnebarramul and for their children to be minded, fed and clothed by Parker and even to be taught the rudiments of the white man's ways, perhaps because they recognised that it was necessary to make some accommodation to the ways of the colonists. However, they were unwilling to allow those ways to supplant their own. The most deep-seated opposition came from the Djadja Wurrung elders who were responsible for upholding their traditions and whose authority the protector sought to undermine. A year after he founded the station Parker reported that they had questioned why he had sat down among them: 'I [was] not born of black woman. Why didn't I not go back to my country, up to "woorer woorer" (i.e. the sky!) where I came from'. One man complained that the white man had stolen their country and that Parker was now stealing their children 'by taking them away to live in huts, and work, and "read the book" like whitefellows'. The following year Parker reckoned that senior Djadja Wurrung men had reproached some of the younger men for

---

18 Parker to Robinson, 24 July 1839, Public Record Office Victoria, VPRS 10, Unit 1; Parker, Quarterly Report, 1 September – 30 November 1840; Parker to Robinson, 31 December 1840, 11 November 1841, and 22 November 1841, Public Record Office Victoria, VPRS 11, Unit 4; Parker to Robinson, 6 May 1842, VPRS 11, Unit 5; Parker, Quarterly Report, 1 March – 31 May 1842; New South Wales Legislative Council, *Votes and Proceedings*, 1845, Report from the Select Committee on the Condition of Aborigines, p. 50; Extract of a Report by Francis Tuckfield, undated, attached to Robinson, Annual Report for 1845, New South Wales State Records, NRS 905, Item 4/2472; Parker, Annual Report for 1845, New South Wales State Records, NRS 905, Item 4/2472; Parker, Report for 1 January – 30 June 1846; Parker, Report for 1 January – 30 June 1848, Public Record Office Victoria, VPRS 10, Unit 9.

becoming so much like whitefellows that they were no longer 'able to hunt game like their forefathers'. Several years later they still attacked Parker's work among the younger Djadja Wurrung and resisted his proselytising. In a report for the first six months of 1848, Parker revealed: 'Others, particularly the older men, ridicule the teaching and try to persuade the younger men that it is all false, saying that many white men and "gentlemen" had told them so'.[19]

In essence the response of the Djadja Wurrung to Larrnebarramul was highly pragmatic in nature. The historical record reveals that they visited Larrnebarramul regularly and left their children at the school for extended periods but that few chose to remain for any length of time. They probably saw the station as a place where they could sit down but also move away to hunt and gather and work for pastoralists, thereby maintaining their association with their traditional lands and preserving their own culture. In other words, it would be a mistake to assume that they intended their coming in to the protectorate station as a break with their traditions (though this could be the consequence of this movement in the long term). As Parker observed several years later, 'You expect that [the Aborigine] will at your bidding give up all his native notions, all his preconceived opinions, and at once fall into your mode of life. He will never do it until he has an adequate motive'. At Larrnebarramul the Djadja Wurrung came and went in a pattern largely determined by the seasonal changes that dictated their need for food, the availability of work for squatters, and what was on offer at the station, particularly rations. They could also leave for reasons connected to their traditional religious beliefs. For

19 Parker, Quarterly Report 1 June 1842 – 31 August 1842, Public Record Office Victoria, VPRS 4410, Unit 2; Parker to Robinson, 1 December 1843; Parker, Report for 1 January – 30 June 1846; Parker, Report for 1 January – 30 June 1848, Public Record Office Victoria, VPRS 4410, Unit 2.

example, considerable sickness caused them to move away. All these factors meant that the Djadja Wurrung's presence at the station fluctuated enormously. Indeed, the total number who visited bore little relationship to their average attendance; for instance, during 1844 316 came but the average was only 62.[20]

It also seems clear that the Djadja Wurrung welcomed the protection that was offered by Larrnebarramul since they felt they needed a refuge. Furthermore, they even professed to regard Parker as their head and master. The affiliation that Aboriginal people came to feel for places such as Larrnebarramul was often rooted in their attachment to the place but also the deeply personal relationships they forged with their white superintendents. There is a sense in which the ideals of paternalism that heavily influenced the approach of those such as Parker coincided with the ideals of reciprocity that were prized by Aboriginal people. In other words, by acting in ways that were in keeping with ideals of paternal government, these missionary superintendents behaved in ways that met the expectations of the Aboriginal people who sought to cultivate a relationship of kinship with them. In the terms of the historian Richard Broome, these superintendents had to conduct themselves in accordance with what Aboriginal people regarded as 'right behaviour'. It is apparent that Parker was considered worthy and won the loyalty of the Djadja Wurrung when he acted in those ways. It is clear, moreover, that Aboriginal people also embraced the notion of protection that

---

20 Parker, Quarterly Journals, 1 March – 31 May 1841, 1 September – 30 November 1841, 1 December 1840 – 28 February 1841, and 1 December 1841 – 28 February 1842; Clark (ed.), *Journals of Robinson*, vol. 3, entry 20 November 1841, p. 19; Parker to Robinson, 28 February 1843, 11 March 1843 and 18 March 1843, Public Record Office Victoria, VPRS 11, Unit 5; Return showing the total numbers of natives visiting the Loddon Aboriginal Station, June 1841 – December 1849, Public Record Office Victoria, VPRS 4410, Unit 2; Parker, *Aborigines of Australia*, p. 28.

government and its officers espoused and that they used it to claim what the Western District pastoralist and guardian of Aborigines William Dawson once called 'proper maintenance and protection'.[21]

At the same time, the Djadja Wurrung sought to maintain the relationships they had with their own country and the nations of the Kulin confederation. This caused considerable tension between the Djadja Wurrung and Parker as he tried to stop them going on and off the station. More especially, he was determined to prevent them going to Melbourne. During the 1840s the Djadja Wurrung were often invited by the Woiwurrung to visit Melbourne for traditional ceremonial purposes, and many took the opportunity to go. Throughout this period many colonists demanded that Aboriginal people be removed from the growing township. For their part the protectors believed that it was imperative that they be excluded from Melbourne in order to protect them from the vices of the white settlers, and they demanded measures to ensure that. William Thomas, the assistant protector responsible for the area that included Melbourne, repeatedly called upon those such as the Djadja Wurrung to stay out or to leave town but he had considerable trouble as they resisted fiercely, on one occasion telling him: 'no good why not blackfellows come and see their friends like white fellows'. On more than one of their visits to Melbourne some of the Djadja Wurrung also complained bitterly about Parker's treatment to Thomas, alleging in one instance that he beat them if they did not work and gave them so little food that they could not stop on Larrnebarramul. (Thomas saw no reason to believe

---

21 Parker, Quarterly Journal, 1 March – 31 May 1841; Bain Attwood, *The Making of the Aborigines*, Allen & Unwin, Sydney, 1989, pp. 25–28; Richard Broome, '"There Were Vegetables Every Year Mr Green was Here": Right Behaviour and the Struggle for Autonomy at Coranderrk Aboriginal Reserve', *History Australia*, vol. 3, no. 2, 2006, pp. 43.1–16.

these allegations.) But they also seem to have made a more general complaint that Thomas would have endorsed: on one occasion a Djadja Wurrung man told him: 'Poor blackfellows[.] White man take blackfellow[']s country and frighten him too'.[22]

At the same time that the Djadja Wurrung came and went from Larrnebarramul they made it clear to Parker that they regarded the reserve as *their* place. On more than one occasion in the early years Parker tried to persuade Aboriginal groups from nations to the north of the Djadja Wurrung to come and settle at the station, but the Djadja Wurrung were unwilling to countenance the presence of large numbers of Aboriginal people whom they regarded as foreign. They only permitted a small number of foreign Aborigines who were seeking sanctuary from their own nations and were willing to acknowledge and accept Djadja Wurrung authority to remain at Larrnebarramul. Parker had to recommend that a further station be created for the vast bulk of these Aboriginal people. At the same time the Djadja Wurrung repeatedly complained to Parker about the

22 Clark (ed.), *Journals of Robinson*, vol. 1, entry 18 March 1840, p. 204; Parker, Quarterly Journals, 1 March – 31 May 1841, 1 September – 30 November 1841, 1 December 1840 – 28 February 1841, 1 December 1841 – 28 February 1842; Parker to Robinson, 28 February 1843, 11 March 1843 and 18 March 1843, Public Record Office Victoria, VPRS 11, Unit 5; Marguerita Stephens (ed.), *The Journal of William Thomas, Assistant Protector of the Aborigines of Port Phillip and Guardian of the Aborigines of Victoria, 1839–1867, vol. 1, 1839 to 1843*, Victorian Aboriginal Corporation for Languages, Melbourne, 2014, entries 25 March 1843, 27 March 1843, and 29 March 1843, pp. 507–08; Thomas, Report for 1 December – 1 March 1844, Public Record Office Victoria, VPRS 4410, Unit 3; Marguerita Stephens (ed.), *The Journal of William Thomas, Assistant Protector of the Aborigines of Port Phillip and Guardian of the Aborigines of Victoria, 1839–1867, vol. 2, 1844 to 1853*, Victorian Aboriginal Corporation for Languages, Melbourne, 2014, entries 27 June 1844, 29 August 1844, 31 August 1844, 1 September 1844, 7 September 1844, 8 September 1844, 12 September 1844, 4 April 1845, 15 April 1845, 18 May 1845, 26 May 1845, 28 May 1845, 3 June 1845, 2 February 1846, 6 February 1846, 8 February 1846, and 8 June 1848, pp. 23, 42–45, 94, 99, 107–10, 154–55, 313; Penelope Edmonds, *Urbanizing Frontiers: Indigenous Peoples and Settlers in 19th-Century Pacific Rim Cities*, University of British Columbia Press, Vancouver, 2010, pp. 125–29, 134–35, 150.

loss of their country to the white man, a charge which Parker found difficult to answer.[23]

The Protectorate under attack

At the same time that Parker battled to hold the Djadja Wurrung on the station and undertake his work of civilising and christianising, the Protectorate continued to be attacked by white critics. In June 1842 a pastoralist by the name of John Hunter Patterson published a pamphlet in which he proposed a radical change in the way government sought to protect Aborigines. Patterson alleged that the worst depredations that pastoralists suffered were caused by those Aborigines under the eye of the assistant protectors. Not surprisingly, Arden reprinted its content in the pages of the *Port Phillip Herald*. Parker was apprehensive that this claim would create an unfavourable opinion about the impact of his station on the Aborigines,[24] and so he wrote to Robinson to contradict Patterson's claim.[25]

Parker received a great fillip when La Trobe visited Larrnebarramul at the end of September 1842 and Parker was able to persuade him that he had convinced the Djadja Wurrung to abandon their customary pattern of movement. La Trobe sent a very favourable report of the station to Gipps the following month: it was benefitting

23 Parker, Quarterly Journals, 1 March – 31 May 1841, 1 December 1841 – 28 February 1842, 1 March – 31 May 1842, 1 June – 31 August 1842, 1 June – 31 August 1848; Parker to Robinson, 1 December 1843, Public Record Office Victoria, VPRS 4410, Unit 2; Parker, *Aborigines of Australia*, p. 13.

24 The following February Parker felt he had to defend himself against further allegations regarding his work on the Loddon River (Parker to Robinson, 8 February 1843, Public Record Office Victoria, VPRS 11, Unit 5).

25 John Hunter Patterson, *Proposed Plan for the Better Treatment of the Aborigines of Australia Felix*, l.c., Melbourne, 1842, reproduced in Victoria Legislative Council, *Votes and Proceedings*, 1858–59, Report of the Select Committee on Aborigines, pp. 100–01; *Port Phillip Herald*, 21 June 1842; Parker to Robinson, 5 October 1842, Public Record Office Victoria, VPRS 11, Unit 5.

the Aborigines and had checked their attacks on the settlers. But Parker remained anxious about the future of the Protectorate and thus his position. In January 1843 he prepared a special report in which he detailed his work at Larrnebarramul and its beneficial effect on the Djadja Wurrung. La Trobe forwarded this to Gipps in March and lent his weight to it by reminding the Governor that he had personally visited the station in recent months and had been impressed by Parker's management and the fact that the property of the pastoralists in the broad area around the station had been exempt from Aboriginal attacks of any kind.[26]

Parker's report probably helped save the Port Phillip Protectorate from being axed. This at least is the opinion of several historians. However, the Protectorate suffered a severe cut in its budget. Between 1839 and 1843 approximately £24,000 had been spent on it, but by 1844 the annual expenditure was little more than £2000. This did not put an end to attacks on the Protectorate. In July 1843 a pastoralist writing under the pseudonym of a settler in the north-west wrote a long letter to a local newspaper in which he criticised the government for failing to provide adequate protection to both Aborigines and settlers and suggested that no benefit had been derived from the costly Protectorate stations. He chose Parker's station as his example. 'I am told that upwards of thirty whites are employed, and two or three hundred blacks are often fed for doing nothing, but I object decidedly to the concentration of the blacks, and I would adopt the principle in civilisation as well as in politics of "divide et impera"', he

---

26 La Trobe to Deas Thomson, 10 October 1842, Charles Joseph La Trobe, Correspondence, 1839–1864, Australian Manuscripts Collection, State Library Victoria, MS 8431 and MS 8454; Parker to Robinson, 5 January 1843, and La Trobe to Thomson, 6 March 1843, New South Wales Legislative Council, *Votes and Proceedings*, 1843, Return to an Address, Dr Thomson, 29 August 1843, pp. 43–46.

wrote. A few months later the editor of this newspaper expressed the hope that the days of the Protectorate were numbered. Parker tried to defend it at a missionary meeting at this time but was actually attacked by one of his former colleagues, Assistant Protector Dredge (who had resigned his post in June 1840), as a special pleader on its behalf given that he received a handsome salary as a protector.[27]

Parker made a passionate defence of the Protectorate in so far as it related to Larrnebarramul in his annual report for 1843. In concluding his report he argued that any change in the Protectorate system would deprive the Aboriginal people of a permanent home. 'They have been taught to regard the station as their home; they have been informed, in answer to their repeated complaints of the loss of their country, that the government gave them provisions and clothing, and furnished them with protection, as a sort of compensation; and that the continuance of these advantages was dependent on their good behaviour', he wrote. Parker argued that ending these arrangements would surely be regarded by the Djadja Wurrung as the breaking of a promise. 'They are peculiarly susceptible to any breach of faith', he explained. 'I may attribute much of the influence I have had with them to the fact that I have been careful never to break a promise or falsify a threat in my intercourse with them.' If the Aboriginal people were forced to return to their traditional ways, warned Parker, there would be attacks on settlers and bloodshed of the kind that characterised the notorious Western District.[28]

---

27 *Geelong Advertiser*, 10 July 1843 and 16 October 1843; E.J.B. Foxcroft, *Australian Native Policy: Its History, Especially in Victoria*, Melbourne University Press, Melbourne, 1941, p. 78; Christie, *Aborigines in Colonial Victoria*, p. 104; Kenny, *The Lamb*, p. 40.

28 Parker to Robinson, 1 December 1843, Public Record Office Victoria, VPRS 12, Unit 4.

The drastic cut in the government's expenditure on the Protectorate crippled the development of stations such as Larrnebarramul. It put an end to any more new building works, prevented Parker engaging a teacher for the school, and forced him to abandon his plan to build a house in which the children would be housed and overseen by a school master and mistress. To make matters worse, the government dismissed the assistant protector who was responsible for the station on the Goulburn River, Albert Le Souef, and called on Parker to add superintendence of it and the surrounding district to his duties. These responsibilities meant that Parker was away from Larrnebarramul for considerable periods of time. Furthermore, Parker suffered a blow when his wife Mary died in October 1842 and while he married again in December 1843 his family responsibilities only grew as he had six more children (four of whom survived infancy) by his second wife, Hannah Edwards. The historian Heather Holst has suggested that these circumstances brought about a shift in Parker's priorities and that he increasingly devoted himself to advancing his own interests rather than working for those of the Djadja Wurrung.[29]

By 1845 the Port Phillip Protectorate was once more under threat. The New South Wales Legislative Council appointed a select committee to assess the effectiveness of the attempts that had been made to protect Aborigines. Parker again made a strong case for it and more especially its reserves. But most of those who gave evidence were

29 Parker, Annual Report for 1844, New South Wales State Records, NRS 906, Item 4/7153; Parker, Report for 1 July – 31 December 1845; Parker, Annual Report for 1845, New South Wales State Records, NRS 905, Item 4/2472; Parker, Report for 1 January – 30 June 1846; Robinson to La Trobe, 26 June 1847, New South Wales State Records, NRS 905, Item 4/2782; Parker to Robinson, 1 October 1847, Victorian Public Record Office, VPRS 11, Unit 5; Heather Holst, '"Save the People": E.S. Parker at the Loddon Aboriginal Station', *Aboriginal History*, vol. 32, 2008, pp. 113–14.

highly critical and had the Committee issued a report it would have sounded the death knell of the Protectorate. However, its chairman, the pastoralist and lawyer Richard Windeyer, who was a scourge of Aboriginal rights, died and the committee ceased its work. The Protectorate or at least Parker also came under assault from a rather unexpected source: the former assistant protector Albert Le Souef. In a petition to the New South Wales Legislative Council in which he attacked both La Trobe and Robinson for injuring his character, he pointed out that Parker had expended three times as much funds on Larrnebarramul as he had on the Goulburn station.[30]

Decline

The massive cut in expenditure on the Protectorate no doubt played a major role in the marked decline in the number of Djadja Wurrung who frequented Larrnebarramul after 1844. Certainly, they expressed their dissatisfaction with the reduction in the supply of provisions. Parker reckoned the station could attract and hold larger numbers if the government would only provide the means to support them. As it was he only had the means to hold large numbers of the Djadja Wurrung on the station for a few months each year. But the station's lack of resources was not the only factor in determining the Djadja Wurrung's presence at Larrrnebarramul. The connection that they seemed to have formed to the station owed much to a personal attachment they had to Parker, and so his frequent absences mattered to them. Indeed, it appears that their absences from the station often coincided with his absences. In 1844 several deaths among the

---

30 Albert Le Souef, Petition to the New South Wales Legislative Council, undated, reproduced in *Port Phillip Patriot*, 5 and 7 March 1845; Parker to Robinson, 8 March 1845, New South Wales State Records, NRS 905, Item 4/2703; Parker, Reply to a Circular Letter, pp. 54–55; Christie, *Aborigines in Colonial Victoria*, p. 105.

Djadja Wurrung also led many to abandon the reserve, saying that they would only return when the ground had become better. Several years later little, if anything, had changed, though in 1847–48 it was sickness and deaths among the whites that convinced many Djadja Wurrung that the ground at Larrnebarramul was malignant. The average attendance fell to 27, which was the lowest since the station had been established.[31]

Fear of attacks by their traditional enemies also played a role in the Djadja Wurrung moving away from Larrnebarramul. In February 1844 they were anxious that the Jardwadjali and Djab Wurrung nations were joining forces in order to destroy them. They called upon Parker to provide them with horses and guns so they could pursue and shoot these Aborigines. It seems they had good reason to be anxious. In January the following year a party of Jardwadjali slaughtered two women and two girls, and wounded a woman, a girl and a boy at Don Simson's Charlotte Plains Station. The Djadja Wurrung continued to attribute most deaths to the work of sorcery by their traditional enemies. In October 1845, after they found one of their kinsmen murdered in the bush near Alfred and George Joyce's Plaistow run, they conducted an investigation to determine the identity of the foreign Aborigine whom they believed had killed him. In the early months of 1848 the hostility of a particular clan

---

31 Parker to Robinson, 1 December 1843; Parker, Annual Report for 1845; Parker, Report for 1 January – 30 June 1846; Parker, Report for 1 July – 30 November 1846, New South Wales State Records, NRS 905, Item 4/2779.3; Robinson, Abstract of Parker Report for 1847, New South Wales State Records, NRS 905, Item 4/2821; Parker to Robinson, 21 January 1848, Documents Collected by Sir William Dixson regarding Aboriginal Australians in Victoria 1 April 1839 – 8 January 1850, Dixson Library, State Library of New South Wales, MS DLADD 90; Robinson to La Trobe, 27 March 1848, Public Record Office Victoria, VPRS 10, Unit 9; Parker, Report for 1 January – 30 June 1848; Parker, Return for June 1841 – December 1849, Public Record Office Victoria, VPRS 4410, Unit 2.

of the Daung Wurrung saw the Djadja Wurrung move as far north and east as they could. Scarcely any remained on the station.[32] (There was also a rise in deadly conflicts among the Djadja Wurrung clans. Munangabum fell victim to one of these in November 1847.)[33]

The Djadja Wurrung might have found it somewhat easier to survive off Larrnebarramul at this time because pastoralists began to take land in the northern reaches of their country. More than one pastoralist reported Djadja Wurrung people begging for food as well as doing casual labour on their runs, while Parker observed that they were frequently employed, especially for seasonal tasks such as washing sheep and harvesting potatoes. Indeed, at times when white labour was scarce, as it was in 1847–48, most of the pastoral runs in the district apparently employed Djadja Wurrung. A small number worked full time as stockmen, shepherds and bullock drivers. They were paid in wages or in kind for their labour but usually got much less than white workers received. (Parker claimed that most white

---

32 Parker to Robinson, 11 January 1845, Public Record Office Victoria, VPRS 11, Unit 5; Parker to Robinson, 12 November 1845, Public Record Office Victoria, VPRS 11, Unit 5; Thomas to Robinson, 29 December 1845, Public Record Office Victoria, VPRS 11, Unit 10; G.F. James (ed.), *A Homestead History: The Reminiscences and Letters of Alfred Joyce, of Plaistow and Norwood Port Phillip 1843 to 1964*, 3rd edn, Melbourne, 1969, p. 75; Parker, Report for 1 January – 30 June 1848; Parker, Report for 6 months ending 31 December 1848, and Return showing the total numbers of natives visiting the Loddon Aboriginal Station, June 1841 – December 1849, Public Record Office Victoria, VPRS 4410, Unit 2; Mary Lillias Drought (comp.), *Extracts from Old Journals Written by Frederick Race Godfrey (Pioneer) of Boort Station, Loddon District, Victoria, 1846–1853*, Tytherleigh Press, Melbourne, 1926, entries 28 May 1849, 5 June 1849 and 14 December 1849, pp. 12–13, 33; Parker, *Aborigines of Australia*, p. 27; Joseph Parker, 'Dialect of the Ja-Jow-Er-Ong Race', in Robert Brough Smyth, *The Aborigines of Victoria*, vol. 2, Government Printer, Melbourne, 1878, pp. 155–56; Marie Fels, *Good Men and True: The Aboriginal Police of the Port Phillip District 1837–53*, Melbourne University Press, Melbourne, 1988, p. 152; Ian D. Clark, *Aboriginal Languages and Clans: An Historical Atlas of Western and Central Victoria, 1800–1900*, Department of Geography and Environmental Science, Monash University, Melbourne, 1990, p. 143.

33 Between 1843 and 1849 eleven deaths arising from conflicts between Aborigines were recorded by Parker: Census 1849, Public Record Office Victoria, VPRS 44, Unit 669.

labourers were averse to Aboriginal men getting work on the pastoral runs for fear that this would cause a drop in the going rate of wages.) At the same time it appears that in some places in their country the Djadja Wurrung were still able to get food by hunting and gathering. In some cases at least they had to supplement these by begging, prostitution and petty theft. The public houses that sprang up in their country were apparently a favoured haunt.[34]

In the mid to late 1840s Parker experienced further problems at Larrnebarramul as the flocks of a couple of the neighbouring pastoralists began to encroach on the reserve. Parker asked Robinson to submit a case to La Trobe requesting that the boundaries of Aboriginal reserves be clearly defined, and he called for legal proceedings to remove sheep from the reserve. More than a year later he expressed a more general concern about the need to secure reserves for Aborigines. 'Another subject deeply affecting the future condition of the Aborigines is the probability that unless suitable reserves are immediately formed for their benefit every acre of their native soil will shortly be leased out and occupied as to leave them, in a legal view, no place for the sole of their feet', Parker told Robinson. He went on to argue: 'If the occupation of Crown Lands is to be settled by the Crown granting a lease for years the natives will be deprived of all legal right to hunt over their own native land, and according to the dicta of certain high legal authorities, may be forcibly excluded by the

---

34 H.E.P. Dana to La Trobe, 5 April 1843, Public Record Office Victoria, VPRS 19, Unit 44; Parker, Reply to a Circular Letter, New South Wales Legislative Council, *Votes and Proceedings*, 1845, Report from the Select Committee on the Condition of Aborigines, pp. 50–51; Parker, Report for 1 July – 31 December 1845; Parker to Robinson, 21 January 1848; Parker, Report for 6 months ending 31 December 1848, Public Record Office Victoria, VPRS 4410, Unit 2; Drought (comp.), *Journals of Godfrey*, entries 12 May 1849, 16 September 1849 and 22 September 1849, pp. 9, 24–25; James (ed.), *Homestead History*, p. 74.

lessee from the tract of country so leased'. Parker was apprehensive that in remote parts of the Port Phillip District the legal rights provided by a lease would be exploited by pastoralists and that the Aboriginal people would be forced or in Parker's words hunted from pastoral run to pastoral run and so never have a place to call their own. Both Parker and Robinson concluded that reserves were urgently needed in every principal locality for the Aborigines' support and benefit.[35]

In the spring of 1847 a neighbouring pastoralist, William Hunter, who had taken over Tarrengower from Mackinnon in 1842, tried to take a large and valuable part of the reserve at Larrnebarramul for his flocks. Parker complained bitterly to Robinson about this, calling it gross aggression. To try and counter it he decided to allow Hepburn to temporarily leave some of his sheep on the reserve until such time as he could form an outstation and remove Hunter's sheep. But in the following year the problem continued and Parker repeatedly complained to Robinson that Hunter's flocks were depastured on the best parts of the reserve, and claimed that several pastoralists in the area had told him that they would begin to occupy parts of the reserve that adjoined their runs if Hunter's encroachment was accepted by the government. In mid April 1848 Parker warned: 'their encroachments if carried into effect will entirely break up the reserve and render it impracticable any longer to depasture the government flocks on the establishment'. In early May Parker reported that Hunter had taken possession of a bark hut on the reserve and called for this seizure of public property to be resisted. In the last week of May he informed Robinson that Hunter's sheep were now within sight of his house.

---

35   Parker to Robinson, 26 June 1845, Public Record Office Victoria, VPRS 11, Unit 5; Parker to Robinson, 21 September 1845, Public Record Office Victoria, VPRS 11, Unit 5; Parker, quoted by Robinson, Annual Report for 1846, New South Wales State Records, NRS 905, Item 4/2780.

'From facts which have come to my knowledge, I am satisfied that this aggression is the result of a deliberate attempt to appropriate as large a portion of the Aboriginal reserve as can be obtained', he wrote. Indeed, he claimed: 'It is in fact an experiment to ascertain how far the government will allow two or three individuals to go in seizing and appropriating the small remnant of the country left to the Aborigines'.[36]

La Trobe called on the Commissioner of Crown Lands for Westernport, Edward Grimes, to investigate. In the meantime Parker moved two flocks containing 2000 sheep to the area of the reserve that Hunter had been encroaching upon and commenced building a hut for a permanent outstation. Hunter told Grimes he had always depastured sheep on the reserve and Grimes concluded that this had not harmed the reserve. La Trobe ruled that Parker had acted improperly in moving sheep onto that part of reserve. More generally, he had come to have grave doubts about Parker's previous claims about what he had managed to achieve at Larrnebarramul and had apparently formed the view that he had done no more than any settler but at a much greater cost and that he should have tried running a school on the reserve rather than trying to cultivate the land. But Parker believed he was in the right in this case, appealed to La Trobe, and once more took possession of the land in dispute. Grimes complained to La Trobe but this time the Superintendent sided with Parker. 'If the Assistant Protector *has* occasion for the ground and can occupy it or depasture it for the benefit and with

---

36 Robinson, Journal, 18 June 1847, Mitchell Library, vol. 20, MS A 7041; Parker to Robinson, 1 October 1847, Public Record Office Victoria, VPRS 11, Unit 5; Parker to Robinson, 17 April 1848, Public Record Office Victoria, VPRS 11, Unit 5; Parker to Robinson, 6 May 1848, Public Record Office Victoria, VPRS 2897, Unit 1; Parker to Robinson, 23 May 1848, Public Record Office Victoria, VPRS 11, Unit 5.

the aid of the Aboriginal natives, I confirm that he must have preference', he wrote. 'Mr Hunter's occupation must always have been held to be on sufferance.' The following March two other pastoralists encroached on the reserve. At this point Parker called on the government to both delineate clearly the boundaries of the reserve and enforce them. The following month La Trobe agreed that this should be done.[37]

Failure?

By this time, however, La Trobe had already recommended that the Protectorate be abandoned. In October 1848 Gipps' successor as Governor of New South Wales, Sir Charles FitzRoy, had asked La Trobe whether the Protectorate should be abolished and La Trobe had told his superior in the most resounding of terms that it should be. 'The result of all this outlay [on Aborigines] may be stated in a few words', he wrote. 'Every one of these plans and arrangements made for the benefit of the aboriginal native, with the exception of the last named, the Native Police, perhaps, has either completely failed, or shows at this date most undoubted sights of failure, in the attainment of the main objects aimed at.' Indeed, La Trobe asserted that the Protectorate had really made no difference to the condition of Aboriginal people: 'if no such establishment had existed the state

---

37 La Trobe, Minute, 30 May 1848, on Robinson to La Trobe, 29 May 1848, Public Record Office Victoria, VPRS 2897, Unit 1; Edward Grimes to La Trobe, 24 July 1848, Public Record Office Victoria, VPRS 2897, Unit 1; Parker to La Trobe, 9 October 1848, Public Record Office Victoria, VPRS 2897, Unit 1; Grimes to La Trobe, 14 October 1848, Public Record Office Victoria, VPRS 2897, Unit 1; La Trobe, Minute, undated, on Grimes to La Trobe, 14 October 1848, his emphasis; Parker to Robinson, 24 March 1849 (two letters), Public Record Office Victoria, VPRS 11, Unit 5; Parker to Robinson, 17 April 1849, Public Record Office Victoria, VPRS 11, Unit 5; La Trobe, Minute, undated, on Robinson to La Trobe, 21 April 1849, Public Record Office Victoria, VPRS 2897, Unit 1.

of the aboriginal native within the [Port Phillip] District would not have differed greatly from what it is now'. He believed that this failure should primarily be attributed to the impracticable nature of the scheme and the inapplicability of its measures to the circumstances of the Aboriginal people. But he also believed there was a further reason, namely its personnel. 'They one and all had their failings', he told FitzRoy. 'They each, under one impulse or other, undertook, and had pretensions to a task, beyond their powers.'[38]

In September 1849 a select committee of the New South Wales Legislative Council put the final nail in the Protectorate's coffin. It, too, argued that the Protectorate had completely failed in its aims: 'Some of the evidence shows it to have been useless, while other witnesses state that its effect has been prejudicial to the objects of its care'. Among those who had contributed to the Select Committee's findings on the Protectorate was a Justice of the Peace at Mount Macedon, J.C. Riddell. 'It was, and has been, a grand mistake from beginning to end', he argued. The Select Committee seems to have made no attempt to seek the opinion of the protectors. By the end of the year the government had closed the Protectorate.[39]

Many historians have followed in the footsteps of the Protectorate's critics, but this is by no means the only story that can be told of the Aboriginal protectorate at Larrnebarramul. Over several years Parker was grown up by the Djadja Wurrung, in the sense that he slowly learned something of their language and kinship system and their notion of right behavior and became aware of those aspects of their culture that held greatest significance for them. Furthermore,

---

38 La Trobe to Deas Thomson, 18 November 1848, New South Wales Legislative Council, *Votes and Proceedings*, 1849, vol. 2, Report of the Select Committee on the Aborigines and Protectorate, pp. 3–10.

39 Report of the 1849 Select Committee on the Aborigines and Protectorate, pp. 1, 30.

there emerged on the station a small core of men and women who were drawn to Parker's world and who became Christians as well as keen and hard-working farmers. They tended to be the children, youths, and young men and women who had few or no affiliations with traditional Djadja Wurrung land and kin groupings. In this small group lay the slender hopes for a Djadja Wurrung future.[40]

---

40 Parker, Reports for 1 July – 31 December 1845 and 1 January – 30 June 1846.

Chapter 6

DECLINE

The abolition of the Port Phillip Protectorate marked the beginning of the end of the Djadja Wurrung as a community, or so it seemed at the time. The New South Wales Select Committee of 1849 made no recommendation for what might replace it, and Governor Charles FitzRoy merely proposed the most general of measures. It was up to Charles Joseph La Trobe, as Superintendent of the Port Phillip District, to make his own arrangements. He did so in a rather ad hoc fashion. He decided to retain one of the assistant protectors, William Thomas, as a Guardian of the Aborigines; to appoint the Commissioners of Crown Lands as honorary protectors with the responsibility of visiting Aboriginal reserves, supplying Aborigines with food, clothes and blankets in cases of emergency, and submitting reports on their condition; and to maintain support for two schools for Aboriginal children, at Merri Creek and the former protectorate station of Larrnebarramul.[1]

---

1   Edward Deas Thomson to Charles Joseph La Trobe, 29 January 1850, Victoria Legislative Council, *Votes and Proceedings*, 1858–59, Report of the Select Committee on Aborigines (henceforth Select Committee 1858–59), pp. 101–02; La Trobe to Frederick Powlett, 8 June 1850, Victoria Legislative Council, *Votes and Proceedings*, 1853–54, vol. 3, Aboriginal Protectorate on the Loddon. Return to Address, Mr Fawkner, 4 November 1853, p. 5; M.F. Christie, *Aborigines in Colonial Victoria 1835–86*, University of Sydney Press, Sydney, 1979, pp. 136–37.

It appears that La Trobe decided to make particular arrangements in regard to Larrnebarramul as a result of representations that Parker made after the assistant protector learned in the middle of 1849 that the Protectorate was going to be abolished. In December that year Parker had sought permission to occupy any land in the reserve that might be vacated. Indeed, he had pleaded with La Trobe to be granted this land without having to compete openly for it: 'I am anxious, less for my own sake as for the sake of the native with whom I have so long been connected, to remain in the district that I may continue to employ such influence and facility of access as I may possess with them for their religious instruction'. It is apparent that personal considerations played a major role in Parker making such a case. Perhaps this is hardly surprising. After all, he had a large family to support. But Parker realised that he had to play these down: 'I should feel myself bound by every obligation to render the utmost aid in my power for the success of any future measures or arrangements that may be adopted by Her Majesty's Government for the benefit of the aborigines', he sought to reassure La Trobe. Indeed, he found it necessary to go so far as to 'disclaim any wish to deprive the aborigines of a single yard of ground that can be occupied by them advantageously'. In January 1850 La Trobe visited Larrnebarramul and seems to have decided to sanction Parker's request in regard to the land on the basis of the arguments the assistant protector had advanced. Later this arrangement was confirmed for three years on the condition that Parker give employment to the Djadja Wurrung and carry out his pastoral and agricultural operations mainly on the basis of their labour.[2]

---

2   Edward Parker to George Augustus Robinson, 20 June 1849 and 12 September 1849, Public Record Office Victoria, VPRS 11, Unit 5; Parker to La Trobe, 17 December 1849, Public Record Office Victoria, VPRS 2897, Unit 1; La Trobe to Powlett, 8 June 1850, p. 5; Parker to La Trobe, 31 August 1850, Public Record Office Victoria,

CHAPTER 6: DECLINE

Three months later, Parker made further representations to La Trobe about the management of the station. Some of these concerned the terms upon which food and clothes might be provided to the Djadja Wurrung: Parker argued that the principles informing the previous system for these should be maintained (which involved Aborigines being required to work) but that less encouragement should be given to the Djadja Wurrung to congregate at the station. Most of Parker's recommendations focused on the young. 'It is', he told La Trobe, 'of great importance that appropriate encouragement should be given to young people to settle there, and detach themselves from their less improvable seniors'. Parker undertook to devote his future efforts to the younger Djadja Wurrung in order to enable them to provide for themselves from the proceeds of their own labour, emphasised the need to support the school, and asked La Trobe to ensure that the children were amply provided with food and clothing. La Trobe seems to have been largely persuaded by the case for the school but asked the Commissioner of Crown Lands for Western Port, Frederick Powlett, to go to Larrnebarramul and investigate. Powlett gave the school a good report. Most importantly, he told La Trobe: 'I have no hesitation in saying that the continuance of [the school] is the only chance left of doing any permanent good to the aborigines in this district'. La Trobe decided to support the school, to leave the oversight of Aborigines on the station with Parker, and to have a medical officer visit it occasionally to treat any Aborigines who might be there.[3]

VPRS 44, Unit 669; La Trobe, Proposed Arrangement with Parker, no date, Victoria Legislative Council, *Votes and Proceedings*, 1853–54, vol. 3, Aboriginal Protectorate on the Loddon. Return to Address, Mr Fawkner, 4 November 1853, p. 6.

3   Parker to La Trobe, 8 April 1850, Public Record Office Victoria, VPRS 44, Unit 669; La Trobe to Powlett, 8 June 1850, p. 6; Powlett to La Trobe, 8 August 1850, Public Record Office Victoria, VPRS 44, Unit 669.

These measures met Parker's needs and perhaps those of the younger Aboriginal people at Larrnebarramul but they represented very little in terms of assistance for most of the Djadja Wurrung. They were acutely aware of this lack of provision for them. A Djadja Wurrung man complained to a local pastoralist: 'Missionary man tell us say Our Fader which art in heaven, and bib us to-day our daily bread; but no gib it daily bread. Gib siftens (siftings) flour, damaged tobacco, and three fellow potato!'. It seems that the same man, who was known by whites as Prince Jamie, often expressed his scorn of the former Protectorate station. A digger on one of the goldfields in the area observed: 'He would commence with an imitation of the chanting of the service, in a reverent attitude, and with an attempt at grave looks. He would then wind up in solemn accents with these words, "As it was in the beginning, is now and ever s'all be, world without end, amen. No give it grog, no give it flour, cabbage, baccy, b------ the money!"'. But it might be a mistake to make too much of this testimony. A pastoralist who knew Prince Jamie well once remarked that he had 'a glib tongue'.[4]

Gold

The government's neglect of Aborigines following the closure of the Protectorate was to have serious consequences in the wake of the gold rushes that began in 1851. The impact of the discovery of gold in Victoria was considerable for those Aboriginal people whose land was invaded once more. Among those most affected were the Djadja Wurrung. Within a few months of the first strike, 10,000 diggers

---

4   William Wilson Dobie, *Recollections of a Visit to Port-Phillip, Australia, in 1852–55*, Thomas Murray and Son, Glasgow, 1857, p. 96; John Hunter Kerr, *Glimpses of Life in Victoria by 'A Resident'* (1872), introduced by Marguerite Hancock, Miegunyah Press, Melbourne, 1996, p. 143–44.

had swept down upon Barkers Creek, Mount Alexander. The Djadja Wurrung's camping areas along creeks and streams became alluvial sites, timber was felled and burned, wildlife shot, plants trampled, and sacred sites violated. Later, the discovery of gold at Yandoit Creek in May 1854 brought a large influx of Europeans close to the centre of Larrnebarramul and the station lost a huge amount of stock to theft. There were demands in parliament that reserves such as Larrnebarramul be broken up in order to encourage agriculture by white settlers and to provide revenue for the government, and by the following year much of the best land in the area of the goldfields was subdivided and sold. This process saw Larrnebarramul being reduced to a mere 640 acres.[5]

Yet, as the historian Fred Cahir has argued recently, the experience of Aboriginal people on the goldfields was not simply one of loss and suffering.[6] They were neither simply pushed to the periphery nor bewildered spectators but instead exhibited considerable entre-preneurial spirit, an eagerness to participate in mining and related activities, and a desire to interact with Europeans in a variety of ways. It has also been noted that the Djadja Wurrung probably knew of the presence of gold in their country prior to its discovery by Europeans. The name in the Djadja Wurrung language for the area that Europeans came to call Avoca, Kara Kara, signified gold; and some leads and mines were named after the Aboriginal people who

5   W.E.P. Dana to Colonial Secretary, 12 November 1851, Public Record Office Victoria, VPRS 2878, Unit 2; Parker to Colonial Secretary, 1 March 1853, Public Record Office Victoria, VPRS 1189, Unit 503; *Argus*, 14 June 1854; Select Committee 1858–59, p. 79; Joseph Parker, 'Boyish Recollections of Victoria Seventy Years Ago', *Mount Alexander Mail*, 24 June 1916; C.C. Culvenor, *The Boundaries of the Mount Franklinford Aboriginal Reserve*, Jim Crow Press, Daylesford, 1992, p. 19.

6   For much of the research for this section of this chapter I am indebted to the painstaking work Cahir has undertaken.

discovered them or because they were connected with them in some way, as for example in the case of Black Protector's Creek.[7]

As a result of the gold rushes there was undoubtedly a marked increase in the demand for Aboriginal labour on pastoral runs. As white labourers went walkabout to the goldfields, Aborigines took their place. Indeed, Parker recalled several years later, with the outbreak of mining there were several runs in the area where the only shepherds were Aborigines. Like other Aborigines elsewhere in the Port Phillip District or what had become Victoria (on 1 July 1851), the Djadja Wurrung got semi-permanent work as stock riders, station hands, shepherds, hutkeepers, and domestic servants, and casual employment, such as sheep washing and stripping bark, and they did a range of tasks that included chopping wood and carrying water. They also found it easier to get better remuneration, which included cash wages, on the pastoral runs than they had done previously.[8]

7   Robert Brough Smyth, *The Aborigines of Victoria*, vol. 2, Government Printer, Melbourne, 1878, p. 195; Fred Cahir, *Black Gold: Aboriginal People on the Goldfields of Victoria, 1850–1870*, Australian National University E Press and Aboriginal History, Canberra, 2012, pp. 1, 8.

8   Mary Lillias Drought (comp.), *Extracts from Old Journals Written by Frederick Race Godfrey (Pioneer) of Boort Station, Loddon District, Victoria, 1846–1853*, Tytherleigh Press, Melbourne, 1926, entries 26 September 1851, 16 June 1852, 25 August 1852, 1 September 1852, 8 September 1852, 22 November 1852, pp. 108, 132, 139, 140, 141, 149, Marguerita Stephens (ed.), *The Journal of William Thomas, Assistant Protector of the Aborigines of Port Phillip and Guardian of the Aborigines of Victoria, 1839-1867, vol. 3, 1854 to 1867*, Victorian Aboriginal Corporation for Languages, Melbourne, 2014, entries 9 November 1855, 13 December 1855, 10 November 1856, pp. 59, 62, 95; G.F. James (ed.), *A Homestead History: The Reminiscences and Letters of Alfred Joyce, of Plaistow and Norwood Port Phillip 1843 to 1964*, 3rd edn, Oxford University Press, Melbourne, 1969, pp. 74, 91; Select Committee 1858–59, pp. 22, 26, 35–36; Report of W.S. Urquhart, Central Board for the Protection of the Aborigines, *First Report*, 1861, p. 18; Richard Broome, 'Aboriginal Workers on South-Eastern Frontiers', *Australian Historical Studies*, vol. 26, no. 103, 1994, p. 212.

Djadja Wurrung stockman
This photograph, taken by the pastoralist John Hunter Kerr (see page 162), might
suggest that some of the young Djadja Wurrung men had come to embrace the ethos
of the white stockman. Dressed in well-fitting European clothes and carrying a
stock-whip, he seems to be relaxed, confident and proud, perhaps even cocky.
(Courtesy State Library of Victoria)

On the goldfields themselves there was also some demand for Aboriginal labour. They performed a range of tasks. These included the role of guides. It is apparent that some miners recognised that the traditional knowledge that Aboriginal people had of the country was invaluable. One miner went so far as to claim that his party would almost have given two Aboriginal men, who were probably Djadja Wurrung, all the gold they had in return for their putting them on the track to the diggings at Castlemaine. There seems no doubt that Aboriginal people also grasped the economic opportunities presented by the goldfields as they sold goods they had manufactured, most notably rugs, baskets, nets and artefacts, and game they had caught, such as birds. It is also evident that Aboriginal people, including Djadja Wurrung, engaged in mining themselves, though they tended to fossick rather than dig. As one remarked after a particularly good find, 'white-fellow dig for gold and black-fellow pick it up'. Indeed, at times they appear to have enjoyed considerable success, or so it was claimed by the author James Bonwick. 'Even the aborigines are wealthy in these times', he argued. 'I met a party of them at Bullock Creek well clothed, with a good supply of food, new cooking utensils and money in their pockets'. Bonwick added: 'One remarked with becoming expression of dignity "me no poor blackfellow now, me plenty rich blackfellow"'.[9]

At the same time it appears that Aboriginal people realised that there was an interest among mining communities in their traditional ceremonies, especially corroborees. On one occasion Aborigines who might have been Djadja Wurrung gave a performance of a corroboree

9   James Bonwick, *Notes of a Gold Digger and Gold Digger's Guide*, R. Connebee, Melbourne, 1852, pp. 18–19; John Sherer (ed.), *The Gold Finder of Australia: How he Went, How he Fared, and How he Made his Fortune*, Clarke, Beeton & Co, London, 1853, p. 131; *Argus*, 3 October 1866; Cahir, *Black Gold*, pp. 22–24, 40, 43, 68, 72–73.

to a large audience at a theatre in Lamplough. It had five acts and in one scene two men killed a third man and buried him under one of the stage's trapdoors, upon which he reappeared from another, smothered in white chalk, having apparently 'jumped up white fellow'. (Readers will recall that a common Aboriginal perception or conception of Europeans at first contact was of their being kinsmen returned from the dead.) As Richard Broome has observed, it is difficult to know what to make of such performances. Were the Aboriginal performers presenting traditional ceremonies and thereby revealing something of their history or culture in an attempt to engage the sympathy of white settlers, or were they simply fashioning a form of theatre in the knowledge that they could earn money from a curious white audience, or something else again? The Aboriginal people responsible for performing the corroboree described above were booked to give a further appearance at Back Creek, ten miles away, and they refused to walk there and demanded that their passage in a Cobb's coach be paid or that they be provided with a special conveyance.[10]

It seems clear, though, that a good deal of how the Djadja Wurrung acted on the gold fields was influenced by traditional concerns. For example, they continued to insist that it was proper for Europeans to share their resources with them. A Welsh miner, Joseph Jenkins, remarked in his diary for September 1873: 'A dark native, that is an Aborigine, paid me a visit. He was looking for bees. He mentioned that when a native discovers a hive, he invites the neighbours to partake of the honey, but when a white Christian discovers it,

---

10   *Mount Alexander Mail*, 21 May 1860; Tom Griffiths, *Hunters and Collectors: The Antiquarian Imagination in Australia*, Cambridge University Press, Melbourne, 1996, p. 53; Broome, *Aboriginal Victorians*, p. 111; Cahir, *Black Gold*, pp. 79–80.

he keeps the produce for himself'. It also seems that the Djadja Wurrung were struck by the frenzied manner in which many miners pursued gold, remarking to one miner at Bendigo that 'whitefellow all gone mad digging holes and washing stones'. Aboriginal people were prepared to undertake work for miners, as we have noted, but it appears that traditional cultural matters could take precedent. One miner reckoned that his party had to delay their departure for a gold field for an evening so that two Aboriginal men who had agreed to act as guides for his party could receive Aborigines of another tribe and conduct a corroboree. On another occasion a party of Aboriginal people, presumably Djadja Wurrung, asked a party of miners to move as their presence interfered with their carrying out some religious business. J.C. Hamilton recalled: 'A party of blacks came and wanted us to shift from the place [we had camped], as they had buried one of their number late the evening before, and wanted to complete their arrangements'.[11]

Among the Europeans whom the Djadja Wurrung encountered on the gold fields there seem to have been some who became genuinely interested in their culture. One miner, J.F. Hughes, recorded some of their language and place names and information about their ceremonies and material culture, and another miner, George Rowe, became conversant with their medicine for treating dysentery. Both men also clearly enjoyed their sharp wit and talent in mimicry. Hughes recalled: 'They had a keen sense of humour, and it afforded them great merriment to get me to shout aloud at

11 Sherer (ed.), *The Gold Finder*, p. 131; J.C. Hamilton, *Pioneering Days in Western Victoria* (1914), Warrnambool Institute Press, Warrnambool, 1981, p. 99; William Evans (comp.), *Diary of a Welsh Swagman, 1869–1894*, MacMillan, Melbourne, 1975, p. 38; John Baldwin Moore to his brother, December 1874, reproduced in Margery and Betty Beavis, *Avoca: The Early Years*, Margery and Betty Beavis, Warrnambool, 1986, p. 22.

night some message in their own language to their comrades across the creek, the reply which reverberated through the woods causing them intense amusement'. He particularly remembered one man: 'One of the tribe, more adventuresome than his fellows, had visited the capital of the colony, and though he ordinarily spoke in broken English he could excellently imitate the language and gesture of a new chum swell he had met at a hotel, pronouncing distinctly, with an affected air, "Waiter, bring me a glass of brandy"'. Rowe was a graphic artist and became sufficiently well acquainted with some Djadja Wurrung that they were willing to allow him to sketch their portraits. In a letter he began writing to his wife at the end of January 1854 he reported that a Djadja Wurrung man, known to Europeans as Billy or King William, and his wife, had sat for him and that he had since 'had a visit from all the tribe every day'. Rowe found that there was a lucrative market among his fellow Europeans on the gold fields for the sketches and paintings he made of the Djadja Wurrung and so he was keen to do more. In the first of the portraits he did Rowe sketched Billy with an opossum rug thrown over his shoulder and the woman with a blanket over her shoulder, which is to say that he depicted them in a way that contrasted savagery with civilisation. If he continued to portray his sitters in this way, this might account for the interest in his sketches and paintings.[12]

It seems that many Aboriginal people were only able to eke out a scanty subsistence on the gold fields, that their main sources of

---

12 George Rowe to his wife, 25 January 1854, and Rowe to his daughter, undated (marked Letter 10), George Rowe, Correspondence, 1852–1854, National Library of Australia, MS 3116; J.F. Hughes, in The Castlemaine Association of Pioneers and Old Residents, *Records of the Castlemaine Pioneers*, Rigby, Adelaide, 1972, p. 225; Cahir, Black Gold: A History of the Role of Aboriginal People on the Goldfields of Victoria, 1850–70, PhD thesis, University of Ballarat, 2006, p. 222; Cahir, *Black Gold*, p. 99.

subsistence were what Europeans tended to regard as begging and prostitution, and that the payment they received for work performed and goods sold was most often in the form of food, clothes and alcohol rather than cash. This at least seems to have been the view of pastoralists and officials in the area. Moreover, these observers reported that alcohol was readily available as bush inns and grog shanties sprang up across the diggings, and claimed that proprietors were keen to exchange grog for whatever cash Aboriginal people could put together. The Djadja Wurrung had previously been able to get alcohol but during the gold rushes it became easier to obtain. It appears that drunkenness became increasingly common among many, that more died as the result of accidents and fights, and that the consumption of alcohol had a pernicious effect on their health.[13]

The Djadja Wurrung had been ravaged by newly introduced diseases in the 1840s. The historical geographer Ian Clark has estimated that their numbers were halved between 1840 and 1852, and by the end of that period they are thought to have numbered only 142. The Djadja Wurrung's health suffered further now as they became increasingly malnourished. In going into white settlement they had started to eat starchy foods such as flour, which were nutritionally poorer than their traditional diet of vegetables, fish and meat. They continued to get the latter where they could but this would have become more difficult as pastoral runs in the areas of

13 Parker to Colonial Secretary, 1 October 1853, Public Record Office Victoria, VPRS 1189, Unit 203; Inquest 8 February 1855, Public Record Office Victoria, VPRS 24, Unit 24; Inquest 18 September 1857, Public Record Office Victoria, VPRS 24, Unit 49; Select Committee 1858–59, pp. 19–20, 26, 28–30, 32–33, 35–36, 54, 79–80; Inquest 30 June 1862, Public Record Office Victoria, VPRS 24, Unit 119; James (ed.), *Homestead History*, pp. 74, 78; Kerr, *Glimpses of Life*, p. 146; Report of Urquhart, Central Board for the Protection of the Aborigines, *First Report*, 1861, p. 18; Inquest 30 June 1862, Public Record Office Victoria, VPRS 24, Unit 119; *Boort Standard*, 23 September 1892.

goldfields were broken up for closer settlement. Besides, it appears that they increasingly preferred to eat the white man's tucker. The Djadja Wurrung also began wearing European clothes and blankets and spent longer periods in the same camping place, and this tended to cause respiratory diseases and gastric problems. Many became too unwell to hunt and gather or work for wages and food. The mortality rates seem to have dramatically worsened during these years of the gold rushes. A resident warden at Avoca believed that they were now only one-tenth of their former numbers. Most observers blamed alcohol consumption. Medical care for Aborigines was largely absent and generally they were excluded from local hospitals. Parker knew of several cases in the course of the 1850s in which Aborigines in his district had died because of a lack of medical help. By 1863 the Djadja Wurrung appear to have numbered a mere 38.[14]

The hardship Djadja Wurrung suffered was aggravated by the humiliating treatment they sometimes received on the goldfields. It appears that some diggers vented their pent-up resentments and frustration upon Aborigines. John Bulmer, a young white man who would later become a missionary and devote the rest of his life to ministering to Aborigines, was on the Bet Bet (Dunolly) diggings in 1854 and reckoned the diggers amused themselves by plying the Aborigines with grog and watching the mayhem that followed. He

---

14 William Thomas to Colonial Secretary, 2 October 1854, Public Record Office Victoria, VPRS 1189, Unit 203; Select Committee 1858–59, pp. 21, 28, 30, 55, 58, 79–80; Report of W.S. Urquhart, Central Board for the Protection of Aborigines, *First Report*, 1861, p. 26; Charles Judkins to William Thomas, 25 June 1862, William Thomas Papers, Mitchell Library, uncatalogued mss, set 214, Item 17; Inquest 12 March 1865, Public Record Office Victoria, VPRS 24, Unit 166; Kerr, *Glimpses of Life*, p. 146; James (ed.), *Homestead History*, p. 78; Edgar Morrison, *The Loddon Aborigines: "Tales of Old Jim Crow"*, s.n., Yandoit, 1971, p. 180; Ian D. Clark, *Aboriginal Languages and Clans: An Historical Atlas of Western and Central Victoria, 1800–1900*, Department of Geography and Environmental Science, Monash University, Melbourne, 1990, p. 150.

recalled: 'On one occasion two men fastened on each other and with mouth and hand tried to injure themselves. One man I noticed had his lower lip bitten off, and this was a scene that made the crowd laugh'. In the light of such encounters many European observers were of the opinion that the further the Djadja Wurrung were from diggings and the grog houses the better. It seems that some of the Djadja Wurrung were of the same mind.[15]

Close relations

Many Djadja Wurrung appear to have moved northwards in their country in the wake of the gold rushes. The pastoral runs they favoured included Alfred Joyce's Plaistow and Norwood, Frederick Race Godfrey's Boort, and John Hunter Kerr's Fernyhurst. Joyce found the Djadja Wurrung useful for some casual tasks and expected them to provide some service in return for the food they demanded. On one occasion at least, a group of Djadja Wurrung performed a ceremonial dance for him, and on another occasion they allowed he and his men to observe the internment of one of their kin who had been murdered by someone they called a wild blackfellow.[16]

A group of Djadja Wurrung dwelt for periods of time at Boort where Godfrey employed a number of the men and came to rely on their help for tasks like ferrying goods across the Loddon River. They seem to have regarded Godfrey as someone upon whom they

15 John Hepburn to Charles Joseph La Trobe, 10 August 1853, in Thomas Francis Bride, *Letters from Victorian Pioneers* (1898), Heinemann, Melbourne, 1969, p. 78; Select Committee 1858–59, pp. 20, 34, 36; Central Board for the Protection of Aborigines, Minutes, 6 August 1860, National Archives of Australia, Series B314, Item 1; John Bulmer Papers, Museum Victoria, South-eastern Australia Ethnographic Collection, Box 11, folder 1, paper 3.

16 James (ed.), *Homestead History*, pp. 72–77; Ian D. Clark, 'The Aboriginal Pioneers of the Shire of Korong', in Korong Historical Society (comp.), *Burrabungle: Mt Korong*, Koorong Historical Society, Wedderburn, 1988, p. 11.

could look for sympathy or help.[17] They no doubt sought to create a relationship of kin with him. On his arrival in the area in the late 1840s they assumed that he must have known of the country previously; indeed, that he was one of their kinsmen who had returned from the dead. In keeping with this they tried to share many aspects of their culture with him. This included performing some ceremonies in his presence. On one occasion they took a large quantity of ochre to him and explained how they used it to decorate their bodies for these ceremonies. Godfrey also seems to have known an Aboriginal man and an Aboriginal woman well enough to mesmerise them one evening, which was part of his interest in experimenting with one of the popular sciences of the day. (He had recently attended a phreno-mesmeric lecture at the Mechanics' Institute in Melbourne.)[18]

There were also pastoralists in the area who acquired a genuine interest in traditional Aboriginal culture. The most notable was probably William Stanbridge, who took a lease for Wombat Run or Wombat Flat (previously called Holcombe) in 1852. He had previously become very interested in learning the language, culture and traditions of the Wergaia people (who were northern neighbours of the Djadja Wurrung), and especially their knowledge of astronomy. In 1861 Stanbridge became a Fellow of the Ethnological Society of

---

17 Godfrey served on the Victorian Board for the Protection of the Aborigines for fifteen years and was a key figure in its affairs in the mid 1870s. In the opinion of the anthropologist and historian Diane Barwick he was a principled man but one who was dictatorial towards Kulin Aborigines at Coranderrk and helped preside over the destruction of that reserve (Diane E. Barwick, *Rebellion at Coranderrk*, Aboriginal History, Canberra, 1998, pp. 108, 111, 143, 158, 304).

18 Drought (comp.), *Journals of Godfrey*, entries 28 May 1849, 5 June 1849, 31 May 1850, 3, 11 and 24 September 1850, 16 June 1852, 25 August 1852, 8 and 11 September 1852, 1 November 1852, 24 November 1852, pp. 12–13, 55, 65, 67, 132, 139, 141, 148, 150; Select Committee 1858–59, p. 60; Fernihurst District History Committee, *Reflections from Kinypaniel: The Early Years of the Fernihurst District*, Fernihurst District History Committee, Maryborough, 1992, p. 12.

London and in 1863 a fellow of the Anthropological Institute in London. In a paper he submitted to the former society's journal he seems to have been concerned to contribute ethnological or anthropological knowledge about Aboriginal people but also to counter the reputation that had been foisted upon them of being the lowest race in the scale of humankind. In concluding this paper he made reference to 'the astonishment that [he] felt, as [he] sat by a little camp fire, with a few boughs for shelter, on a large plain, listening for the first time to two [Wergaia] aboriginals, speaking of Yurree, Wanjel, Larnan-kurrk, Kulkun-bulla, as they pointed to those beautiful stars'. It is unclear whether Stanbridge established a similar relationship with the Djadja Wurrung but he did become an honorary correspondent for Aborigines for the Upper Loddon for the Central Board for the Protection of Aborigines (which will be discussed later) in 1862.[19]

The closest relationship between any pastoralist and the Djadja Wurrung was that forged at Fernyhurst where some Djadja Wurrung spent considerable periods of time. They performed many tasks for Kerr, which included ferrying goods across the river, but they also invited him to join in hunting expeditions for native game, attend some of their ceremonies, and observe the burial of a senior man, all of which suggests that they sought to establish a relationship with Kerr in which he would assume the responsibilities of a kinsman, which included that of sharing his resources with them. For his part Kerr had a lively sense of curiosity and was a keen observer of the world around him at Fernyhurst. Most importantly from a historian's point of view he was interested in documenting how British colonisation

---

19 W.E. Stanbridge, 'Some Particulars of the General Characteristics, Astronomy, and Mythology of the Tribes in the Central Part of Victoria, Southern Australia', *Transactions of the Ethnological Society of London*, new series, vol. 1, 1861, pp. 286, 304; *Argus*, 9 July 1862.

Djadja Wurrung artefacts

In the 1850s there was growing interest among settlers in Aboriginal culture as a new science of anthropology emerged. In July 1854 the organisers of an exhibition of industry in the Central Victorian town of Sandhurst (later Bendigo) called for examples of the resources and industry of the colony of Victoria. John Hunter Kerr responded quickly, forwarding a large and wide range of material made by Djadja Wurrung, which he had commissioned from them at Fernyhurst. It not only included weapons and tools such as shields, waddies, spears and boomerangs, which is what most European hunters of Aboriginal artefacts collected at the time, but also possum rugs and examples of work made by Djadja Wurrung women, such as a bag, and some children's play sticks and three items of ceremonial significance. It seems that Kerr took this photograph of some of this material before sending it to the exhibition, and he later included a lithograph based on this photograph in a book he wrote, *Glimpses of Life in Victoria*. After the Bendigo Exhibition closed, these artefacts were displayed at the Melbourne Exhibition of the same year and the Exposition Universelle de Paris the following year.

(Courtesy State Library of Victoria)

was transforming the culture of the Djadja Wurrung. He did this by writing about them, drawing them and taking their photographs, and collecting their artefacts.[20]

These days Kerr is probably best known for his photographs. He was among the first amateur photographers in the Australian colonies and seems to have been genuinely interested in taking photographs that showed Aboriginal people as they were, rather than trying to represent Aborigines as noble savages, as many photographers did. It is believed that he took at least 36 photographs of Aboriginal people at Fernyhurst. The historian Elizabeth Willis, who has examined Kerr's photographs carefully, has argued that the Djadja Wurrung willingly participated in the process of having their photographs taken and that each photograph was clearly the result of a transaction between a photographer and a subject who lived in close proximity and knew each other pretty well. Certainly, by Kerr's own account, once they overcome their fear of the new technology the Djadja Wurrung proved to be willing sitters. In fact, as the anthropologist Nicolas Peterson has pointed out, any photograph of Aboriginal people taken prior to the invention of the snapshot actually required a significant degree of co-operation from them. The Djadja Wurrung also took a keen interest in the results, though they were reluctant to see any photographs of any of their deceased kin. Once both photographer and sitters became more confident with the technology, Kerr took a series of photographs in which the Djadja Wurrung people, and especially the men, were more obviously posed. On one occasion

---

20 Drought (comp.), *Journals of Godfrey*, entries 16 September 1849, 20 July 1850, 27 September 1851, 22 November 1852, pp. 24, 61, 108, 149; Kerr, *Glimpses of Life*, pp. 12, 113, 137, 142–43, 146–49, 161, 174–75, 178, 186–87; Elizabeth Willis, "'People Undergoing Great Change': John Hunter Kerr's Photographs of Indigenous People at Fernyhurst, Victoria, 1850s', *La Trobe Library Journal*, no. 76, 2005, p. 49.

Aboriginal ceremony at Fernyhurst

This is the best known of a series of photographs John Hunter Kerr took of a ceremonial dance that Djadja Wurrung performed at his request. Kerr later reproduced a lithograph based on this photograph in his *Glimpses of Life in Victoria*.

(Courtesy State Library of Victoria)

Kerr prevailed upon several Djadja Wurrung men and three or four Djadja Wurrung boys to perform a corroboree in daylight so that he could photograph it. Apparently they only agreed to do this after he promised a considerable gift in exchange and on the condition that none of their women kin witnessed their performance.[21]

Christian converts

At the time the Protectorate was abolished six Aboriginal families amounting to some 20-30 people chose to remain at Larrnebarramul. They included several whom Parker had adopted as young children soon after he arrived in the Port Phillip District. Among them was Kolain, the boy whom the Wesleyan missionary Francis Tuckfield had baptised at Larrnebarramul in the early 1840s, and the group of Christian converts whom we noted in the previous chapter. In regard to the latter, historians are best able to recover something of the lives of two men, Yerrebulluk or Dicky, who was born in 1827, and Beernbarmin or Tommy Farmer, who seems to have been born in 1831.

Yerrebulluk and Beernbarmin were typical of many Aboriginal converts to Christianity in the early to mid-nineteenth century in the sense that they were both orphans and had been raised by a missionary figure since they were very young boys, having joined Parker after a Daung Wurrung raid had left many of their kin dead. Soon after the abolition of the Protectorate, Dicky and Farmer made application to

---

21 Kerr, *Glimpses of Life*, pp. 16–17, 149–50; Nicolas Peterson, 'The Changing Photographic Contract: Aborigines and Image Ethics', in Christopher Penney and Nicolas Peterson (eds), *Photograph's Other Histories*, Duke University Press, Durham, 2003, p. 124; Willis, '"People Undergoing Great Change"', pp. 50–51, 54, 59, 62–63; Willis, 'Re-Working a Photographic Archive: John Hunter Kerr's Portraits of Kulin People, 1850s–2004', *Journal of Australian Studies*, vol. 35, no. 2, 2011, p. 236.

government to occupy a section of the reserve as their own, following in the footsteps of those such as the Woiwurrung headman Billibellary who had told William Thomas in July 1843 that his people would stop on their country and cultivate the soil, and whose people had recently gained a grant of nearly 2000 acres. Dicky and Farmer were granted permission to hold some land at Larrnebarramul. From 1852 they farmed 21 acres of land on their own account, erecting houses for themselves, cultivating several crops, running stock, and selling their produce to the diggings that bordered Larrnebarramul. (The land they occupied was clearly marked on a surveyor's drawing of the station that was made in 1854 [see p. 112].) In March 1853 Parker claimed that they had probably earned a hundred pounds in the previous year and that their success had had a marked influence on some of the other young men. Several years later, Parker also noted that the Christian converts at Larrnebarramul attended church every Sunday and that their children were receiving instruction in the school. He claimed that they were no different from those he called ordinary peasants. Parker's observations suggest the ways in which these men had actually come to have a sense of themselves as both farmers and Christians.[22] Yet Parker probably exaggerated the extent of cultural change, not least because he overlooked their obligation to share their earnings and care for their kin.

---

22 Parker to Colonial Secretary, 1 March 1853 and 1 October 1853, Public Record Office Victoria, VPRS 1189, Unit 203; Parker to Colonial Secretary, 9 January 1854, Public Record Office Victoria, VPRS 4415, Unit 1; Inquest 23 April 1855, Public Record Office Victoria, VPRS 24, Unit 25; Select Committee 1858–59, p. 19; Charles Judkins to William Thomas, 28 February 1862, 11 March 1862 and 19 July 1862, William Thomas Papers, Mitchell Library, uncatalogued mss, set 214, Item 17; Victoria, Legislative Assembly, *Votes and Proceedings*, 1877–78, vol. 3, Royal Commission on the Aborigines (henceforth Royal Commission 1877), pp. 24, 31–32; Edgar Morrison, *Frontier Life in the Loddon Protectorate: Episodes from Early Days, 1837–42*, Advocate, Daylesford, 1967, p. 95; Richard Broome, *Aboriginal Victorians: A History Since 1800*, Allen & Unwin, Sydney, 2005, pp. 33, 107.

Facing page: At Larrnebarramul

These photographs are believed to be the work of a geologist, Richard Daintree, who collaborated with an artist, Antoine Fauchery, to produce a collection of photographs called *Sun Pictures of Victoria*. Daintree took these photographs at Larrnebarramul in 1858 or 1859. The first shows the houses or huts the young Aboriginal farmers had built there some years earlier. The second features several of these men, among whom are probably Farmer, Dicky and Lankey. The former photograph appeared in *Sun Pictures of Victoria* under the title of *Group of Civilised Blacks*.

(Courtesy State Library of Victoria)

In 1857 William Westgarth, a former member of the Victorian Legislative Assembly, claimed that Beernbarmin (whom he had met a couple of years earlier) confessed that he had not liked Europeans or European customs at first. Beernbarmin also told Westgarth that his people had been greatly diminished in number since the coming of the Europeans: they had once numbered 500 but there were now only sixty of them. Beernbarmin's embrace of Christianity no doubt owed something to this fact. As the historian Robert Kenny has reminded us, Christianity is an especially consoling religion for those living in the midst of sickness and death because it is a religion that has suffering at its core.[23]

The livelihood of these Aboriginal farmers and their families was precarious. They got relatively little help from the government and their land holdings were insecure. The author and traveller William Howitt reported in 1858 that they were dissatisfied with merely having the reserve as a home to which they might resort and had asked to be granted some land in their own right. But the main problem they faced was disease. For example, Farmer married in 1854 and had two children but they both died in infancy and his

---

23 William Westgarth, *Victoria and the Australian Gold Mines in 1857*, Smith, Elder and Co, London, 1857, pp. 223–24; Robert Kenny, *The Lamb Enters the Dreaming: Nathanael Pepper & the Ruptured World*, Scribe, Melbourne, 2007, p. 192.

wife died soon afterwards. One of the other farmers, Lankey, was to die of a mishap in 1855, falling down a digger's hole as he made his way home one night. The inquest recorded that he was drunk.[24]

As far as the school at Larrnebarramul is concerned, Parker tried to increase the number of pupils by persuading parents in the area to allow their children to be taken. Godfrey told a Victorian select committee in 1858 that Aboriginal people could seldom be induced to give up their children to whites. 'They say, invariably, "When jump up, you man him", [that is] when the child is grown up, you may then have him'. But Parker had some success after the teacher and the overseer at Larrnebarramul toured the wider area and met some 300 Aborigines. By the middle of 1853 there were apparently twenty pupils in the school. The children were taught for several years by a Wesleyan clergyman, Joseph Carvasso, but he resigned after complaining that the government was failing to provide enough support, and his place was taken by Charles and Margaret Judkins.[25]

By the late 1850s settlers in Victoria increasingly argued that the Aboriginal people were a dying race. For example, an artist who visited Larrnebarramul in April 1858 claimed that the Djadja Wurrung were rapidly passing away. 'The grave will soon close over the last of the race', he blithely asserted. Indeed, the notion that the

---

24 Inquest 23 April 1855, Public Record Office Victoria, VPRS 24, Unit 25; William Howitt, *Land, Labour, and Gold: Or Two Years in Victoria*, 2nd edn, vol. 2, Longman, Brown, Green, Longmans, and Roberts, London, 1858, p. 179; Judkins to Thomas, 28 February 1862, Thomas Papers, Mitchell Library, uncatalogued mss, set 214, Item 17; Royal Commission 1877, p. 31.

25 Parker to Colonial Secretary, 1 March 1853, 1 October 1853 and 19 October 1853, Public Record Office Victoria, VPRS 1189, Unit 203; *Argus*, 30 June 1853; Parker to Norman Campbell, 3 October 1853 and 19 October 1853, Public Record Office Victoria, VPRS 1189, Unit 203; Parker to Joseph Kaye, 20 January 1855 and 6 June 1855, Public Record Office Victoria, VPRS 1189, Unit 203; Select Committee 1858–59, pp. 43, 51.

CHAPTER 6: DECLINE

Men and children at Larrnebaramul
This was the last of the three Daintree photographs of Djadja Wurrung that appeared in *Sun Pictures of Victoria*. He captioned it *Civilised Blackfellows at Parker's Protectorate, Mount Franklyn.*
(Courtesy State Library of Victoria)

Djadja Wurrung and the Aborigines more generally were dying out in accordance with the law of nature became a commonplace, uttered even by those who were sympathetic to their plight. 'For a few years after [the beginning of the gold rush] a few of them would occasionally visit the station I was on, but they soon disappeared altogether', Joyce would write. 'It is not so very surprising that these poor creatures, so low in the scale of civilisation or rather in the entire absence of it, should succumb to the inundation of the white population when we see the half-civilised Maoris of New Zealand gradually receding under the same influence', he mused. But Joyce was more troubled by the rapid depopulation of the Djadja Wurrung than these comments might suggest. 'A general impression has prevailed that the colony, as a nation, has been guilty of a great wrong in so utterly sweeping them out of existence, or at any rate not making better provision for their preservation', he noted. Joyce, like so many colonists, seems to have found it necessary to pin the blame on the Aboriginal people themselves: '[T]heir nomadic habits were the great difficulty in any systematic plan of settlement on their behalf. At the very foundation of the colony some well-meaning missionary efforts were made to evangelise and civilise them, but they all failed'.[26]

It appears that some whites sought to distance themselves from this troubling past by turning Aborigines into scientific curiosities. Certainly, scientific interest in Australian Aborigines grew enormously under the influence of evolutionary ideas as they were perceived to be a type of early humanity. A case in point is R.E. Johns, who was clerk of petty sessions at Moornambel, near Avoca. He collected almost a hundred Aboriginal artefacts, including skulls, and hung some of these on the wall of his living room, which he described as a museum.[27]

The 1858–59 Select Committee

Joyce probably expressed the sentiments noted above as the Victorian Select Committee on Aborigines was appointed to consider the future of the Aborigines of the colony. This committee was the outcome

26 *The Age*, 6 May 1858; Select Committee 1858–59, pp. 41, 43, 71; James (ed.), *Homestead History*, pp. 5, 77–79; Kerr, *Glimpses of Life*, p. 11; Broome, *Aboriginal Victorians*, p. 93.

27 See Griffiths, *Hunters and Collectors*, chapter 2.

of concern expressed over the previous few years by pastoralists, philanthropists, and ethnologists, including Parker. These men believed that Europeans were superior to Aborigines and had a duty to colonise what they called the waste places of the earth. But, unlike the vast majority of settlers, they acknowledged the fact that the Aboriginal people were the original possessors of the soil and that Europeans were intruders who had stolen their land. Most of all they recognised that the white invasion had deprived the Aboriginal people of their former means of existence and had almost exterminated them. Consequently, they believed that Aborigines had an inalienable right to obtain the necessities of life and a claim upon the settlers. Indeed, they argued that the very first charge upon the colonial government was due compensation for the Aborigines.[28]

Parker was the last witness to give evidence to the Select Committee and his testimony proved to be very telling. He vigorously argued that it was possible to reclaim the Aboriginal people by bringing them under the influence of Christianity, and urged that this be done on stations that should be established at various places throughout the colony and placed under the authority of religious bodies rather than government. He also insisted that the provision of schooling for the young was vitally important. Finally, he argued that some part of the colony should be reserved so that the Aboriginal people had a place where they could rest their feet knowing that they had a

---

28 *Argus,* 17 March 1856, 2 April 1856, 27 October 1858, 28 October 1858, 3 February 1859; Victoria Legislative Assembly, *Votes and Proceedings,* 1856–57, vol. 3, Petition of the United Church of England and Ireland in Victoria; *Age,* 28 October 1858; Christie, *Aborigines in Colonial Victoria,* pp. 152–55; Kenny, *The Lamb,* pp. 32–33; Anne O'Brien, 'Humanitarianism and Reparation in Colonial Australia', *Journal of Colonialism and Colonial History,* vol. 12, no. 2, 2011, DOI: 10.1353/cch.2011.0016.

right to be there. By and large, the Select Committee adopted these suggestions in its recommendations to the government.[29]

However, twelve months were to pass before a parliamentarian, Richard Heales, suggested that the government create a number of local committees under the supervision of a central board for the protection of the Aborigines. The government agreed but gave this board no commission to act. However, after the Board's members applied some pressure, the government granted it a commission to advise it on the amount of moneys to be voted year by year, control the expenditure of these funds, suggest the proclamation of reserves, supply rations and the like, recommend the appointment of agents, officers and local committees in connection with the Board, and outline and oversee the duties of all such people.[30]

At its early meetings the Board discussed the recommendations of the 1858–59 Select Committee and decided to seek more information and suggestions for future plans by sending a circular letter to members of the local committees. In the advice they received it is apparent that there was a growing tendency to see Aboriginal people as children who needed protection because they were unable to look after themselves. It was also evident that there was a common belief that any hope of civilising the Aborigines lay in teaching the young, preferably apart from their parents and kin. In turn the Board recommended that permanent reserves be made for Aboriginal people in the areas where sufficient numbers remained and placed under the care of missionaries. These reserves resembled the stations of the Protectorate but the Board urged that the Aboriginal people should be confined to them as much as possible. In the case of the

---

29 Select Committee 1858–59, pp. v, 18–20.
30 Central Board for the Protection of Aborigines, *First Report*, 1861, p. 3.

Beembarmin (Tommy Farmer)
This photograph, taken by Charles Walter at Coranderrk in 1866, is a result of a
commission by the Melbourne Intercolonial Exhibition to make a series of portraits
of the Aboriginal people on that reserve.
(Courtesy State Library of Victoria)

young but most especially orphaned children, it recommended that
the government should acquire the power to send them to a special,
central school. As the historian Michael Christie has noted, what
the Board was suggesting amounted to a significant shift towards
a coercive form of paternalism. Its plans had serious implications

for the Djadja Wurrung (though the Board was only to acquire the powers it sought in 1869).[31]

At much the same time, it appears that the farmers at Larrne-barramul began to struggle. Beernbarmin lost nearly all of his bullock team and was unable to harvest his crops. Several years later he was to claim that the loss of his bullocks had caused his farming to fail: 'That broke me down, and I could not get on'. Yet the Board agreed at one of its first meetings to grant 100 guineas to allow Beernbarmin and Yerrebulluk to buy a team of bullocks as well as tools and seeds to grow wheat. The more important cause of the failure of these farmers seems to have lain elsewhere, namely in their poor health. In October 1862 Yerrebulluk died after a severe bout of tuberculosis. He was only 35 years old. This meant that Beernbarmin was now the only surviving man of those who had begun farming on their own account after the Protectorate was abolished.[32]

The closing of Larrnebarramul

In February 1863 the Guardian of the Aborigines, William Thomas, visited Larrnebarramul and was dismayed to find that its buildings were in a very dilapidated condition and the cemetery in an even worse state. He urged the Board to replace the school house and to

---

31 *Ibid.*, pp. 5–6, 11, 18–23, 34; Central Board for the Protection of Aborigines, Minutes, 11 June 1860, National Archives of Australia, CRS B314, Item 1; Christie, *Aborigines in Colonial Victoria*, p. 164.

32 Central Board for the Protection of Aborigines, Minutes, 7 June 1860 and 25 June 1860, National Archives of Australia, CRS B314, Item 1; Central Board for the Protection of Aborigines, *First Report*, 1861, p. 6; Judkins to Thomas, 25 October 1862, Thomas Papers, Mitchell Library, uncatalogued mss, set 214, Item 17; Thomas to Brough Smyth, 28 February 1863, William Thomas Papers, Mitchell Library, uncatalogued mss, set 214, Item 19; John Green to Robert Brough Smyth, 4 March 1864, National Archives of Australia, CRS B312, Item 8; William Thomas to Brough Smyth, 5 March 1864, National Archives of Australia, CRS B312, Item 8; Royal Commission 1877, pp. 31, 86–87.

develop the station more generally. 'I trust the Central Board will with the least delay make this Aboriginal Station not an eyesore and a byword which it is at present, but a credit to the Board', he wrote in his journal. However, several months later the Board's secretary, Robert Brough Smyth, insisted that the Djadja Wurrung should be moved to a new reserve called Coranderrk, which had been founded near Healesville in May 1863 by John Green and the Woiwurrung and Taungurong. In July the Board accepted this recommendation but it was only in December that it began to investigate the practicality of removing the Aboriginal people at Larrnebarramul to Coranderrk. In February 1864 the Central Board for the Protection of Aborigines asked Thomas and Green, who was not only the manager of Coranderrk but had become the Board's inspector, to inspect the station, the school and the children at Larrnebarramul and assess the merit or otherwise of removing all the people to Coranderrk. By this time the number of children had dwindled considerably and it only had seven children. The station's condition had also deteriorated seriously. Green was dismayed. He reported that the farms had been completely abandoned, claimed that all the buildings on the reserve were in a deplorable state, and suggested they should be razed to the ground. He recommended that the Board close the reserve and the school and remove the children to Coranderrk as soon as possible.[33]

---

33 Central Board for the Protection of Aborigines, *Second Report*, 1862, p. 7; Stephens (ed.), *Journal of Thomas*, entries 7 and 8 February 1863, pp. 407–08; Thomas to Brough Smyth, 28 February 1863; Central Board for the Protection of Aborigines, Minutes, 14 July 1863, National Archives of Australia, CRS B312, Item 1; Thomas to Parker, 5 October 1863, National Archives of Australia, CRS B312, Item 8; Parker to Brough Smyth, 28 January 1864, National Archives of Australia, CRS B312, Item 8; Central Board for the Protection of Aborigines, Minutes, 8 February 1864, National Archives of Australia, CRS B312, Item 1; Brough Smyth to Thomas, 17 February 1864, William Thomas Papers, Mitchell Library, uncatalogued mss, set 214, Item 19; Brough Smyth, Minute, 17 February 1864, on Parker to Brough Smyth, 28 January 1864, National Archives of Australia, CRS B312, Item 8; Brough Smyth to Thomas,

However, Thomas was reluctant to endorse Green's recommend-ation to close the school. He had been impressed by Yerrebulluk's widow Eliza (who was Daung Wurrung), describing her as indust-rious and shrewd and well able to look after herself, her twelve-year-old daughter Ellen (of whom more shortly), and the children in the school. Thomas was also opposed to removing the Djadja Wurrung to Coranderrk since he realised that this would involve the breaking up of the station and could provoke general discontent. 'We may justly say in the interior "Other refuges have they none"', he wrote to Smyth. 'If this station is broken up where are the poor afflicted blacks to crawl to?', he wanted to know. Thomas went on to complain: 'Since the Board has been [established], there have been concessions I would never have anticipated. *Maffra* [a reserve in Gippsland] *is gone, and will they take Franklinford also?*'. He also called on the Board 'to secure to the heirs of the deceased farmers their rights'. (Thomas seems to have had in mind the cattle, horses and bullocks they owned.)[34]

The Board was unmoved. It decided to remove the children and as many of the Aboriginal men and women who were willing to accompany them from Larrnebarramul to Coranderrk. Smyth told the Chief Secretary James McCulloch that these steps were necessary because Larrnebarramul had been poorly managed and that it was a useless expense to maintain a school there since the children could be taught at Coranderrk.[35]

---

17 February 1864, William Thomas Papers, Mitchell Library, uncatalogued mss, set 214, Item 20; John Green to Brough Smyth, 4 March 1864, National Archives of Australia, CRS B312, Item 8; *Mount Alexander Mail*, 20 April 1864.

34 Thomas to Brough Smyth, 5 March 1864, National Archives of Australia, CRS B312, Item 8, his emphases.

35 Central Board for the Protection of Aborigines, Minutes, 7 March 1864, National Archives of Australia, CRS B312, Item 1; Brough Smyth to James McCulloch, 16 March 1864, National Archives of Australia, CRS B312, Item 8.

In December 1863 Parker had got wind of these plans and protested to the Board. He argued that the Aboriginal people at Larrnebarramul belonged to the country north and northwest of there and that they would oppose removal to Coranderrk as they regarded it as a foreign country. Indeed, he claimed that the removal of the Aboriginal people at Larrnebarramul, though he especially seems to have had the Djadja Wurrung in mind, could only be done by the use of coercive means. However, it appears that Parker was ignorant of the fact that there were some kinship ties between the Djadja Wurrung and their fellow Kulin in the country where Coranderrk lay. Many of the Djadja Wurrung actually had kin at Coranderrk and members of two of the Djadja Wurrung clans had made marriages with Woiwurrung and Taungurong there. Consequently, they were willing to move to Coranderrk. Besides, Beernbarmin had already decided to go there. The school at Coranderrk might have played a crucial role in the decision of the Djadja Wurrung to leave their own country given that they wanted their children to master new skills.[36]

On 12 April 1864 John Green arrived at Larrnebarramul to shift the people to Coranderrk. Apparently many of them had already moved there. Green took a party of twelve comprising seven children and five men and women. Eliza, Ellen and Kolain were among their number. There is some evidence to suggest that Green used coercion or made threats. One Djadja Wurrung man, James Edgar, told a parliamentary inquiry several years later that he was forced to go to Coranderrk by Green: 'He told me I would have to come or else he would give me in charge'. However, the Woiwurrung leader Robert Wandin, who gave evidence at a later parliamentary

---

36 Parker to Brough Smyth, 28 January 1864; Royal Commission 1877, p. 31; Barwick, *Rebellion at Coranderrk*, pp. 72, 122, 263, 266.

inquiry, was adamant that Green never forced anyone against their will to move to the reserve. Furthermore, in a letter Ellen wrote to Parker a few months after she and her fellow Djadja Wurrung moved to Coranderrk she spoke of the great sadness they felt when they remembered Larrnebarramul but remarked that they liked Coranderrk very much (and Green undoubtedly believed that this was the case). Moreover, eighteen months or so later, several of the Djadja Wurrung who had remained at Larrnebarramul agreed to a proposition by Green that they move to Coranderrk after he visited them at Kangaroo Flat, near Bendigo.[37]

The moving of most of the Djadja Wurrung to Coranderrk might be said to mark the end of the Djadja Wurrung as a community. However, it can also be argued that this ensured their survival. The recent research of a team of demographic historians led by Len Smith and Janet McCalman has uncovered the striking fact that those who chose to stay away from supervised reserves such as Coranderrk have no living descendants today.[38]

Prior to some of the Djadja Wurrung moving to Coranderrk a further connection had been forged between the Djadja Wurrung and the Woiwurrung and Taungurong. In May 1863 the Governor of Victoria, Sir Henry Barkly, had held a levee on the banks of the Yarra

---

37 *Daylesford Express*, 14 April 1864; Judkins to Brough Smyth, 19 April 1864, National Archives of Australia, CRS B312, Item 8; Green to Brough Smyth, 21 April 1864, National Archives of Australia, CRS B312, Item 8; Ellen to Parker, 10 June 1864, Parker Family Papers, State Library of Victoria, MS 8174; Green to Thomas, 23 June 1864, Thomas Papers, Mitchell Library, uncatalogued mss, set 214, Item 20; *Bendigo Advertiser*, 16 March 1865 and 5 April 1865; Thomas, Journal, entry 6 January 1866, Thomas Papers, Mitchell Library, uncatalogued mss, set 214, Item 5; Royal Commission 1877, pp. 26, 28; Victoria, Legislative Assembly, *Votes and Proceedings*, 1882–83, vol. 2, Board Appointed to Inquire into Coranderrk Aboriginal Station, p. 89; Morrison, *Loddon Aborigines*, p. 96; Barwick, *Rebellion at Coranderrk*, p. 72.

38 Len Smith et al., 'The Political Arithmetic of Aboriginal Victorians', *The Journal of Interdisciplinary History*, vol. 38, no. 4, 2008, pp. 547, 550–51.

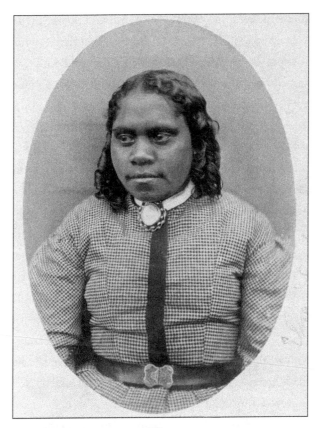

Ellen

This is one of two photographs Charles Walter took of Ellen at Coranderrk in 1865.
The other photograph Walter took of her appeared in a popular monthly news
magazine, *The Illustrated Australian News*. In both these photographs Ellen appeared
as a neatly dressed young woman. According to the photographic historian Jane
Lydon, they were readily pressed into service by the Central Board for the Protection
of Aborigines and its allies to support a story about the acquisition of the virtues of
civilisation by Aboriginal people. Walter also included Ellen's portrait in every set of
photographs that survives of his work at Coranderrk. He sent it to the Commissioners
of the Melbourne Intercolonial Exhibition of 1866 as an example of his work, and it
was one of many Aboriginal portraits they displayed.
(Courtesy Museum Victoria)

to celebrate the wedding of the Prince of Wales two months earlier. The Woiwurrung and Taungurong had presented the Governor with an address to Queen Victoria in both English and Kulin, pledged themselves to become her loyal subjects, and presented a number of gifts for her and her children, which included a large possum rug, several weapons and a crocheted collar. The collar had been made a year earlier by Ellen and sent to Susannah Thomas, and she and her husband, William Thomas, seem to have suggested that it be included in these gifts for the royal family. Ellen also penned two letters to the Queen in which she probably expressed her people's attachment and loyalty to Her Majesty, and Barkly's wife sent the Queen a doily Ellen had crocheted. The gift giving on the Yarra that afternoon was part of a ceremony that the Kulin performed in order to bring into being or cement a relationship of reciprocity between themselves and the British Crown. Each party was to give, and receive in return, access to one another's resources. By the end of June Governor Barkly had gazetted the reserve at Coranderrk, and in September and October the Secretary of State for the Colonies, the Duke of Newcastle, had conveyed the satisfaction with which she had received the Kulin's assurances of their attachment and loyalty to the Crown and a promise of her interest in their advancement and welfare. (In doing this the Queen requested that Ellen be told that she had accepted the crocheted collar with much pleasure.) Not surprisingly, the Kulin interpreted both the Governor and the Queen's responses as a confirmation that the British Crown had entered into a relationship of reciprocity with them, and this established a belief that they had been permanently granted the land at Coranderrk.[39]

---

39 *Illustrated Melbourne Post*, 25 June 1863; *Victorian Government Gazette*, no. 69, 3 July 1863, p. 1474; Judkins to Thomas, 7 August 1863, Thomas Papers, Mitchell Library,

Among those who moved to Coranderrk was a young Djadja Wurrung boy by the name of Thomas Dunolly. He was to make something of a name for himself in the fight that the Aboriginal people mounted to save the reserve from being closed in the 1870s and 1880s. The Kulin headman William Barak led this protest but in keeping with Kulin tradition he gave his words to younger men such as Dunolly who acted as his speakers. Dunolly, using the skills of reading and writing he had been taught in the school at Larrne-barramul, acted as Barak's principal scribe as well, and Barak hoped the young man would be one of those who would succeed him as headman. Three other Djadja Wurrung men, Tommy Avoca, John Charles and Martin Simpson, also played a role in the famous protest or rebellion that was mounted at Coranderrk in a bid to stop the Board closing the station. As it turned out, they were not the only Djadja Wurrung to play a political role in the coming years. Caleb Morgan, the child of a Djadja Wurrung woman who had moved to Coranderrk in the mid 1860s, would become a member of one of the first Aboriginal political organisations to be formed in Australia, the Australian Aborigines' League, founded by William Cooper in 1933–34.[40]

---

uncatalogued mss, set 214, Item 19; Duke of Newcastle to Governor Sir Charles Darling, 18 September 1863 and 24 October 1863, Central Board for the Protection of Aborigines, *Third Report*, 1864, p. 11; Brough Smyth to Thomas, 9 December 1863, Thomas Papers, Mitchell Library, uncatalogued mss, set 214, Item 19; Smyth to Thomas, 16 February 1864, Thomas Papers, Mitchell Library, uncatalogued mss, set 214, Item 20; Central Board for the Protection of Aborigines, *Fourth Report*, 1864, p. 20; Morrison, *Loddon Aborigines*, pp. 98–99; Barwick, *Rebellion at Coranderrk*, p. 66.

40 Ann Bon, 'Barak: An Aboriginal Statesman', *Argus*, 28 November 1931; Morrison, *Loddon* Aborigines, p. 96; Marie Fels, Research Notes, held Bendigo Dja Dja Wurrung Aboriginal Association; Nicholas Clark (ed.), Trackback: Aboriginal History and Archaeology in Djadja *Wurrung* Country (Central Victoria) Examining Mount Kooyoora, Mount Alexander and Mount Tarrengower, March 1995, section 5; Barwick, *Rebellion at Coranderrk*, pp. 74, 96, 125, 128, 131, 145, 161, 190, 221, 265, 272, 303, 307.

Thomas Dunolly

Photograph taken by Charles Walter at Coranderrk in 1866. It appears that Walter gave the results of his work to his subjects. Certainly, they took a great interest in having photographs of themselves and their kin.

(Courtesy Museum Victoria)

By contrast, Beernbarmin appears to have moved back and forth between Coranderrk and his own country. He had no claim to the land at Coranderrk through descent or intermarriage and lacked the ritual knowledge considered proper for a senior man, and so he had no influence there.[41] In fact several Djadja Wurrung seem to have remained or returned to their own country after the closure of Larrnebarramul. In July 1865 a local newspaper suggested that even though some of the Aboriginal people in the area were very impoverished they nevertheless preferred to live there because they 'distrust[ed] the good intentions of the white men'. The desire to live off government reserves such as Coranderrk was in fact a common one. A census taken in March 1877 revealed that half of the Aboriginal people in Victoria were living off them at the time. Four of that number were residing in Castlemaine. However, it was very difficult to survive off the reserves, and those who did so were severely impoverished and they came under a good deal of pressure from local officials to move or return to Coranderrk and stay there.[42]

At the same time these Aborigines could achieve considerable prominence in settler communities. In 1865 a local newspaper reported that a man it called King Billy, and whom it figured as the last of the Loddon tribe, had declared that he was going to erect a toll

---

41 In July 1867 Beernbarmin was one of five Aboriginal men that the Chief Commissioner of Police for Victoria engaged as black trackers to search for three small boys who were lost near Daylesford, and was later awarded an oval shaped silver plate by the Central Board for the Protection of Aborigines for his efforts (Heather Holst, *Making a Home: A History of Castlemaine*, Australian Scholarly Publishing, Melbourne, 2014, p. 26).

42 Inquest 12 March 1865, Public Record Office Victoria, VPRS 24, Unit 166; *Argus*, 6 June 1865; *Bendigo Advertiser*, 20 July 1865; *Argus*, 3 October 1866; Central Board for the Protection of the Aborigines, *Sixth Report*, 1869, p. 20; Inquest 9 September 1872, Public Record Office Victoria, VPRS 24, Unit 283; *Avoca Mail*, 8 December 1874; Royal Commission 1877, p. 95; Barwick, *Rebellion at Coranderrk*, pp. 73, 154; Broome, *Aboriginal Victorians*, p. 147.

gate at a new bridge at Laanecorrie over the Loddon River on the grounds that his ancestors had enjoyed such rights since the age of antiquity. King Billy was making a political point, but the newspaper that reported this incident dismissed his declaration. And in July 1887 a Djadja Wurrung man, seeking charity from the government, asserted his title to land in petitioning the commissioners of the colony's railways: 'Gentlemen and brothers too, I am the last of the Aborigines tribe in these parts. I do humbly compare two lots of title deeds. I received mine from the Author of Nature, while the land occupied by all the railways is titled by the white man's lawyers'.[43]

But seldom did settler communities truly empathise with the plight of these Aboriginal people. Instead, the notion of the last local Aborigine was a popular one in the Australian colonies in the second half of the nineteenth century, symbolising the succession of the races. This seems to have been especially the case when the Aborigines could be depicted as a king or a queen and thus deemed to be somehow emblematic of their race. Often settler communities presented the Aboriginal men with what were called king plates, which were crescent shaped plates engraved with their status and name, and called upon them to play a role at public events where they wanted them to provide a sense of novelty or a sense of contrast between an apparent primitive past and a progressive present. At the opening of the railway at Dunolly in April 1879 King Tommy carried a banner on a long pole and danced in front of the train engine. Yet the Aboriginal people on whom the status of king or queen had been bestowed could turn this to their advantage. On the occasion just mentioned King Tommy apparently told a heart-rending account of

---

43 *Bendigo Advertiser*, 20 July 1865; Petition, 28 July 1887, reproduced in Evans (comp.), *Diary of a Welsh Swagman*, p. 156.

the earlier days of his people to the Governor of Victoria, Sir George Bowen, and the Governor was sufficiently moved to give him some money.[44]

The notion that particular Aboriginal men or women were the last of their race was extraordinarily powerful. Settler Australians came to regard this as a matter of common sense. Yet it was simply a fantasy. There is no doubt that Aboriginal people had been devastated by British colonisation, but it was one thing to note the catastrophic decline in their numbers and quite another to claim that they were doomed to die out. And so time would tell. A hundred years or so later, Aboriginal people including the Djadja Wurrung would return to prominence and do so with all the power of the oppressed and the repressed.

---

44 James Flett, *Dunolly: Story of an Old Gold Diggings*, 2nd edn, Hawthorn Press, Melbourne, 1974, pp. 3, 8; Griffiths, *Hunters and Collectors*, pp. 111, 199; Broome, *Aboriginal Victorians*, p. 102; Cahir, *Black Gold*, p. 19.

EPILOGUE

On 28 March 2013 the Victorian government and the Dja Dja Wurrung Clans Aboriginal Corporation on behalf of what was called the Dja Dja Wurrung traditional owner group announced they had reached an agreement that formally recognised the Djadja Wurrung people as the traditional owners of the land for part of central Victoria and settled four claims to native title that representatives of the Djadja Wurrung had made for some 266,532 hectares of Crown land. The terms of the agreement granted in fee simple (i.e. freehold ownership) to the Corporation two properties deemed to be of particular cultural significance, and transferred to it Aboriginal title to two national parks, one regional park, two state parks, and one reserve, which meant that those parks and reserves would be jointly managed by the State and the Corporation and that the Djadja Wurrung would be entitled to take certain natural resources from them within agreed limits. The settlement also provided $9.65 million of funding to enable the Djadja Wurrung to meet its obligations under the agreement and to advance their cultural and economic goals. The agreement was one of a number of settlements that the Victorian government made with Aboriginal claimants to native title at this time.[1]

---

1   State Government of Victoria and the Djadja Wurrung Clans Aboriginal Corporation, Fact Sheet: Settlement Between the Dja Dja Wurrung Traditional Owner Group and the State of Victoria, 28 March 2013, <http://ntsv.com.au/ntsvwp-content/uploads/2013/05/Dja-Dja-Wurrung-Settlement-Factsheet.pdf>; History of Native Title in Victoria, <http://www.ntsv.com.au/native-title-in-victoria/>. For full details of the agreement, see Dja Dja Wurrung Clans Aboriginal Corporation and the State of Victoria, *Recognition and Settlement Agreement*, 2 vols, <http://www.justice.vic.gov.au/home/your+rights/native+title/dja+dja+wurrung+settlement+commences>.

This was an event that no one could have anticipated in the mid to late nineteenth century: Aboriginal peoples such as the Djadja Wurrung had ceased to exist as tribal communities in the areas of Australia that had been subject to rapid colonisation by British settlers, and settler communities were proclaiming that Aboriginal people were a dying race and assuming that those they called half-castes would be assimilated and thereby disappear as a recognisable group of people.[2] The story of this astonishing turn-around in the fortunes of groups such as the Djadja Wurrung deserves a book in itself.[3] All I can do here is sketch the principal forces that were responsible for this dramatic change.

The post-war period in Australia saw the gradual rise of a movement calling for rights for Aborigines.[4] By the late 1960s this movement had increasingly begun to demand what were called *Aboriginal rights*, that is, rights that could only be claimed by Aboriginal people. These claims for Aboriginal rights had two dimensions. One was to rights on a permanent basis on the grounds of an assertion that Aboriginal people today were the descendants of the original or indigenous peoples of the country. The other was to rights for the foreseeable future on the grounds of an assertion that Aboriginal people had suffered enormous loss as the consequence of British colonisation. Both were inherently historical in nature since they concerned the past as well as the relationship between the past and the present. But, more to the point, the making of these claims required history

---

2   For an overview of the history of Aboriginal people in Victoria between 1886 and 1970, see Richard Broome, *Aboriginal Victorians: A History Since 1800*, Allen & Unwin, Sydney, 2005, Part 3.

3   For an account of these changes in respect of Victorian Aboriginal people, see *ibid.*, Chapter 17.

4   See my book *Rights for Aborigines*, Allen & Unwin, Sydney, 2003, Parts 3 and 4.

because they needed to be legitimised by stories that told of the past. Consequently, they provoked a demand for history among Aboriginal claimants. Indeed, by the mid 1980s an Aboriginal history movement could be said to be sweeping across Australia, just as, more generally, an Aboriginal cultural renaissance was taking place.

The kinds of history required by many Aboriginal people were far-reaching, especially in those parts of Australia where colonisation had been especially disastrous for the indigenous inhabitants. At its most basic, many Aboriginal people needed family history and genealogy in order to recover connections to Aboriginal family and kin and reconstruct communities that had been destroyed or dissolved. Beyond this, they required ethnographical accounts of traditional or classical Aboriginal culture as well as histories of the dispossession, displacement and destruction and the resistance and survival of Aboriginal people in order to recover or revive a sense of Aboriginality or what it meant to be Aboriginal. More specifically, they needed these in order to be able to make legal claims to rights in property in land, such as native title, and legal claims in regard to what was increasingly called heritage, such as rights to cultural property that included Aboriginal remains and artefacts. In the wake of the decimation of Aboriginal people and the devastation of Aboriginal culture, the knowledge of which lay in oral forms and was therefore highly vulnerable, Aboriginal people, especially in the most colonised parts of the country, have had to draw largely on knowledge produced by settler Australians, in particular the work of anthropologists, archaeologists and historians. By these means, many have increasingly renewed a store of cultural and historical knowledge that they had lost, and over time new generations of Aboriginal people have come to understand themselves and identify themselves in terms of what is now called Aboriginal culture and heritage.

At the same time Australian governments began to realise that the economic costs of implementing a policy of assimilation were enormous, became more apprehensive about the political costs of international criticism of Australia's treatment of Aboriginal people, and started to acknowledge the terrible impact of colonisation on Aboriginal people and the need to right the wrongs of the past. This led to a dramatic shift in direction. Settler governments had long assumed that Aboriginal communities would not have a permanent presence in Australia; moreover, they had at times acted in ways that served to undermine and even destroy the communities that provided the locus of Aboriginality, as we have seen was the case with Larrnebarramul. Now the Australian state decided to nurture Aboriginality. In order to be able to do this it needed to legitimise treating Aboriginal people differently to the way it treated other Australian citizens. It found one rationale in the argument that the Australian state had a moral obligation to right the historical wrongs Aboriginal people had suffered and that addressing those wrongs would in due course resolve this problem. But this rationale alone was insufficient because Aboriginal people were claiming Aboriginal rights in perpetuity. Consequently, the Australian state sought to further justify its special treatment of Aboriginal people by claiming that they were *culturally* different and that that difference was invaluable to the Australian nation. This claim saw the Australian state championing the value of Aboriginal cultural difference in terms of an ancient or deep past. Under this new dispensation, Aboriginal people were to be recognised (and the term *recognition* became one of the new key words in Australian culture) as a people or group of peoples (though not as a nation or nations) and were granted special rights to things such as land (but not compensation). At the same time, the Australian state sought to nurture Aboriginality by creating new forums for Aboriginal political representation, establishing new forms of bureaucracy in which Aboriginal people would be employed, and funding new projects in which Aboriginal people could be helped to produce and present art, theatre, dance, music, literature, history and so forth.[5]

The two developments I have been discussing – Aboriginal people's demands for Aboriginal rights and the manner in which the Australian state responded to these – have led to a certain kind of history being produced so that both parties are able to realise their various economic, cultural and political goals. The kind of history that has been forged has tended to have the following characteristics. Aboriginal claimants seek to show that they are indeed culturally different; this difference is couched largely in terms of what is called *tradition*; and the difference is conceived in terms of classical or traditional Aboriginal culture as this was once defined by Australian anthropologists. Consequently, this history-making places considerable emphasis on matters such as land, religion and language. Furthermore, Aboriginal claimants seek to demonstrate that they have historically *continuous* links with that traditional culture, especially in making claims to native title (since the relevant legislation states that such title can only exist where 'traditional connection' to land has been maintained). Finally, claimants produce histories that stress on the one hand the overwhelming power of the settler state and settler peoples, and their dispossession, destruction

---

5 Jeremy Beckett, 'Aboriginality, Citizenship and Nation State', *Social Analysis*, no. 24, 1988, pp. 3–18.

and displacement of Aboriginal people and culture, and hence their responsibility for what has happened and their obligation to provide redress, and on the other hand the powerlessness and lack of agency of Aboriginal people in these historical circumstances, though also their resistance, including, most importantly, their maintenance of tradition (however paradoxical this might seem).[6]

In many parts of Australia and especially those most affected by the course of colonisation these ways of representing Aboriginal culture and history have involved what the historian Eric Hobsbawm famously called the invention of tradition (which is a common phenomenon in the construction of groups such as nations). Certainly, the Aboriginal histories that many Aboriginal people want to produce and which the Australian state has demanded they present have differed markedly in form from those that have long been created by the practitioners of the discipline of history. Most importantly, these histories are not committed to empirical procedures for verifying the claims they make to historical truth.[7]

What I have been describing was evident in various statements that were made in March 2013 on the announcement of the recognition and settlement agreement between the Djadja Wurrung Clans Aboriginal Corporation and the Victorian government. For example, the Djadja Wurrung were called the traditional owners of

6   For a discussion of these matters, see Jeremy R. Beckett (ed.), *Past and Present: The Construction of Aboriginality*, Aboriginal Studies Press, Canberra, 1988.

7   Eric Hobsbawm, 'Introduction: Inventing Traditions', in his and Terence Ranger (eds), *The Invention of Tradition*, Cambridge, 1983. For a discussion of these matters, see Peter Sutton, 'Myth as History, History as Myth', in Ian Keen (ed.), *Being Black: Aboriginal Cultures in 'Settled' Australia*, Aboriginal Studies Press, Canberra, 1988; Bain Attwood, 'Portrait of an Aboriginal as an Artist: Sally Morgan and the Construction of Aboriginality', *Australian Historical Studies*, vol. 25, no. 99, 1992, pp. 302–18; and Gillian Cowlishaw, 'On "Getting it Wrong": Collateral Damage in the History Wars', *Australian Historical Studies*, vol. 37, no. 127, 2006, pp. 181–202.

the country at stake; it was asserted that Aboriginal people had lived in this part of Australia for a very long time (a thousand generations); it was claimed that the Djadja Wurrung had a special relationship to their country and that this had been shaped by principles embedded in kinship, language, spirituality and mythic law, and imprinted by Dreaming stories, totemic relationships, ceremonies and ancestral spirits; it was argued that the Djadja Wurrung had been forced from their traditional country and that their economic resources and cultural places had been damaged or destroyed by Europeans; it was claimed that the Djadja Wurrung were forced to take refuge at Larrnebarramul and that the government and its agencies as well as other organisations had later obstructed their practice of traditional law and customs and prevented their access to their country and its resources by placing them on reserves and missions where managers enforced tight restraints on movement, employment and cultural practices; but it was also asserted that the Djadja Wurrung had continued to reside on or near their traditional country, maintain their culture and customs, and uphold their law.[8]

At the same time that the Djadja Wurrung have made claims to land, they have made claims in regard to cultural artefacts that have been held by museums in Australia and overseas. The most important case has involved three artefacts (two bark etchings and a ceremonial figure) that were made by Aboriginal people in 1854 and which have long been held by two British Museums. In 2004 Museum Victoria borrowed these artefacts for a small exhibition it staged, *Etched on Bark 1854: Kulin Barks from Northern Victoria*. Shortly after this exhibition closed, representatives of the Djadja Wurrung led

8   Dja Dja Wurrung Clans Aboriginal Corporation and the State of Victoria, *Recognition and Settlement Agreement*, vol. 1, pp. 1–2.

by Gary Murray and Rodney Carter called for the artefacts to be repatriated. In the first instance, they sought to prevent the objects being returned to Britain on the basis of a claim that they belonged rightfully to the people whose ancestors had made them and that they had been stolen by the museums that held them. In other words, in the eyes of the Djadja Wurrung representatives, the history of these artefacts symbolised the dispossession of their people and thus stood for a larger history of wrongs. At the same time the Djadja Wurrung made particular cultural claims regarding the nature of the artefacts, namely that the barks had been produced as part of traditional practices and that the nature of the ceremonial piece was sacred and perhaps even secret. Most importantly, perhaps, the Djadja Wurrung regarded the matter at stake as one that concerned their right to determine the historical and cultural meaning and significance of these artefacts, and so involved an attempt to put an end to what they saw as the misrepresentation of their people and culture, both in the past and the present. In turn they saw the matter as one that could help restore their culture and people. To demonstrate how this could occur some of the younger members of the Djadja Wurrung began to produce new bark etchings that resembled the historical ones that were at stake in the dispute.[9]

---

9   [Elizabeth Willis], *Etched on Bark 1854: Kulin Barks from Northern Victoria*, Melbourne Museum, Melbourne, 2005. For a discussion of this matter and its outcomes at the time, that serves in part to present and account for the position adopted by the Djadja Wurrung, see Pamie Fung and Sara Wills, 'There's So Much in Looking at those Barks', in Chris Healy and Andrea Witcomb (eds), *South Pacific Museums: Experiments in Culture*, Monash University ePress, 2006. More recently, one of the old bark etchings has appeared alongside one of the new ones online in an exhibition staged at the National Museum of Australia called *Encounters: Revealing Stories of Aboriginal and Torres Strait Islander Objects from the British Museum*. See <www.nma.gov.au/exhibitions/encounters/mapping/fernyhurst>, and National Museum of Australia, *Encounters: Revealing Stories of Aboriginal and Torres Strait Islander Objects from the British Museum*, National Museum of Australia Press, Canberra, 2015, pp. 127–33.

Perhaps it goes without saying that the story that the Djadja Wurrung representatives told about the history of the three artefacts differed in important respects from the one that might be and indeed has been told by a historian working in keeping with the conventions of the discipline of history: Elizabeth Willis, the curator of the exhibition at Museum Victoria. In contrast to the story the Djadja Wurrung tell of dispossession, powerlessness and exploitation, Willis has recounted a story that depicts negotiation, perhaps even friendship, and which features Aboriginal agency and adaptation. On the basis of the historical research she conducted Willis has suggested that the artefacts in question were made by the Djadja Wurrung in response to a special request by the pastoralist John Hunter Kerr, on whose pastoral property they lived during the 1850s (as we saw in Chapter 6) and who wished to be able to display them at exhibitions in Sandhurst (Bendigo) and Melbourne. Willis points out that work such as these artefacts was traditionally done by Aboriginal men on the inside of their bark shelters but that the ones in question were on shorter pieces of bark that were too small to have ever been part of a bark shelter. Moreover, she argues that the Djadja Wurrung men welcomed Kerr's interest in their bark etchings and were happy to oblige him, given the nature of the relationship that had developed between them at Fernyhurst and given that Aboriginal people had come by this time to realise that items like these had a commercial value to European collectors. Consequently, Willis argues, it is likely that the material at stake was acquired by Kerr in 1854 in exchange for some kind of payment that he and the Djadja Wurrung had agreed upon. Moreover, Willis contends, it is possible that the Aboriginal people at Fernyhurst might have worked with Kerr in deciding which aspects of their culture could be presented to a European audience.[10]

Yet, as Willis concedes and indeed as she has shown in some of her writings, with the passing of time these artefacts as well as the photographs that Kerr took of the Djadja Wurrung slipped out of Aboriginal control and were stripped of the particular meanings and significance they had for them as they were appropriated by Europeans who misrepresented the makers of the artefacts and the subjects of the photographs by fabricating a story of a primitive people and a dying race.[11]

The fact remains, however, that in this case there are major differences between the story the Aboriginal claimants have told and the one presented by a scholarly historian and museum curator. This represents what has become an increasingly common problem in democratic nation states. The historian Dipesh Chakrabarty has pinpointed its nature in the following way. The discipline of history has placed enormous emphasis on the importance of being able to defend on rational grounds the stories it tells. '[An] author's position may reflect an ideology, a moral choice, or a political philosophy, but the choices are not unlimited', Chakrabarty has noted. 'A madman's narrative is not history. Nor can a preference that is arbitrary or just personal – based on sheer taste, say – give us rationally defensible principles for narration (at best it will count as fiction and not

10 Elizabeth Willis, 'History, Strong Stories and New Traditions: The Case of "Etched on Bark 1854"', *History Australia*, vol. 4, no. 1, 2007, 13.1–11. See also her 'Exhibiting Aboriginal Industry: A Story Behind a "Re-Discovered" Bark Drawing From Victoria', *Aboriginal History*, vol. 27, 2003, pp. 39–58, and '"People Undergoing Great Change": John Hunter Kerr's Photographs of Indigenous People at Fernyhurst, Victoria, 1850s', *La Trobe Library Journal*, no. 76, 2005, pp. 49–70.

11 Elizabeth Willis, 'Re-Working a Photographic Archive: John Hunter Kerr's Portraits of Kulin People, 1850s–2004', *Journal of Australian Studies*, vol. 35, no. 2, 2011, pp. 235–49.

history)'. In settling disputes about the past the discipline of history has insisted on certain procedures for assessing historical narratives according to whether they meet its conception of what is real and its evidentiary rules for determining what is reality, and these privilege scientific rationality. However, as a result of the kind of democratisation of history that has occurred in recent decades, some Aboriginal people and other groups have been encouraged and urged to tell their histories and, as we have just noted, they do not tend to tell these in ways that conform to the protocols demanded by the discipline of history or which meet the conditions for rationality that are demanded by it and the democratic nation state it serves. The Aboriginal history making is an example of what Chakrabarty has called subaltern pasts or minority histories. They provide narratives that do not meet the dominant understandings of what constitutes fact and evidence and so history's particular principle of rationality. Consequently, in the past they have been assigned an inferior position in historical discourse. Indeed, often they have not been treated as history but cast out as mere myth or legend.[12]

Here we come to the nub of the problem. 'If minority histories go to the extent of questioning the very idea of a fact or evidence, then, [traditionalists] ask, how would one find ways of adjudicating between competing claims in public life?', Chakrabarty points out. 'Would not the absence of a certain minimum agreement about what constitutes fact and evidence seriously fragment the body politic and would not that in turn impair the capacity of the nation to function as a whole?' Traditionalists insist that a shared, rational understanding of what constitutes historical facts and evidence *must* be maintained in order

---

12 Dipesh Chakrabarty, *Provincialising Europe: Postcolonial Thought and Historical Difference*, Princeton University Press, Princeton, 2000, pp. 98, 100–01.

for state institutions to be able to adjudicate between conflicting historical narratives and to be able to operate effectively. Some would say that their apprehension is by no means unreasonable. But one might ask whether in the interests of representative democracy and social justice it is appropriate to insist that minority peoples present histories that meet the rules of the dominant group when they are often unable to do so. Some traditionalists fear that the abandonment of history's particular rules for determining what is real and unreal, true and untrue, will lead to an outbreak of what they regard as hapless relativism or postmodern irrationalism, which will sweep through Historyland and the nation. As Chakrabarty suggests, these fears are probably extreme. Historical practice in both the academy and the public realm, at least in the case of Australia, still respects what we might call the objectivist impulses of the instruments of executive government, the bureaucracy and the judiciary. This is to suggest that some traditionalists exaggerate the deleterious consequences of the kind of history told by the Djadja Wurrung in the bark etchings case. They appear to lack confidence and trust that public institutions can handle difference and the conflict it often causes. Moreover, they seem to be unduly anxious about what might befall their people or the nation as a result of *their* story or *their* way of telling a story no longer being accepted as *the* truth.[13]

This said, it probably makes sense for there to be some commonly understood ground rules to guide the reception of diverse historical narratives in most circumstances and contexts. Crucial to this is a notion we might call *sharing histories*. Its premises differ from those

---

13 *Ibid.*, pp. 99, 107. For a discussion of an example of this, see my 'Contesting Frontiers: History, Memory and Narrative in a National Museum', *Recollections*, vol. 1, no. 2, 2006, pp. 103–14.

that inform a project that has been called *shared history*, which informed a good deal of the work undertaken by the Council for Aboriginal Reconciliation in Australia in the 1990s. Whereas shared history largely conceives of history as a body of historical facts presented as a singular story compiled by an anonymous narrator, sharing histories tends to regard history as a collection of narratives told by differently situated or positioned peoples and hence contingent on who the teller is, what their purpose is, the context in which they tell their story, and who their audience is. In conceiving of history in this way, sharing histories highlights the conjunction between past and present as the ground upon which all history-making occurs. It thus counters the tendency of much academic history to create a sense of distance rather than proximity between present and past. In doing this, it performs the useful function of prompting people to reflect on the nature of the relationship they have to the history they are telling, hearing, reading or seeing.[14]

This approach also encourages us to accept that much historical knowledge is a matter of perspective and interpretation. This is not a relativist position, contrary to what is sometimes claimed. It does not hold that all historical accounts are true or equal, that anything goes. It merely acknowledges that the most significant parts of historical narratives are always contingent, limited and partial. In sharing histories one might hope that a narrator or narrators will assert vigorously the value of their interpretation and challenge those of others, but also acknowledge that other interpretations also have

14 See Council for Aboriginal Reconciliation, *Addressing the Key Issues for Reconciliation*, <www.austlii.edu.au/other/IndigLRes/car/1993/9/2>; Heather Goodall, 'Too Early or Not Soon Enough? Reflections on Sharing Histories as Process', *Australian Historical Studies*, vol. 33, no. 118, 2002, pp. 7–24; Bain Attwood, 'Unsettling Pasts: Reconciliation and History in Settler Australia', *Postcolonial Studies*, vol. 8, no. 3, 2005, pp. 243–59.

value. In this way the notion of sharing histories can provide forums in which there is an exchange of views between differently situated or positioned people, a place where they both tell their histories and listen to others, and a place of robust but courteous debate. Here, the vital work of cross-cultural communication can occur so that people might understand and respect other people's histories and history-making even though they will probably continue to differ about the interpretations presented.

Sharing histories assumes that democracies such as Australia will continue to be peopled by groups with diverse histories and identities, presumes that there will continue to be contestation and conflict, and recommends that this situation be accepted. Communities need not require that all conflicts be resolved and full consensus be reached on all matters. One should not expect reconciliation between Aboriginal and settler Australians to involve agreement on every aspect of the histories that are told. It is more sensible to admit the ongoing presence of different pasts or histories and seek to accommodate these through a shared commitment to certain democratic principles. Most importantly, as I have been saying, this would allow for different forms of historical knowledge, thereby providing for a measure of equality between academic history and Aboriginal ways of relating the past.

LIST OF ILLUSTRATIONS

ACKNOWLEDGEMENTS

This book might be said to have had an earlier incarnation. In 1996–97 Nicholas Clark, Marie Fels and I undertook research for the Dja Dja Wrung Aboriginal Association as part of a broader historical study which was conceived by the Association's Cultural Officer Jim Remedio and sponsored by the National Estate. This resulted in a small book I wrote, published in 1999. In the years since, many scholars have undertaken research that is pertinent to its subject matter. Recently, I decided to return to this in the light of that scholarship and to conduct more research of my own. What appears between these covers constitutes such a thoroughgoing revision of what I wrote previously that it amounts to a new book. I would not have returned to this work had not a Reconciliation leader in Castlemaine, Vic Say, repeatedly urged me to get the earlier book I wrote about the Djadja Wurrung back into print, and had not a Djadja Wurrung elder, Gary Murray, insisted that more recent research meant that that book would have to be revised considerably. I am indebted to them both.

I also wish to acknowledge my debt to Nicholas Clark and Marie Fels for their earlier research and their generous assistance, Barbara Younger and Anisa Puri for their research assistance, and Fred Cahir for his generous help with references. I must also thank the wonderful staff of the National Archives of Australia, the National Archives of the United Kingdom, the New South Wales State Records, the Public Record Office Victoria, the State Library of New South Wales, the Matheson and Law Libraries at Monash University, the

Royal Historical Society of Victoria, the State Library of Victoria, and Museum Victoria.

I am especially indebted to the historians Richard Broome, Charles Fahey and Liz Reed for reading the manuscript of the book and offering invaluable comments and suggestions, which have served to make it a much better book than would otherwise have been the case. I am grateful to Paul Mullaly and Alex Roginski for clarifying particular matters for me. I also wish to acknowledge a small grant from the School of Philosophical, Historical and International Studies at Monash University which provided me some teaching relief to allow me to complete revisions to the manuscript.

The Dja Dja Wurrung Clans Aboriginal Corporation, Museum Victoria, and the State Library of Victoria gave permission to reproduce the drawings and photographs that appear in the book. I wish to thank Rodney Carter and Maxine Briggs for their role in facilitating those permissions. The late Gary Swinton of the School of Geography and Environmental Science, Monash University, and Helen McFarlane of the School of Earth, Atmosphere and Environment, Monash University, expertly drew the maps. One of these maps first appeared in Ian Clark's book, *Aboriginal Language and Clans: An Historical Atlas of Western and Central Victoria, 1800–1900*, and another in Ian Clark and Fred Cahir, *Tanderrum 'Freedom of the Bush': The Djadja Wurrung Presence on the Goldfields of Central Victoria*, and I thank them for allowing me to reproduce them here.

Finally, I have dedicated this book to the memory of my PhD suprevisor, John Hirst, who was a remarkable historian, a wonderful provocateur, a superb teacher, and a generous man.

November 2016

BIBLIOGRAPHY

Primary sources

Official achives

National Archives of Australia, Melbourne

CRS B312 Central Board for the Protection of Aborigines, Correspondence Files
CRS B314 Central Board for the Protection of Aborigines, Minutes of Meetings

National Archives of the United Kingdom

CO 201/39, CO 201/47 and CO 201/382, Colonial Office files for New South Wales

Public Record Office Victoria

VPRS 4 Police Magistrate Port Phillip District Inward Registered Correspondence
VPRS 10 Registered Inward Correspondence to the Superintendent of Port Phillip District relating to Aboriginal Affairs
VPRS 11 Unregistered Inward Correspondence to the Chief Protector of Aborigines: Reports and Returns
VPRS 12 Aboriginal Protectorate Returns
VPRS 19 Superintendent of Port Phillip District Inward Registered Correspondence
VPRS 21 Superintendent of Port Phillip District Inward Unregistered Correspondence
VPRS 24 Inquest Deposition Files
VPRS 44 Superintendent of Port Phillip District Inward Registered and Unregistered Correspondence
VPRS 1189 Colonial Secretary of Victoria Inward Registered Correspondence I
VPRS 2878 Colonial Secretary of Victoria Inward Registered Correspondence II
VPRS 2897 Registered Inward Correspondence of the Land Branch, Superintendent of Port Phillip District Relating to Aboriginal Stations
VPRS 4410 Aboriginal Protectorate Weekly, Monthly, Quarterly and Annual Reports and Journals
VPRS 4415 Victorian Chief Secretary Registered Inward Correspondence Relating to Aboriginal Affairs Transferred to the Department of Crown Lands and Survey
VPRS 4399 Duplicate Annual Reports of the Chief Protector of Aborigines
VPRS 6915 Loddon Aboriginal Station Files
VPRS 13172 Aboriginal Protectorate Records

State Records Authority of New South Wales
NRS 905, Colonial Secretary, Main series of letters received, 1826+
Item 4/1013
Item 4/2423.3
Item 4/2472.1
Item 4/2510
Item 4/2511
Item 4/2512
Item 4/2589B
NRS 906, Special bundles, 1826–1982
Item 4/7153

Manuscripts

Bulmer, John, Papers, Museum Victoria
Documents Collected by Sir William Dixson regarding Aboriginal Australians in
    Victoria 1 April 1839 – 8 January 1850, Dixson Library, State Library of New
    South Wales, MS DLADD 86 and 90
Ercildoun Homestead, 1830–1860, Thomas and Somerville Learmonth Station
    Diary 1839–43, State Library of Victoria, MS Box 102/9
La Trobe, Charles Joseph, Correspondence, 1839–1864, State Library of Victoria,
    MS 8431 and MS 8454
Johns, R.E., Scrapbook, vol. 1, Museum Victoria,
Mollison, Alexander Fullerton, Station Day Book, Royal Historical Society of
    Victoria, MS 2506, Box 1, Item 2
Orton, Reverend Joseph, Papers 1825–42, Mitchell Library, State Library of New
    South Wales, MS A 1715
Parker, Edward Stone, Papers, 1831–40, State Library of Victoria, MS Box
    133/8(3)
Parker Family Papers, State Library of Victoria, MS 8174
Pohlman, Robert William, Diaries, Royal Historical Society of Victoria, MSS
    000026, Box 12, Item 1
Robinson, George Augustus, Correspondence and Related Papers, Mitchell Library,
    State Library of New South Wales, vol. 20, MS A 7041, and vol. 57, MS A 7078
Rowe, George, Letters, 1853–54, State Library of Victoria, MS 8185
Thomas, William, Papers, Mitchell Library, State Library of New South Wales,
    uncatalogued MSS, set 214, Items 3, 9, 18, 19 and 20
Willis, John Walpole, Case books, 1838–1843, Royal Historical Society of
    Victoria, MS 5181

Parliamentary papers

British House of Commons Debates
British House of Commons, *Sessional Papers*, 1837, vol. 7, no. 425, Select
    Committee on aborigines in British settlements
British House of Commons, *Sessional Papers*, 1842, vol. 31, no. 231, Return to an
    Address on Emigration and Crown Lands

BIBLIOGRAPHY

British House of Commons, *Sessional Papers*, 1844, vol. 34, no. 627, Aborigines (Australian Colonies), Return to an Address

New South Wales Legislative Council, *Votes and Proceedings*, 1841, Report from the Committee on Immigration

New South Wales Legislative Council, *Votes and Proceedings*, 1843, Return to an Address, Dr Thomson, 29 August 1843

New South Wales Legislative Council, *Votes and Proceedings*, 1845, Report from the Select Committee on the Condition of Aborigines

New South Wales Legislative Council, *Votes and Proceedings*, 1849, vol. 2, Report of the Select Committee on the Aborigines and Protectorate

Victoria Legislative Council, *Votes and Proceedings*, 1853–54, vol. 3, Aborigines. Return to Address, Mr Parker, 21 October 1853

Victoria Legislative Council, *Votes and Proceedings*, 1853–54, vol. 3, Aboriginal Protectorate on the Loddon. Return to Address, Mr Fawkner, 4 November 1853

Victoria Legislative Assembly, *Votes and Proceedings*, 1856–57, vol. 3, Petition of the United Church of England and Ireland in Victoria

Victoria Legislative Council, *Votes and Proceedings*, 1858–59, Report of the Select Committee on Aborigines

Victoria, Legislative Assembly, *Votes and Proceedings*, 1877–78, vol. 3, Royal Commission on the Aborigines

Victoria, Legislative Assembly, *Votes and Proceedings*, 1882–83, vol. 2, Board Appointed to Inquire into Coranderrk Aboriginal Station

Victorian Central Board for the Protection of Aborigines, Annual Reports, 1861–69

Newspapers

The Age
Argus
Australian
The Banner
Bendigo Advertiser
Boort Standard
Colonist
Daylesford Advocate
Daylesford Express
Geelong Advertiser
Illustrated Melbourne Post
Mount Alexander Mail
Port Phillip Gazette
Port Phillip Herald
Port Phillip Patriot
Sydney Gazette
Sydney Herald
Sydney Monitor
Victorian Government Gazette

Books

Bonwick, James, *Notes of a Gold Digger and Gold Digger's Guide*, R. Connebee, Melbourne, 1852

Bride, Thomas Francis, *Letters from Victorian Pioneers* (1898), Heinemann, Melbourne, 1969

Castlemaine Association of Pioneers and Old Residents, *Records of the Castlemaine Pioneers*, Rigby, Adelaide, 1972

Clark, Ian D. (ed.), *The Journals of George Augustus Robinson, Chief Protector, Port Phillip Aboriginal Protectorate*, 6 vols, Heritage Matters, Melbourne, 1998–2000

———, *The Port Phillip Journals of George Augustus Robinson: 8 March – 7 April 1842 and 18 March – 29 April 1843*, Monash Publications in Geography, Melbourne, 1988

Dobie, William Wilson, *Recollections of a Visit to Port-Phillip, Australia, in 1852–55*, Thomas Murray and Son, Glasgow, 1857

Drought, Mary Lillias (comp.), *Extracts from Old Journals Written by Frederick Race Godfrey (Pioneer) of Boort Station, Loddon District, Victoria, 1846–1853*, Tytherleigh Press, Melbourne, 1926

Evans, William (comp.), *Diary of a Welsh Swagman, 1869–1894*, MacMillan, Melbourne, 1975

Hamilton, J.C., *Pioneering Days in Western Victoria* (1914), Warrnambool Institute Press, Warrnambool, 1981

Historical Records of Australia, series 1, vol. 19

Historical Records of Victoria, vol. 2A, Victorian Government Printing Office, Melbourne, 1982

Historical Records of Victoria, vol. 2B, Victorian Government Printing Office, Melbourne, 1983

Historical Records of Victoria, vol. 7, Melbourne University Publishing, Melbourne, 1998

Howitt, William, *Land, Labour, and Gold: Or Two Years in Victoria*, 2nd edn, vol. 2, Longman, Brown, Green, Longmans, and Roberts, London, 1858

James, G.F. (ed.), *A Homestead History: The Reminiscences and Letters of Alfred Joyce, of Plaistow and Norwood Port Phillip 1843 to 1964*, 3rd edn, Oxford University Press, Melbourne, 1969

Kerr, John Hunter, *Glimpses of Life in Victoria by 'A Resident'* (1872), introduced by Marguerite Hancock, Miegunyah Press, Melbourne, 1996

Lang, John Dunmore, *Phillipsland: Or the Country Hitherto Designated Port Phillip: Its Present Condition and Prospects*, Longman, Brown, Green, and Longmans, London, 1847

Leavitt, T.W.H. and W.D. Lilburn, *Jubilee History of Victoria and Melbourne*, vol. 2, Duffus Bros, Melbourne, 1888

Mitchell, T.L., *Three Expeditions into the Interior of Eastern Australia*, vol. 1, T. & W. Boone, London, 1839

National Museum of Australia, *Encounters: Revealing Stories of Aboriginal and Torres Strait Islander Objects from the British Museum*, National Museum of Australia Press, Canberra, 2015

Parker, Edward Stone, *The Aborigines of Australia: A Lecture delivered in the Mechanics' Hall, Melbourne, Before the John Knox Young Men's Association, on Wednesday 10 May 1854*, Hugh McColl, Melbourne, 1854

Sherer, John (ed.), *The Gold Finder of Australia: How he Went, How he Fared, and How he Made his Fortune*, Clarke, Beeton & Co, London, 1853

Smyth, Robert Brough, *The Aborigines of Victoria*, 2 vols, Government Printer, Melbourne, 1878

Stephens, Marguerita (ed.), *The Journal of William Thomas, Assistant Protector of the Aborigines of Port Phillip and Guardian of the Aborigines of Victoria, 1839-1867*, 3 vols, Victorian Aboriginal Corporation for Languages, Melbourne, 2014

Westgarth, William, *Victoria and the Australian Gold Mines in 1857*, Smith, Elder and Co, London, 1857

Journal articles

Stanbridge, W.E., 'Some Particulars of the General Characteristics, Astronomy, and Mythology of the Tribes in the Central Part of Victoria, Southern Australia', *Transactions of the Ethnological Society of London*, new series, vol. 1, 1861, pp. 286–304

Websites

Council for Aboriginal Reconciliation, *Addressing the Key Issues for Reconciliation*, <www.austlii.edu.au/other/IndigLRes/car/1993/9/2>

Dja Dja Wurrung Clans Aboriginal Corporation and the State of Victoria, *Recognition and Settlement Agreement*, 2 vols, <http://www.justice.vic.gov.au/home/your+rights/native+title/dja+dja+wurrung+settlement+commences>

History of Native Title in Victoria, <http://www.ntsv.com.au/native-title-in-victoria/>

National Museum of Australia, *Encounters*, <http://www.nma.gov.au/exhibitions/encounters/mapping/fernyhurst>

State Government of Victoria and the Djadja Wurrung Clans Aboriginal Corporation, Fact Sheet: Settlement Between the Dja Dja Wurrung Traditional Owner Group and the State of Victoria, 28 March 2013, <http://ntsv.com.au/ntsvwp-content/uploads/2013/05/Dja-Dja-Wurrung-Settlement-Factsheet.pdf>

Secondary sources

Books

Arkley, Lindsey, *The Hated Protector: The Story of Charles Wightman Sievwright, Protector of Aborigines 1839–42*, Orbit Press, Melbourne, 2000.

Atkinson, Alan, *The Europeans in Australia: A History*, vol. 2, Oxford University Press, Melbourne, 2004.

Atkinson, Alan and Marian Aveling (eds), *Australians 1838*, Fairfax, Syme & Weldon, Sydney, 1987.

Attwood, Bain, *The Making of the Aborigines*, Allen & Unwin, Sydney, 1989.

_____, *'My Country': A History of the Djadja Wurrung 1837–1864*, Monash Publications in History, Melbourne, 1999.

_____, *Possession: Batman's Treaty and the Matters of History*, Miegunyah Press, Melbourne, 2009.

_____, *Rights for Aborigines*, Allen & Unwin, Sydney, 2003.

_____, *Telling the Truth about Aboriginal History*, Allen & Unwin, Sydney, 2005.

Attwood, Bain and S.G. Foster (eds), *Frontier Conflict: The Australian Experience*, National Museum of Australia, Canberra, 2003.

Barwick, Diane E., *Rebellion at Coranderrk*, Aboriginal History, Canberra, 1998.

Beavis, Margery and Betty, *Avoca: The Early Years*, Margery and Betty Beavis, Warrnambool, 1986.

Beckett, Jeremy R. (ed.), *Past and Present: The Construction of Aboriginality*, Aboriginal Studies Press, Canberra, 1988.

Belich, James, *Replenishing the Earth: The Settler Revolution and the Rise of the Anglo-World, 1783–1939*, Oxford University Press, New York, 2009.

Benton, Lauren, *Law and Colonial Cultures: Legal Regimes in World History*, Cambridge University Press, New York, 2002.

Blake, Steven, *George Rowe, Artist and Lithographer 1796–1864*, Cheltenham Art Gallery and Museum, Cheltenham, 1982.

Boucher, Leigh and Lynette Russell (eds), *Settler Colonial Governance in Nineteenth-Century Victoria*, Australian National University Press and Aboriginal History, Canberra, 2015.

Broome, Richard, *Aboriginal Victorians: A History Since 1800*, Allen & Unwin, Sydney, 2005.

Butlin, N.G., *Our Original Aggression: Aboriginal Populations of Southeastern Australia 1788–1850*, Allen & Unwin, Sydney, 1983.

_____, *Economics and the Dreamtime: A Hypothetical History*, Cambridge University Press, Melbourne, 1993.

Cahir, Fred, *Black Gold: Aboriginal People on the Goldfields of Victoria, 1850–1870*, Australian National University E Press and Aboriginal History, Canberra, 2012.

Cannon, Michael, *Who Killed the Koories?* William Heinemann, Melbourne, 1990.

Chakrabarty, Dipesh, *Provincialising Europe: Postcolonial Thought and Historical Difference*, Princeton University Press, Princeton, 2000.

Christie, M.F., *Aborigines in Colonial Victoria 1835–86*, University of Sydney Press, Sydney, 1979.

Clark, Ian D., *Aboriginal Languages and Clans: An Historical Atlas of Western and Central Victoria, 1800–1900*, Department of Geography and Environmental Science, Monash University, Melbourne, 1990.

_____, *Scars in the Landscape: A Register of Massacre Sites in Western Victoria, 1803–1859*, Australian Institute of Aboriginal and Torres Strait Islander Studies, Canberra, 1995.

_____, *'That's My Country Belonging to Me': Aboriginal Land Tenure and Dispossession in Nineteenth Century Western Victoria*, Heritage Matters, Melbourne, 1998.

BIBLIOGRAPHY

Clark, Ian D. and David A. Cahir, *Tanderrum 'Freedom of the Bush': The Djadja Wurrung Presence on the Goldfields of Central Victoria*, Friends of the Mount Alexander Dwellings, Castlemaine, 2004.

Connor, John, *The Australian Frontier Wars 1788–1838*, University of New South Wales Press, Sydney, 2002.

Corris, Peter, *Aborigines and Europeans in Western Victoria*, Australian Institute of Aboriginal Studies, Canberra, 1968.

Critchett, Jan, *A Distant Field of Murder: Western District Frontiers 1834–1848*, Melbourne University Press, Melbourne, 1990.

Culvenor, C.C., *The Boundaries of the Mount Franklinford Aboriginal Reserve*, Jim Crow Press, Daylesford, 1992.

Denholm, David, *The Colonial Australians*, Penguin, Melbourne, 1979.

Dwyer, Philip G. and Lyndall Ryan (eds), *Theatres of Violence: Massacre, Mass Killing and Atrocity throughout History*, Berghahn Books, New York, 2012.

Edmonds, Penelope, *Urbanizing Frontiers: Indigenous Peoples and Settlers in 19th-Century Pacific Rim Cities*, University of British Columbia Press, Vancouver, 2010.

Fels, Marie, *Good Men and True: The Aboriginal Police of the Port Phillip District 1837–53*, Melbourne University Press, Melbourne, 1988.

———, *'I Succeeded Once': The Aboriginal Protectorate on the Mornington Peninsula 1839–40*, Aboriginal History, Canberra, 2011.

Fernihurst District History Committee, *Reflections from Kinypaniel: The Early Years of the Fernihurst District*, Fernihurst District History Committee, Maryborough, 1992.

Flett, James, *Dunolly: Story of an Old Gold Diggings*, 2nd edn, Hawthorn Press, Melbourne, 1974.

Ford, Lisa and Tim Rowse (eds), *Between Indigenous and Settler Governance*, Routledge, New York, 2013.

Foster, Robert et al., *Fatal Collisions: The South Australian Frontier and the Violence of Memory*, Wakefield Press, Adelaide, 2001.

Foxcroft, E.J.B., *Australian Native Policy: Its History, Especially in Victoria*, Melbourne University Press, Melbourne, 1941.

Gammage, Bill, *The Biggest Estate on Earth: How Aborigines Made Australia*, Allen & Unwin, Sydney, 2011.

Goodall, *Invasion to Embassy: Land in Aboriginal Politics in New South Wales, 1770–1972*, Allen & Unwin in association with Black Books, Sydney, 1996.

Griffiths, Tom, *Hunters and Collectors: The Antiquarian Imagination in Australia*, Cambridge University Press, Melbourne, 1996.

Haldane, Robert, *The People's Force: A History of the Victorian Police*, 2nd edn, Melbourne University Press, Melbourne, 1995.

Holst, Heather, *Making a Home: A History of Castlemaine*, Australian Scholarly Publishing, Melbourne, 2014.

Johnston, Anna, *Paper War: Morality, Print Culture, and Power in Colonial New South Wales*, University of Western Australian Press, Perth, 2012.

Kenny, Robert, *The Lamb Enters the Dreaming: Nathanael Pepper and the Ruptured World*, Scribe, Melbourne, 2007.

Lester, Alan and Fae Dussart, *Colonization and the Origins of Humanitarian Governance: Protecting Aborigines Across the Nineteenth-Century British Empire*, Cambridge University Press, Cambridge, 2014.

Milliss, Roger, *Waterloo Creek: The Australia Day Massacre of 1838, George Gipps and the British Conquest of New South Wales*, McPhee Gribble, Melbourne, 1992.

Mitchell, Jessie, *In Good Faith? Governing Indigenous Australia through God, Charity and Empire, 1825–1855*, Aboriginal History, Canberra, 2011.

Morrison, Edgar, *Early Days in the Loddon Valley: Memoirs of Edward Stone Parker 1802–1865*, s. n., Daylesford, 1966.

———, *Frontier Life in the Loddon Protectorate: Episodes from Early Days, 1837–42*, Advocate, Daylesford, 1967.

———, *The Loddon Aborigines: "Tales of Old Jim Crow"*, s.n., Yandoit, 1971.

Moses, Dirk A. (ed.), *Empire, Colony, Genocide: Conquest, Occupation and Subaltern Resistance in World History*, Berghahn Books, New York, 2008.

——— (ed.), *Genocide and Settler Society: Frontier Violence and Stolen Indigenous Children in Australian History*, Berghahn Books, New York, 2004.

——— and Dan Stone (eds), *Colonialism and Genocide*, Routledge, London, 2007.

Mullaly, Paul R., *Crime in the Port Phillip District 1835–51*, Hybrid Publishers, Melbourne, 2008.

Powell, J.M., *The Public Lands of Australia Felix: Settlement and Land Appraisal in Victoria 1834–91 with Special Reference to the Western Plains*, Oxford University Press, Melbourne, 1970.

Rae-Ellis, Vivienne, *Black Robinson: Protector of Aborigines*, Melbourne University Press, Melbourne, 1988.

Randell, J.O., *Pastoral Settlement in Northern Victoria*, vol. 1, Queensberry Press, Melbourne, 1979.

———, *Pastoral Settlement in Northern Victoria*, vol. 2, Chandos, Melbourne, 1982.

Reece, R.H.W., *Aborigines and Colonists: Aborigines and Colonial Society in New South Wales in the 1830s and 1840s*, Sydney University Press, Sydney, 1974.

Reilly, Diane and Jennifer Carew, *Sun Pictures of Victoria: The Fauchery-Daintree Collection 1858*, Currey O'Neill Ross on behalf of the Library Council of Victoria, Melbourne, 1983.

Reynolds, Henry, *Forgotten War*, New South Publishing, Sydney, 2013.

———, *Frontier: Aborigines, Settlers and Land*, Allen & Unwin, Sydney, 1987.

———, *The Other Side of the Frontier*, History Department, James Cook University, Townsville, 1981.

———, *The Law of the Land*, Penguin, Melbourne, 1987.

———, *This Whispering in our Hearts*, Allen & Unwin, Sydney, 1998.

———, *With the White People*, Penguin, Melbourne, 1990.

Richards, Jonathan, *The Secret War*, University of Queensland Press, St Lucia, 2008.

Roberts, Tony, *Frontier Justice: A History of the Gulf Country to 1900*, University of Queensland Press, St Lucia, 2005.

Roginski, Alexandra, *The Hanged Man and the Body Thief: Finding Lives in a Museum Mystery*, Monash University Publishing, Melbourne, 2015.

Shaw, A.G.L., *A History of the Port Phillip District: Victoria Before Separation*, Miegunyah Press, Melbourne, 1996.

BIBLIOGRAPHY

Smith, M.A., *Peopling the Cleland Hills: Aboriginal History in Western Central Australia*, Aboriginal History, Canberra, 2005.

Swain, Tony, *A Place for Strangers: Towards a History of Australian Aboriginal Being*, Cambridge University Press, Melbourne, 1993.

Tindale, Norman B., *Aboriginal Tribes of Australia: Their Terrain, Environmental Controls, Distribution, Limits and Proper Names*, Australian National Press, Canberra, 1974.

Veracini, Lorenzo, *Settler Colonialism: A Theoretical Overview*, Palgrave Macmillan, Basingstoke, 2010.

[Willis, Elizabeth], *Etched on Bark 1854: Kulin Barks from Northern Victoria*, Melbourne Museum, Melbourne, 2005.

Woollacott, Angela, *Settler Society in the Australian Colonies: Self-Government and Imperial Culture*, Oxford University Press, Oxford, 2015.

Yarwood, A.T. and M.J. Knowling, *Race Relations in Australia: A History*, Methuen Australia, Melbourne, 1982.

Journal articles, essays, and chapters in books

Atkinson, Alan, 'A Slice of the Sydney Press', *Push from the Bush*, no. 1, 1978, pp. 82–99.

_____, 'Tasmania and the Multiplicity of Nations', *Tasmanian Historical Research Association Papers and Transactions*, vol. 52, no. 4, 2005, pp. 189–200.

Attwood, Bain, 'Contesting Frontiers: History, Memory and Narrative in a National Museum', *Recollections*, vol. 1, no. 2, 2006, pp. 103–14.

_____, 'The Founding of *Aboriginal History* and the Forming of Aboriginal History', *Aboriginal History*, vol. 36, 2012, pp. 119–71.

_____, 'Historical Controversy and the History Wars in Australia', in Russell West-Pavlov and Jennifer Wawrzinek (eds), *Frontier Skirmishes: Literary and Cultural Debates in Australia after 1992*, Universitätsverlag Winter, Heidelberg, 2010, pp. 33–44.

_____, 'Portrait of an Aboriginal as an Artist: Sally Morgan and the Construction of Aboriginality', *Australian Historical Studies*, vol. 25, no. 99, 1992, pp. 302–18.

_____, 'Remembering, Forgetting, and Denial in a Settler Society: The Australian Case', *History Workshop Journal*, no. 84, 2017 forthcoming.

_____, 'Unsettling Pasts: Reconciliation and History in Settler Australia', *Postcolonial Studies*, vol. 8, no. 3, 2005, pp. 243–59.

Barta, Tony, '"They Appear Actually to Vanish from the Face of the Earth": Aborigines and the European Project in Australia Felix', *Journal of Genocide Research*, vol. 10, no. 4, 2008, pp. 519–39.

Barwick, Diane, 'Changes in the Aboriginal Population of Victoria, 1863–1966', in Jack Golson and D.J. Mulvaney (eds), *Aboriginal Man and Environment in Australia*, Australian National University Press, Canberra, 1971.

Beckett, Jeremy, 'Aboriginality, Citizenship and Nation State', *Social Analysis*, no. 24, 1988, pp. 3–18.

Broome, Richard, 'Aboriginal Workers on South-Eastern Frontiers', *Australian Historical Studies*, vol. 26, no. 103, 1994, pp. 202–20.

_____, '"There Were Vegetables Every Year Mr Green was Here": Right Behaviour and the Struggle for Autonomy at Coranderrk Aboriginal Reserve', *History Australia*, vol. 3, no. 2, 2006, pp. 43.1–16.

_____, 'The Struggle for Australia: Aboriginal-European Warfare, 1770–1930', in Michael McKernan and Margaret Browne (eds), *Australia: Two Centuries of War and Peace*, Australian War Memorial/Allen & Unwin, Canberra/Sydney, 1988.

Cahir, Fred et al., '*Winda Lingo Parugoneit* or Why Set the Bush [on] Fire? Fire and Victorian Aboriginal People on the Colonial Frontier', *Australian Historical Studies*, vol. 47, no. 2, 2016, pp. 225–40.

Carey, Hilary M., 'Lancelot Threlkeld, Biraban, and the Colonial Bible in Australia', *Comparative Studies in Society and History*, vol. 52, no. 2, 2010, pp. 447–78.

Clark, Ian D., 'The Aboriginal Pioneers of the Shire of Korong', in Korong Historical Society (comp.), *Burrabungle: Mt Korong*, Koorong Historical Society, Wedderburn, 1988.

Clendinnen, Inga, 'Reading Mr Robinson', in her *Tiger's Eye: A Memoir*, Text Publishing, Melbourne, 2000.

Cooper, Carol, 'Early Photographs of Aborigines in the Picture Collection', *La Trobe Library Journal*, no. 43, 1989, pp. 33–35.

_____, 'Traditional Visual Culture in South-East Australia', in Andrew Sayers, *Aboriginal Artists of the Nineteenth Century*, Oxford University Press, Melbourne, 1994.

Cowlishaw, Gillian, 'On "Getting it Wrong": Collateral Damage in the History Wars', *Australian Historical Studies*, vol. 37, no. 127, 2006, pp. 181–202.

Critchett, Jan, 'Encounters in the Western District', in Bain Attwood and S.G. Foster (eds), *Frontier Conflict: The Australian Experience*, National Museum of Australia, 2003.

Curthoys, Ann, and Jessie Mitchell, 'The Advent of Self-Government, 1840s– 1890', in Alison Bashford and Stuart Macintyre (eds), *The Cambridge History of Australia*, Cambridge University Press, Melbourne, 2013.

Davies, Suzanne, 'Aborigines, Murders, and the Criminal Law in Early Port Phillip, 1840-1851', *Australian Historical Studies*, vol. 22, no. 88, 1987, pp. 313–36.

Dwyer, Philip and Lyndall Ryan, 'Reflections on Genocide and Settler-Colonial Violence', *History Australia*, vol. 13, no. 3, 2016, pp. 335–50.

Elbourne, Elizabeth, 'Exploration, Conquest and the African "Frontier"', in *Frontier, Settlement & Borderland Encounters*, <www.amdigital.co.uk>, 2016.

_____, 'Imperial Politics in the Family Way: Gender, Biography and the 1836–37 Select Committee on Aborigines', in Bain Attwood and Tom Griffiths (eds), *Frontier, Race, Nation: Henry Reynolds and Australian History*, Australian Scholarly Publishing, Melbourne, 2009.

_____, 'The Sin of the Settler: The 1835–36 Select Committee on Aborigines and Debates Over Virtue and Conquest in the Early Nineteenth-Century British White Settler Empire', *Journal of Colonialism and Colonial History*, vol. 4, no. 3, 2003, <http://muse.jhu.edu/journals/journal_of_colonialism_and_colonial_history/v004/4.3elbourne.html>.

_____, 'Violence, Moral Imperialism and Colonial Borderlands, 1770s–1820s: Some Contradictions of Humanitarianism', *Journal of Colonialism and Colonial History*, vol. 17, no. 1, 2016, <https://muse.jhu.edu/article/613282>.

Ferry, John, 'The Failure of the New South Wales Missions to the Aborigines Before 1845', *Aboriginal History*, vol. 3, pt 2, 1979, pp. 25–36.

Ford, Lisa, 'Protecting the Peace on the Edges of Empire: Commissioners of Crown Lands in New South Wales', in Lauren Benton et al. (eds), *Protection and Empire*, Cambridge University Press, Cambridge, 2017.

Ford, Lisa and David Roberts, 'Expansion, 1820–50', in Alison Bashford and Stuart Macintyre (eds), *The Cambridge History of Australia*, Cambridge University Press, Melbourne, 2013.

Foster, Robert, '"Don't Mention the War": Frontier Violence and the Language of Concealment', *History Australia*, vol. 6, no. 3, 2009, pp. 68.1–15.

Foster, S.G., 'Aboriginal Rights and Official Morality', *Push from the Bush*, no. 11, 1981, pp. 68–98.

Fung, Pamie and Sara Wills, 'There's So Much in Looking at those Barks', in Chris Healy and Andrea Witcomb (eds), *South Pacific Museums: Experiments in Culture*, Monash University ePress, 2006.

Goodall, Heather, 'Too Early or Not Soon Enough? Reflections on Sharing Histories as Process', *Australian Historical Studies*, vol. 33, no. 118, 2002, pp. 7–24.

Griffiths, Tom, 'The Language of Conflict', in Bain Attwood and S.G. Foster (eds), *Frontier Violence: The Australian Experience*, National Museum of Australia, Canberra, 2003.

Hallam, Sylvia J., 'A View from the Other Side of the Western Frontier: Or "I Met a Man Who Wasn't There ..."', *Aboriginal History*, vol. 7, pt 2, 1983, pp. 134–56.

Harrison, Brian, 'The Myall Creek Massacre', in Isabel McBryde (ed.), *Records of Times Past*, Australian Institute of Aboriginal Studies, Canberra, 1978.

Holst, Heather, '"Save the People": E.S. Parker at the Loddon Aboriginal Station', *Aboriginal History*, vol. 32, 2008, pp. 109–27.

Johnson, Miranda, 'Writing Indigenous Histories Now', *Australian Historical Studies*, vol. 45, no. 3, 2014, pp. 317–30.

Laidlaw, Zoë, '"Aunt Anna's Report": The Buxton Women's Political and Intellectual Contribution to the Aborigines Select Committee, 1835-37', *Journal of Imperial and Commonwealth History*, vol. 32, no. 2, 2004, pp. 1–28.

Lester, Alan, 'British Settler Discourse and the Circuits of Empire', *History Workshop Journal*, no. 54, 2002, pp. 25–48.

_____, 'Colonial Networks, Australian Humanitarianism and the History Wars', *Geographical Research*, vol. 44, no. 3, 2006, pp. 229–41.

_____, 'George Augustus Robinson and Imperial Networks', in Anna Johnston and Mitchell Rolls (eds), *Reading Robinson: Companion Essays to Friendly Mission*, Monash University Publishing, Melbourne, 2012.

_____, 'Indigenous Engagements with Humanitarian Governance: The Port Phillip Protectorate of Aborigines and "Humanitarian Space"', in Jane Carey and Jane Lydon (eds), *Indigenous Networks: Mobility, Connections and Exchange*, Routledge, London, 2014.

Lester, Alan and Fae Dussart, 'Masculinity, "Race", and Family in the Colonies: Protecting Aborigines in the Early Nineteenth Century', *Gender, Place and Culture*, vol. 16, no. 1, 2009, pp. 65–76.

Lydon, Jane, 'The Experimental 1860s: Charles Walter's Images of Coranderrk Aboriginal Station, Victoria', *Aboriginal History*, vol. 26, 2002, pp. 78–130.

McBryde, Isabel, 'Exchange in South-East Australia: An Ethnographic Perspective', *Aboriginal History*, vol. 8, pt 2, 1984, pp. 132–53.

_____, 'Kulin Greenstone Quarries: The Social Contexts of Production and Distribution for the Mount William Site', *World Archaeology*, vol. 16, no. 2, 1984, pp. 267–85.

_____, 'Wil-im-ee Moor-ring: Or Where do Axes Come From? Stone Axe Distribution and Exchange Patterns in Victoria', *Mankind*, vol. 11, no. 3, 1978, pp. 354–82.

McLisky, Claire, '"Due Observance of Justice, and the Protection of their Rights": Philanthropy, Humanitarianism and Moral Purpose in the Aborigines Protection Society circa 1837 and its Portrayal in Australian Historiography, 1883–2003', *Limina*, vol. 11, 2005, pp. 57–66.

Mitchell, Jessie, '"Country Belonging to Me": Land and Labour on Aboriginal Missions and Protectorate Stations, 1830-1850, *Eras Journal*, vol. 6, 2004, <http://artsonline.monash.edu.au/eras/country-belonging-to-me-land-and-labour-on-aboriginal-missions-and-protectorate-stations-1830-1850/>.

Nance, Beverley, 'The Level of Violence: Europeans and Aborigines in Port Phillip 1835-51', *Historical Studies,* vol. 19, no. 77, 1981, pp. 532–52.

Nelson, Hank, 'The Missionaries and the Aborigines in the Port Phillip District', *Historical Studies*, vol. 12, no. 45, 1965, pp. 56–67.

_____, 'Parker, Edward Stone', *Australian Dictionary of Biography*, vol. 5, Melbourne University Press, Melbourne, 1974, <http://adb.anu.edu.au/biography/parker-edward-stone-4363>.

Nettelbeck, Amanda, '"A Halo of Protection": Colonial Protectors and the Principle of Aboriginal Protection through Punishment', *Australian Historical Studies*, vol. 43, no. 3, 2012, pp. 396–411.

_____, 'Proximate Strangers and Familiar Antagonists: Violence on an Intimate Frontier', *Australian Historical Studies*, vol. 47, no. 2, 2016, pp. 209–24.

O'Brien, Anne, 'Humanitarianism and Reparation in Colonial Australia', *Journal of Colonialism and Colonial History*, vol. 12, no. 2, 2011, <DOI: 10.1353/cch.2011.0016>.

O'Donnell, N.M., 'The Australian Career of Henry Fysche Gisborne', *Victorian Historical Magazine*, vol. 5, no. 19, 1917, pp. 112–35.

Peterson, Nicolas, 'The Changing Photographic Contract: Aborigines and Image Ethics', in Christopher Penney and Nicolas Peterson (eds), *Photograph's Other Histories*, Duke University Press, Durham, 2003.

Powell, J.M., 'Squatting Expansion in Victoria, 1834–1860', in Robert Spreadborough and Hugh Anderson (comps), *Victorian Squatters*, Red Rooster Press, Melbourne, 1983.

Prest, Wilfrid, 'Antipodean Blackstone', in Wilfrid Prest (ed.), *Reinterpreting Blackstone's Commentaries: A Seminal Text in National and International Contexts*, Hart Publishing, Oxford, 2014.

Price, Richard A., 'The Colonial Frontier in Nineteenth-Century History and Beyond', in *Frontier, Settlement & Borderland Encounters*, <www.amdigital. co.uk>, 2016.

Reece, Bob, 'Inventing Aborigines', *Aboriginal History*, vol. 11, pt 1, 1987, pp. 14–23.

Reynolds, Henry, 'Racial Thought in Early Colonial Australia', *Australian Journal of Politics and History*, vol. 20, no. 1, 1974, pp. 45–53.

_____, 'The Written Record', in Bain Attwood and S.G. Foster (eds), *Frontier Violence: The Australian Experience*, National Museum of Australia, Canberra, 2003.

Roberts, David, 'Bells Falls Massacre and Bathurst's History of Violence: Local Tradition and Australian Historiography', *Australian Historical Studies*, vol. 26, no. 105, 1995, pp. 615–33.

Rowse, Tim, 'Indigenous Heterogeneity', *Australian Historical Studies*, vol. 45, no. 3, 2014, pp. 297–310.

Ryan, Lyndall, 'Settler Massacres on the Port Phillip Frontier, 1836–1851', *Journal of Australian Studies*, vol. 34, no. 3, 2010, pp. 257–73.

Say, Madeleine, 'John Hunter Kerr: Photographer', *La Trobe Library Journal*, no. 76, 2005, pp. 71–76.

Shaw, A.G.L., 'British Policy Towards the Australian Aborigines, 1830–1850', *Australian Historical Studies*, vol. 25, no. 99, 1992, pp. 265–85.

Smandych, Russell, 'Contemplating the Evidence of "Others": James Stephen, the Colonial Office, and the Fate of the Australian Aboriginal Evidence Acts, circa 1839–1849', *Australian Journal of Legal History*, vol. 8, no. 2, 2004, pp. 237–83.

Smith, Len, 'How Many People Had Lived in Australia Before it was Annexed by the English in 1788', in Gordon Briscoe and Len Smith (eds), *The Aboriginal Population Revisited: 70 000 Years to the Present*, Aboriginal History, Canberra, 2002.

Smith, Len et al., 'The Political Arithmetic of Aboriginal Victorians', *The Journal of Interdisciplinary History*, vol. 38, no. 4, 2008, pp. 533–51.

Standfield, Rachel, 'Protection, Settler Politics and Indigenous Politics in the Work of William Thomas', *Journal of Colonialism and Colonial History*, vol. 13, no. 1, 2012, <https://muse.jhu.edu/article/475171>.

Stone, Russell, 'Auckland's Political Opposition in the Crown Colony Period, 1841–53', in Len Richardson and W. David McIntyre (eds), *Provincial Perspectives: Essays in Honour of W.J. Gardner*, University of Canterbury Press, Christchurch, 1980.

Sutton, Peter, 'Myth as History, History as Myth', in Ian Keen (ed.), *Being Black: Aboriginal Cultures in 'Settled' Australia*, Aboriginal Studies Press, Canberra, 1988.

White, Richard, 'Indian Peoples and the Natural World: Asking the Right Questions', in Donald L. Fixico (ed.), *Rethinking American Indian History*, University of New Mexico Press, New Mexico, 1997.

Willis, Elizabeth, 'Exhibiting Aboriginal Industry: A Story Behind a "Re-Discovered" Bark Drawing From Victoria', *Aboriginal History*, vol. 27, 2003, pp. 39–58.

_____, 'History, Strong Stories and New Traditions: The Case of "Etched on Bark 1854"', *History Australia*, vol. 4, no. 1, 2007, 13.1–11.

_____, '"People Undergoing Great Change": John Hunter Kerr's Photographs of Indigenous People at Fernyhurst, Victoria, 1850s', *La Trobe Library Journal*, no. 76, 2005, pp. 49–70.

_____, 'Re-Working a Photographic Archive: John Hunter Kerr's Portraits of Kulin People, 1850s–2004', *Journal of Australian Studies*, vol. 35, no. 2, 2011, pp. 235–49.

Wood, Rebecca, 'Frontier Violence and the Bush Legend: The *Sydney Herald*'s Response to the Myall Creek Massacre Trials and the Creation of Colonial Identity', *History Australia*, vol. 6, no. 3, 2009, pp. 67.1–19.

Wolfe, Patrick, 'Settler Colonialism and the Elimination of the Native', *Journal of Genocide Research*, vol. 8, no. 4, 2006, pp. 387–409.

Theses

Cahir, David 'Fred', Black Gold: A History of the Role of Aboriginal People on the Goldfields of Victoria, 1850–70, PhD thesis, University of Ballarat, 2006.

Madden, Helen, The Loddon District Aboriginal Protectorate, BA Honours thesis, La Trobe University, 1976.

Manuscripts

Clark, Nicholas (ed.), Trackback: Aboriginal History and Archaeology in Djadja Wurrung Country (Central Victoria) Examining Mount Kooyoora, Mount Alexander and Mount Tarrengower, 1995.

Fels, Marie, 'The Collision at Monro's Station', in Nicholas Clark (ed.), Aboriginal History and Archaeology in Djadja Wurrung Country (Central Victoria) Examining Mount Kooyoora, Mount Alexander and Mount Tarrengower, a report for the Bendigo Dja Dja Wrung Aboriginal Association, 2nd draft, 1995.

Websites

Carey, Hilary M., 'Missionaries, Dictionaries and Australian Aborigines, 1820–1850, <https://downloads.newcastle.edu.au/library/cultural%20collections/awaba//language/linguistics.html>.

INDEX

Note: *i* = illustration; *n* = footnote

CPSIA information can be obtained
at www.ICGtesting.com
Printed in the USA
JSHW022300290623
43979JS00002B/165